world is though

Bundaberg ?

Northwestern University

STUDIES IN *Phenomenology &*

Existential Philosophy

The Primacy of Perception

Maurice Merleau-Ponty

Edited, with an Introduction by

The Primacy of Perception

And Other Essays on Phenomenological Psychology,

the Philosophy of Art, History and Politics

JAMES M. EDIE

NORTHWESTERN UNIVERSITY PRESS

1964

Acknowledgments

I WISH TO THANK Madame Merleau-Ponty and the editors of the *Bulletin de la société française de philosophie* for permission to publish my translation of "Le primat de la perception et ses conséquences philosophiques," which appeared in that journal in December, 1947, pp. 119–53. I also wish to thank the editors of the *Revue de métaphysique et de morale* for permission to publish a translation of "Un inédit de Maurice Merleau-Ponty" (December, 1962, pp. 401–9), the directors of the Centre de documentation universitaire for *Les sciences de l'homme et la phénoménologie* and *Les relations avec autrui chez l'enfant*, and Editions Gallimard for *L'Oeil et l'esprit* as well as for the chapters from *Humanisme et terreur* and *Les aventures de la dialectique* reproduced below. Finally, my sincere thanks go out to all those who, under varying degrees of duress, contributed their translations to this volume.

J. M. E.

Contents

Introduction

THE PURPOSE OF this volume is to bring together and to present to the English-speaking world a number of important and hitherto scattered studies by Maurice Merleau-Ponty which appeared in various publications from 1947 to 1961. It is a mark of the increasing influence of Merleau-Ponty's thought in American philosophy that within a few years of his death virtually all his writings will be available in English. The content of the present volume was dictated solely by the fortuitous circumstance that the studies included here represent the most important of Merleau-Ponty's writings which still remained untranslated.[1] Since each of these studies was occasioned by a different and particular set of circumstances, since each one deals with a different question, and since they are of very unequal length, this volume cannot but appear to be a somewhat heteroclite and miscellaneous collection.

Nevertheless I think it is possible to arrange these studies, disregarding their chronological sequence, according to a plan which will give a fairly systematic introduction to the major themes of Merleau-Ponty's philosophy. The first chapter, though published posthumously, was written at the time Merleau-Ponty announced his candidacy for the chair of philosophy at the Collège de France and gives a general introduction to his work as a whole, as he conceived it at that time. It is followed by the title-chapter of this volume, "The Primacy of Perception," which is, in essence, a presentation of the underlying thesis of his

1. All the major works published by Merleau-Ponty during his lifetime have been translated though some have not yet been published. Richard C. McCleary's translation of *Signes* will appear concomitantly with this volume in the Northwestern University Studies in Phenomenology and Existential Philosophy, as will Hubert L. Dreyfus' translation of *Sens et non-sens*. Plans are being made at the present time for a translation of his first posthumous volume, *Le visible et l'invisible* (Paris, 1964).

Phenomenology of Perception. It is an extremely interesting and valuable text both because it gives the most concise statement ever produced by Merleau-Ponty of his general philosophical position and also because, in the discussion which followed the reading of this paper to the *Société française de philosophie*, we are given the basic elements of Merleau-Ponty's response to the major objections his position immediately evokes.

Chapters three and four reproduce two courses given by Merleau-Ponty at the Sorbonne on phenomenological psychology. The first, "Phenomenology and the Sciences of Man," is a statement of some methodological importance, which clarifies in many ways Merleau-Ponty's unique interpretation of the phenomenological method. The second is an application of his ideas to a concrete problem of psychology. Finally, in "Eye and Mind" and the concluding chapters, we are presented with applications of Merleau-Ponty's ideas to the realm of art, the philosophy of history and politics. "Eye and Mind," completed only a few months before his death, is considered by some to be one of Merleau-Ponty's most important works, standing apart as one of the richest, most synthetic (and most difficult) presentations of his thought which we have.[2] The last two chapters are taken from two works of political polemic which, because of their dated and topical character, will probably never be published in English in their entirety.[3] These chapters were chosen because they are among the best and most typical statements of Merleau-Ponty's political ideas,[4] the first with reference to Max Weber and the second in criticism of Arthur Koestler, and because they give a first introduction to his (never developed) conception of the existential dialectic of history.

It has not been sufficiently clear to all readers of Merleau-Ponty's first works, *The Structure of Behavior* and the *Phenomenology of Perception*, that in these volumes Merleau-Ponty is presenting a *thesis*, a program for phenomenological research, which would have to be developed, criticized, and tested over a considerable period of time and

2. This is the judgment of Sartre ("Merleau-Ponty vivant" in *Les Temps Modernes*, no. 184–85, 1961, p. 372) and of Alphonse de Waehlens ("Merleau-Ponty, philosophe de la peinture" in *Revue de métaphysique et de morale*, no. 4, 1962).

3. *Humanisme et terreur* (Paris, 1947) and *Les aventures de la dialectique* (Paris, 1955).

4. This is true only up to a certain point. After his break with Sartre and his criticism of communism in *Les aventures de la dialectique* we have little in the way of any systematic political philosophy from the pen of Merleau-Ponty. He never answered the attack which this book evoked on the part of Simone de Beauvoir ("Merleau-Ponty et le pseudo-sartrisme," *Les Temps Modernes*, no. 114–15, 1955) or that of his former Communist friends (*Mésaventures de l'anti-marxisme, Les malheurs de M. Merleau-Ponty*, Paris, 1956).

which should not be taken as prematurely established. Many readers of the *Phenomenology of Perception* have taken it to be the *definitive* expression of Merleau-Ponty's philosophy and have begun to write books for or against his views on this basis alone. They see his philosophy as a middle road between traditional empiricism and traditional idealism and as an attempt to elaborate a "philosophy of ambiguity" through a kind of empiricist-idealist dialectic which continually oscillates between these two poles in its definitions of "lived corporality," "lived space," "lived time," etc. The elaboration of the key notions of the *Phenomenology of Perception* is taken to be the specific contribution of Merleau-Ponty and to establish the originality of his position. This is no doubt true in part. But it is true only to the extent that we can make Merleau-Ponty to be the man of *one book* (as others have tended simply to identify Kant with the first critique or Husserl with the first volume of the *Ideen* and will not hear of any further development or nuances in their thought). The *Phenomenology of Perception* is clearly Merleau-Ponty's greatest single achievement and the book of his which is most likely to become a classic of twentieth-century philosophy, yet even in interpreting this work taken alone and in isolation from his other writings, we must take seriously its *programmatic character*. In this work it was Merleau-Ponty's intention to lay down a solid basis for phenomenological research which would take him forward from the phenomenology of perception to studies on imagination, language, culture, reason, and on aesthetic, ethical, political, and even religious experience. That he was able to do no more than begin this work during his own lifetime is something that he was painfully aware of; his program must now be either abandoned or assumed by others.

But the very existence and nature of this project is infrequently adverted to and is badly misunderstood. The principal value of the first two chapters of this volume is that they make clearly evident the programmatic character of Merleau-Ponty's early work. This program was stated in terms of the thesis of the "Primacy of Perception," defined as follows:

By these words, the "primacy of perception," we mean that the experience of perception is our presence at the moment when things, truths, values are constituted for us; that perception is a nascent *logos*; that it teaches us, outside all dogmatism, the true conditions of objectivity itself; that it summons us to the tasks of knowledge and action. It is not a question of reducing human knowledge to sensation, but of assisting at the birth of this knowledge, to make it as sensible as the sensible, to recover the consciousness of rationality.[5]

5. "The Primacy of Perception," below, p. 25.

These words define a position and launch a program in philosophy which Merleau-Ponty has described in many different ways but which he has at least twice forthrightly called "phenomenological positivism." [6] When he presented his thesis to the *Société française de philosophie* he was both congratulated by M. Lenoir for his resolute "realism" and chided by M. Beaufret for having remained too "idealistic," at least in the formulation of his position. We know that he completely rejects both the metaphysics and the epistemology of traditional naturalism and positivism, with arguments now too well known to need repetition here. We know also that he never discusses any meaning-structure or value-structure in "things" independently of the consciousness *for whom* these things have meaning and value. Like all phenomenologists, Merleau-Ponty claims to be neither a realist nor an idealist but a phenomenologist.

By advancing the thesis of the "primacy of perception" or of "phenomenological positivism," Merleau-Ponty means to assert, first of all, that the perceived life-world is the primary reality, the really real, true being, the primary analogon. The structures of what he calls "perceptual consciousness" are our first route of access to being and truth, and these structures underlie and accompany all the structures of higher-level "intellectual consciousness." What distinguishes this "positivism" from the classical doctrines which go under that name is that Merleau-Ponty does not claim that higher-order experiences can ever be *reduced* to perception, nor does he define perception in terms of a few privileged qualia or sense-data like traditional empiricism. The world which is given in perception according to Merleau-Ponty is the concrete, intersubjectively constituted life-world of immediate experience. It is a world of familiar natural and cultural objects, of other people, the world in which I act. Perception itself is defined in terms of a sensory-motor *behavior* through which the world is constituted for man as the world of human consciousness prior to any explicit or reflexive thought about it.

But man does not live only in the "real" world of perception. He also lives in the realms of the imaginary, of ideality, of language, culture, and history. In short there are various *levels of experience,* and phenomenology is open to all of them and recognizes in each its own irreducible specificity, its own meaning and value structures, its own qualitatively distinctive characteristics. Thus from a phenomenology of perception it is necessary to proceed to a phenomenology of intersubjectivity, a phenomenology of truth or rationality, a phenomenology of aesthetic experience, etc. What is distinctive of Merleau-Ponty's inter-

6. *Phenomenology of Perception,* trans. Colin Smith (New York, 1962), p. xvii, and "Phenomenology and the Sciences of Man," below, p. 50.

pretation of phenomenology is the belief that in all these other levels or realms of experience we will rediscover the fundamental structures of perceptual consciousness, but transformed and enriched and therefore qualitatively irreducible to perception *as such*. But though there are "many ways for consciousness to be conscious," as he says in a famous phrase,[7] we *never* completely escape from the realm of perceptual reality, and even the seemingly independent structures of categorial thought (of "rationality") are ultimately founded in perception. We are always immersed in the world and perceptually present to it.

This is Merleau-Ponty's *thesis* of the primacy of perception. It is not a dogmatic *doctrine* which he has fully *demonstrated,* but a program of phenomenological research which he left incomplete at his death. He spoke more than once of the "immense task"[8] which faced him of showing that "ideal truth" was founded in "perceived truth"—that the idea of truth itself is an "ideal" implied in the least perception and is not the free creation or independent intuition of a "pure," fully-reflexive consciousness detached from the real world of perceptual experience. In attacking this "task" Merleau-Ponty undertook a vast phenomenology of expression, particularly artistic expression, of which only fragments, like "Eye and Mind" in this volume, were completed at his death. His ideas on history and culture, examples of which are also included in this volume, remained much more embryonic and incomplete, and the other realms of experience were approached only indirectly or not at all.

Another way of approaching the underlying intention of Merleau-Ponty's philosophical program would be to compare it with that of his major predecessors in phenomenology. He claims to be continuing the project begun by Edmund Husserl, particularly the *Rückgang auf die Lebenswelt*[9] of Husserl's later writings. In his course on "Phenomenology and the Sciences of Man," included in this volume, Merleau-Ponty gives a good presentation of his position vis-à-vis Husserl. He admits going beyond Husserl but claims to be developing Husserlian phenomenology in the direction which Husserl's own "maturing" thought had led him toward the end of his life.[10] The major difference

---

7. *Phenomenology of Perception, op. cit.,* p. 124.
8. "The Primacy of Perception," below, p. 20.
9. Cf. especially *Erfahrung und Urteil* (Hamburg, 1954), pp. 38 ff.
10. That Merleau-Ponty's interpretation of Husserl has been and will continue to be contested is beyond doubt. Maurice Natanson has spoken of this and similar interpretations of Husserl's later work in terms of "the myth of the *Lebenswelt.*" For a fuller discussion of this controversy in recent American philosophy, see my article, "Recent Developments in Phenomenology" in *American Philosophical Quarterly,* April, 1964. Herbert Spiegelberg has pointed out that some of the citations and doctrines Merleau-Ponty professes to find in Husserl's later writings have not been discovered by anyone else, as, for instance, his quotation "Transcendental subjec-

between Husserl and Merleau-Ponty is that, whereas Husserl spent most of his life elaborating a phenomenology of reason and categorial thought and only then turned to perceptual consciousness as the foundational mode of experience, Merleau-Ponty begins with perception and, in his published works, does no more than pose the problem of a phenomenology of rationality. His project to write a volume entitled *L'Origine de la vérité* was never completed. To what extent he can claim to be a true and authentic continuator of Husserlian phenomenology is thus a question which has only begun to be posed. Certainly it cannot be answered satisfactorily except through a development and continuation of his own project.

At first glance Merleau-Ponty would seem much closer to Heidegger, especially to the Heidegger of *Sein und Zeit*, than to any other major phenomenologist, and they clearly agree on the unitary character of "human reality" as a world-directed, active intentionality in whose experience the world is constituted as the human life-world. But what radically separates Merleau-Ponty's "existential analysis" from Heidegger's is precisely his thesis of the primacy of perception, and his acceptance of the perceived world as the primary reality, as giving us the first and truest sense of "real." For Heidegger, on the contrary, it is not this world but the Being of beings which is the primary reality, and any analysis of human experience, perceptual or otherwise, is only a means to pose the more fundamental question of this Being. Heidegger's "thought of Being" escapes the methods of phenomenology altogether and certainly has nothing whatever to do with perceptual consciousness.

Finally, throughout his writings, Merleau-Ponty's chief, though usually silent, interlocutor is his lifelong friend-enemy, Jean-Paul Sartre. Sartre's radical dichotomization of reality into being-in-itself and being-for-itself poses the fundamentally insoluble problem of the dialectical (or "ambiguous") interrelations which *in fact* pertain between consciousness and the world, between consciousness and the body. Even more than Husserl, Sartre conceives of consciousness as "pure" consciousness, utterly independent of being, absolutely free, without content or structure. It was against this view that Merleau-Ponty developed his philosophy of the "incarnate *cogito*" whose most fundamental behavior is precisely the perceptual constitution of a world of which it is nevertheless always a part and participant. To the interpretation and

---

tivity is an intersubjectivity," which appears in this volume (cf. below, p. 51), in *Phenomenology of Perception*, and in other places. (Cf. Herbert Spiegelberg, *The Phenomenological Movement*, II, The Hague, 1960, p. 517, note.) Philosophically speaking, of course, the fidelity of Merleau-Ponty to Husserl's ultimate intentions is not necessarily decisive; his own direction could very well be a more fruitful one, even if it could be shown that it has no basis in Husserl at all.

criticism of Husserl which Sartre first elaborated in *The Transcendence of the Ego* and consistently followed in his later works, Merleau-Ponty opposes the interpretation of Husserl as the philosopher of the *Lebenswelt*.

It is because of Sartre and Merleau-Ponty that Husserlian phenomenology has become the dominant philosophical influence in postwar French philosophy and is now beginning to exercise an even broader influence. The fact that their interpretations of Husserl's thought and intentions are almost diametrically opposed serves to point up the antinomies which face present-day phenomenologists. The working-out of these (and other) conflicting interpretations of Husserl's thought is a task to which Merleau-Ponty will make no further contribution. It is his own philosophical progeny who will have to work out the internal logic of his thesis of the primacy of perception. Whether this effort will ultimately end in a series of retreats, redefinitions, and an ultimate failure similar to that of contemporary positivism, or whether it will lead to the elaboration of phenomenologies of the other realms of experience which Merleau-Ponty envisaged, and thus to a full development and "demonstration" of his thesis, is a question which will be answered only in the future. It is hoped that this English translation of these important chapters from Merleau-Ponty's corpus will help clarify this question and this challenge and bring it to the attention of American philosophers.

JAMES M. EDIE

Northwestern University

PART I

Questions of Epistemology and Method
Phenomenological Psychology

1 / An Unpublished Text by Maurice Merleau-Ponty: A Prospectus of His Work[1]

Translated by Arleen B. Dallery

WE NEVER CEASE LIVING in the world of perception, but we go beyond it in critical thought—almost to the point of forgetting the contribution of perception to our idea of truth. For critical thought encounters only *bare propositions* which it discusses, accepts or rejects. Critical thought has broken with the naive evidence of *things,* and when it affirms, it is because it no longer finds any means of denial. However necessary this activity of verification may be, specifying criteria and demanding from our experience its credentials of validity, it is not aware of our contact with the perceived world which is simply there before us, beneath the level of the verified true and the false. Nor does critical thought even define the positive steps of thinking or its most valid accomplishments.

My first two works sought to restore the world of perception. My works in preparation aim to show how communication with others, and thought, take up and go beyond the realm of perception which initiated us to the truth.

The perceiving mind is an incarnated mind. I have tried, first of all, to re-establish the roots of the mind in its body and in its world, going against doctrines which treat perception as a simple result of the action of external things on our body as well as against those which

1. "Un inédit de Maurice Merleau-Ponty," *Revue de métaphysique et de morale,* no. 4 (1962), 401–409. This text was preceded by the following "Introductory Note" signed by Martial Gueroult: "The text given below was sent to me by Merleau-Ponty at the time of his candidacy to the Collège de France, when I was putting together a report of his qualifications for presentation to the assembly of professors. In this report Merleau-Ponty traces his past and future as a philosopher in a continuous line, and outlines the perspectives of his future studies from *L'Origine de la vérité* to *L'Homme transcendental.* In reading these unpublished and highly interesting pages, one keenly regrets the death which brutally interrupted the élan of a profound thought in full possession of itself and about to fulfill itself in a series of original works which would have been landmarks in contemporary French philosophy."

insist on the autonomy of consciousness. These philosophies commonly forget—in favor of a pure exteriority or of a pure interiority—the insertion of the mind in corporeality, the ambiguous relation which we entertain with our body and, correlatively, with perceived things. When one attempts, as I have in *The Structure of Behavior*, to trace out, on the basis of modern psychology and physiology, the relationships which obtain between the perceiving organism and its milieu one clearly finds that they are not those of an automatic machine which needs an outside agent to set off its pre-established mechanisms. And it is equally clear that one does not account for the facts by superimposing a pure, contemplative consciousness on a thinglike body. In the conditions of life—if not in the laboratory—the organism is less sensitive to certain isolated physical and chemical agents than to the constellation which they form and to the whole situation which they define. Behaviors reveal a sort of prospective activity in the organism, as if it were oriented toward the meaning of certain elementary situations, as if it entertained familiar relations with them, as if there were an "*a priori* of the organism," privileged conducts and laws of internal equilibrium which predisposed the organism to certain relations with its milieu. At this level there is no question yet of a real self-awareness or of intentional activity. Moreover, the organism's prospective capability is exercised only within defined limits and depends on precise, local conditions.

The functioning of the central nervous system presents us with similar paradoxes. In its modern forms, the theory of cerebral localizations has profoundly changed the relation of function to substrate. It no longer assigns, for instance, a pre-established mechanism to each perceptual behavior. "Coordinating centers" are no longer considered as storehouses of "cerebral traces," and their functioning is qualitatively different from one case to another, depending on the chromatic nuance to be evoked and the perceptual structure to be realized. Finally, this functioning reflects all the subtlety and all the variety of perceptual relationships.

The perceiving organism seems to show us a Cartesian mixture of the soul with the body. Higher-order behaviors give a new meaning to the life of the organism, but the mind here disposes of only a limited freedom; it needs simpler activities in order to stabilize itself in durable institutions and to realize itself truly as mind. Perceptual behavior emerges from these relations to a situation and to an environment which are not the workings of a pure, knowing subject.

In my work on the *Phenomenology of Perception* we are no longer present at the emergence of perceptual behaviors; rather we install ourselves in them in order to pursue the analysis of this exceptional relation between the subject and its body and its world. For contemporary psychology and psychopathology the body is no longer merely *an object in the world,* under the purview of a separated spirit. It is on the side of the subject; it is our *point of view on the world,* the place where the spirit takes on a certain physical and historical situation. As Descartes once said profoundly, the soul is not merely in the body like a pilot in his ship; it is wholly intermingled with the body. The body, in turn, is wholly animated, and all its functions contribute to the perception of objects—an activity long considered by philosophy to be pure knowledge.

We grasp external space through our bodily situation. A "corporeal or postural schema" gives us at every moment a global, practical, and implicit notion of the relation between our body and things, of our hold on them. A system of possible movements, or "motor projects," radiates from us to our environment. Our body is not in space like things; it inhabits or haunts space. It applies itself to space like a hand to an instrument, and when we wish to move about we do not move the body as we move an object. We transport it without instruments as if by magic, since it is ours and because through it we have direct access to space. For us the body is much more than an instrument or a means; it is our expression in the world, the visible form of our intentions. Even our most secret affective movements, those most deeply tied to the humoral infrastructure, help to shape our perception of things.

Now if perception is thus the common act of all our motor and affective functions, no less than the sensory, we must rediscover the structure of the perceived world through a process similar to that of an archaeologist. For the structure of the perceived world is buried under the sedimentations of later knowledge. Digging down to the perceived world, we see that sensory qualities are not opaque, indivisible "givens," which are simply exhibited to a remote consciousness—a favorite idea of classical philosophy. We see too that colors (each surrounded by an affective atmosphere which psychologists have been able to study and define) are themselves different modalities of our co-existence with the world. We also find that spatial forms or distances are not so much relations between different points in objective space as they are relations between these points and a central perspective—our body. In short, these relations are different ways for external stimuli to test, to solicit, and to vary our grasp on the world, our horizontal and vertical anchorage in a place and in a here-and-now. We find that perceived things, unlike geometrical objects, are not bounded entities whose laws of construction we possess *a priori,* but that they are open, inexhaustible systems which we recognize through a certain style of development, although we are never able, in principle, to explore them entirely, and even though they never give us more than profiles and perspectival views of themselves. Finally, we find that the perceived world, in its turn, is not a pure object of thought without fissures or lacunae; it is, rather, like a universal style shared in by all perceptual beings. While the world no doubt co-ordinates these perceptual beings, we can never presume that its work is finished. Our world, as Malebranche said, is an "unfinished task."

If we now wish to characterize a subject capable of this perceptual experience, it obviously will not be a self-transparent thought, absolutely present to itself without the interference of its body and its history. The perceiving subject is not this absolute thinker; rather, it functions according to a natal pact between our body and the world, between ourselves and our body. Given a perpetually new natural and historical situation to control, the perceiving subject undergoes a continued birth; at each instant it is something new. Every incarnate subject is like an open notebook in which we do not yet know what will be written. Or it is like a new language; we do not know what works it will accomplish but only that, once it has appeared, it cannot fail to say little or much, to have a history and a meaning. The very productivity or freedom of human life, far from denying our situation, utilizes it and turns it into a means of expression.

This remark brings us to a series of further studies which I have undertaken since 1945 and which will definitively fix the philosophical significance of my earlier works while they, in turn, determine the route and the method of these later studies.

I found in the experience of the perceived world a new type of relation between the mind and truth. The evidence of the perceived thing lies in its concrete aspect, in the very texture of its qualities, and in the equivalence among all its sensible properties—which caused Cézanne to say that one should be able to paint even odors. Before our undivided existence the world is true; it exists. The unity, the articulations of both are intermingled. We experience in it a truth which shows through and envelops us rather than being held and circumscribed by our mind.

Now if we consider, above the perceived world, the field of knowledge properly so called—i.e., the field in which the mind seeks to possess the truth, to define its objects itself, and thus to attain to a universal wisdom, not tied to the particularities of our situation—we must ask: Does not the realm of the perceived world take on the form of a simple appearance? Is not pure understanding a new source of knowledge, in comparison with which our perceptual familiarity with the world is only a rough, unformed sketch? We are obliged to answer these questions first with a theory of truth and then with a theory of intersubjectivity, both of which I have already touched upon in essays such as "Le doute de Cézanne," "Le Roman et la métaphysique," [2] and, on the philosophy of history, in *Humanisme et terreur* [1947]. But the philosophical foundations of these essays are still to be rigorously elaborated. I am now working on two books dealing with a theory of truth.

It seems to me that knowledge and the communication with others which it presupposes not only are original formations with respect to the perceptual life but also they preserve and continue our perceptual life even while transforming it. Knowledge and communication sublimate rather than suppress our incarnation, and the characteristic operation of the mind is in the movement by which we recapture our corporeal existence and use it to symbolize instead of merely to coexist. This metamorphosis lies in the double function of our body. Through its "sensory fields" and its whole organization the body is, so to speak, predestined to model itself on the natural aspects of the world. But as an active body capable of gestures, of expression, and finally of language, it turns back on the world to signify it. As the observation of apraxics shows, there is in man, superimposed upon actual space with its self-identical points, a "virtual space" in which the spatial values that a point *would receive* (for any other position of our corporal co-ordinates) are also recognized. A system of correspondence is established between our spatial situation and that of others, and each one comes to symbolize all the others. This insertion of our factual situation as a particular case within the system of other possible situations begins as soon as we *designate* a point in space with our finger. For this pointing gesture, which animals do not understand, supposes that we are already installed in virtual space—at the end of the line prolonging our finger in a centrifugal and cultural space. This mimic usage of our body is not yet a conception, since it does not cut us off from our corporeal situation; on the contrary, it assumes all its meaning. It leads us to a concrete theory of the mind which will show the mind in a relationship of reciprocal exchange with the instruments which it uses, but uses only while rendering to them what it has received from them, and more.

In a general way expressive gestures (in which the science of physiognomy sought in vain for the sufficient signs of emotional states) have a univocal meaning only with respect to the situation which they underline and punctuate. But like phonemes, which have no meaning by themselves, expressive gestures have a diacritical value: they announce the constitution of a symbolical system capable of redesigning an infinite number of situations. They are a first language. And re-

2. These are the first two essays in *Sens et non-sens* (Paris, 1948).—*Trans.*

ciprocally language can be treated as a gesticulation so varied, so precise, so systematic, and capable of so many convergent expressions [*recoupements*] that the internal structure of an utterance can ultimately agree only with the mental situation to which it responds and of which it becomes an unequivocal sign. The meaning of language, like that of gestures, thus does not lie in the elements composing it. The meaning is their common intention, and the spoken phrase is understood only if the hearer, following the "verbal chain," goes beyond each of its links in the direction that they all designate together.

It follows that even solitary thought does not cease using the language which supports it, rescues it from the transitory, and throws it back again. Cassirer said that thought was the "shuttlecock" of language. It also follows that perhaps, taken piece by piece, language does not yet contain its meaning, that all communication supposes in the listener a creative re-enactment of what is heard. Language leads us to a thought which is no longer ours alone, to a thought which is presumptively universal, though this is never the universality of a pure concept which would be identical for every mind. It is rather the call which a situated thought addresses to other thoughts, equally situated, and each one responds to the call with its own resources. An examination of the domain of algorithm would show there too, I believe, the same strange function which is at work in the so-called inexact forms of language. Especially when it is a question of conquering a new domain for exact thought, the most formal thought is always referred to some qualitatively defined mental situation from which it extracts a meaning only by applying itself to the configuration of the problem. The transformation is never a simple analysis, and thought is never more than relatively formal.

Since I intend to treat this problem more fully in my work *L'Origine de la vérité*, I have approached it less directly in a partially written book dealing with literary language. In this area it is easier to show that language is never the mere clothing of a thought which otherwise possesses itself in full clarity. The meaning of a book is given, in the first instance, not so much by its ideas as by a systematic and unexpected variation of the modes of language, of narrative, or of existing literary forms. This accent, this particular modulation of speech—if the expression is successful—is assimilated little by little by the reader, and it gives him access to a thought to which he was until then indifferent or even opposed. Communication in literature is not the simple appeal on the part of the writer to meanings which would be part of an *a priori* of the mind; rather, communication arouses these meanings in the mind through enticement and a kind of oblique action. The writer's thought does not control his language from without; the writer is himself a kind of new idiom, constructing itself, inventing ways of expression, and diversifying itself according to its own meaning. Perhaps poetry is only that part of literature where this autonomy is ostentatiously displayed. All great prose is also a re-creation of the signifying instrument, henceforth manipulated according to a new syntax. Prosaic writing, on the other hand, limits itself to using, through accepted signs, the meanings already accepted in a given culture. Great prose is the art of capturing a meaning which until then had never been objectified and of rendering it accessible to everyone who speaks the same language. When a writer is no longer capable of thus founding a new universality and of taking the risk of communicating, he has outlived his time. It seems to me that we can also say of other institutions that they have ceased to live when they show themselves incapable of carrying on a poetry of human relations—that is, the call of each individual freedom to all the others.

Hegel said that the Roman state was the prose of the world. I shall entitle my book *Introduction à la prose du monde*.[3] In this work I shall elaborate the category of prose beyond the confines of literature to give it a sociological meaning.

For these studies on expression and truth approach, from the epistemological side, the general problem of human interrelations—which will be the major topic of my later studies. The linguistic relations among men should help us understand the more general order of symbolic relations and of institutions, which assure the exchange not only of thoughts but of all types of values, the co-existence of men within a culture and, beyond it, within a single history. Interpreted in terms of symbolism, the concept of history seems to escape the disputes always directed to it because one ordinarily means by this word— whether to accept it or to reject it—an external Power in the name of which men would be dispossessed of consciousness. History is no more external to us than language. There *is* a history of thought: the succession of the works of the spirit (no matter how many detours we see in it) is really a single experience which develops of itself and in whose development, so to speak, truth capitalizes itself.[4] In an analogous sense we can say that there is a history of humanity or, more simply, *a* humanity. In other words, granting all the periods of stagnation and retreat, human relations are able to grow, to change their avatars into lessons, to pick out the truth of their past in the present, to eliminate certain mysteries which render them opaque and thereby make themselves more translucent.

3. This work was never published as such, though some of the studies it occasioned are the basis of the early chapters of *Signes* (Paris, 1960).—*Trans.*
4. That is, truth becomes Truth by "building up its capital."—*Trans.*

The idea of a single history or of a logic of history is, in a sense, implied in the least human exchange, in the least social perception. For example, anthropology supposes that civilizations very different from ours are comprehensible to us, that they can be situated in relation to ours and vice-versa, that all civilizations belong to the same universe of thought, since the least use of language implies an idea of truth. Also we can never pretend to dismiss the adventures of history as something foreign to our present action, since even the most independent search for the most abstract truth has been and is a factor of history (the only one, perhaps, that we are sure is not disappointing). All human acts and all human creations constitute a single drama, and in this sense we are all saved or lost together. Our life is essentially universal.

But this methodological rationalism is not to be confused with a dogmatic rationalism which eliminates historical contingency in advance by supposing a "World Spirit" (Hegel) behind the course of events. If it is necessary to say that there is a total history, a single tissue tying together all the enterprises of simultaneous and successive civilizations, all the results of thought and all the facts of economics, it must not be in the guise of a historical idealism or materialism—one handing over the government of history to thought; the other, to matter. Because cultures are just so many coherent systems of symbols and because in each culture the modes of work, of human relations, of language and thought, even if not parallel at every moment, do not long remain separated, cultures can be compared and placed under a common denominator. What makes this connection of meaning between each aspect of a culture and all the rest, as between all the episodes of history, is the permanent, harmonious thought of this plurality of beings who recognize one another as "semblables," even when some seek to enslave others, and who are so commonly situated that adversaries are often in a kind of complicity.

Our inquiries should lead us finally to a reflection on this *transcendental man,* or this "natural light" common to all, which appears through the movement of history—to a reflection on this Logos which gives us the task of vocalizing a hitherto mute world. Finally, they should lead us to a study of the Logos of the perceived world which we encountered in our earliest studies in the evidence of things. Here we rejoin the classical questions of metaphysics, but by following a route which removes from them their character as *problems*—that is to say, as difficulties which could be solved cheaply through the use of a few metaphysical entities constructed for this purpose. The notions of Nature and Reason, for instance, far from explaining the metamorphoses which we have observed from perception up to the more complex modes of human exchange, make them incomprehensible. For by relating them to separated principles, these notions mask a constantly experienced moment, the moment when an existence becomes aware of itself, grasps itself, and expresses its own meaning.

The study of perception could only teach us a "bad ambiguity," a mixture of finitude and universality, of interiority and exteriority. But there is a "good ambiguity" in the phenomenon of expression, a spontaneity which accomplishes what appeared to be impossible when we observed only the separate elements, a spontaneity which gathers together the plurality of monads, the past and the present, nature and culture into a single whole. To establish this wonder would be metaphysics itself and would at the same time give us the principle of an ethics.

2 / The Primacy of Perception

and Its Philosophical Consequences[1]

Translated by James M. Edie

PRELIMINARY SUMMARY OF THE ARGUMENT

1. *Perception as an original modality of consciousness*

THE UNPREJUDICED STUDY of perception by psychologists has finally revealed that the perceived world is not a sum of objects (in the sense in which the sciences use this word), that our relation to the world is not that of a thinker to an object of thought, and finally that the unity of the perceived thing, as perceived by several consciousnesses, is not comparable to the unity of a proposition [*théorème*], as understood by several thinkers, any more than perceived existence is comparable to ideal existence.

As a result we cannot apply the classical distinction of form and matter to perception, nor can we conceive the perceiving subject as a consciousness which "interprets," "deciphers," or "orders" a sensible matter according to an ideal law which it possesses. Matter is "pregnant" with its form, which is to say that in the final analysis every perception takes place within a certain horizon and ultimately in the "world." We experience a perception and its horizon "in action" [*pratiquement*] rather than by "posing" them or explicitly "knowing" them. Finally the quasi-organic relation of the perceiving subject and the

1. This address to the Société française de philosophie was given shortly after the publication of Merleau-Ponty's major work, the *Phenomenology of Perception*, and it represents his attempt to summarize and defend the central thesis of that work. The following translation gives the complete text of Merleau-Ponty's address and the discussion which followed it, with the exception of a few incidental remarks unrelated to the substance of the discussion. These minimal omissions are indicated by the insertion of suspension points in the text. The discussion took place on November 23, 1946, and was published in the *Bulletin de la société française de philosophie*, vol. 49 (December, 1947), pp. 119–53.—*Trans.*

world involves, in principle, the contradiction of immanence and transcendence.

2. The generalization of these results

Do THESE RESULTS have any value beyond that of psychological description? They would not if we could superimpose on the perceived world a world of ideas. But in reality the ideas to which we recur are valid only for a period of our lives or for a period in the history of our culture. Evidence is never apodictic, nor is thought timeless, though there is some progress in objectification and thought is always valid for more than an instant. The certainty of ideas is not the foundation of the certainty of perception but is, rather, based on it—in that it is perceptual experience which gives us the passage from one moment to the next and thus realizes the unity of time. In this sense all consciousness is perceptual, even the consciousness of ourselves.

3. Conclusions

THE PERCEIVED WORLD is the always presupposed foundation of all rationality, all value and all existence. This thesis does not destroy either rationality or the absolute. It only tries to bring them down to earth.

REPORT OF THE SESSION

. . . .

M. Merleau-Ponty. The point of departure for these remarks is that the perceived world comprises relations and, in a general way, a type of organization which has not been recognized by classical psychology and philosophy.

If we consider an object which we perceive but one of whose sides we do not see, or if we consider objects which are not within our visual field at this moment—i.e., what is happening behind our back or what is happening in America or at the South Pole—how should we describe the existence of these absent objects or the nonvisible parts of present objects?

Should we say, as psychologists have often done, that I *represent* to myself the sides of this lamp which are not seen? If I say these sides are representations, I imply that they are not grasped as actually existing; because what is represented is not here before us, I do not actually perceive it. It is only a possible. But since the unseen sides of this lamp are not imaginary, but only hidden from view (to see them it suffices to move the lamp a little bit), I cannot say that they are representations.

Should I say that the unseen sides are somehow anticipated by me, as perceptions which would be produced necessarily if I moved, given the structure of the object? If, for example, I look at a cube, knowing the structure of the cube as it is defined in geometry, I can anticipate the perceptions which this cube will give me while I move around it. Under this hypothesis I would know the unseen side as the necessary consequence of a certain law of the development of my perception. But if I turn to perception itself, I cannot interpret it in this way because this analysis can be formulated as follows: It is *true* that the lamp has a back, that the cube has another side. But this formula, "It is true," does not correspond to what is given to me in perception. Perception does not give me truths like geometry but presences.

I grasp the unseen side as present, and I do not affirm that the back of the lamp exists in the same sense that I say the solution of a problem exists. The hidden side is present in its own way. It is in my vicinity.

Thus I should not say that the unseen sides of objects are simply possible perceptions, nor that they are the necessary conclusions of a kind of analysis or geometrical reasoning. It is not through an intellectual synthesis which would freely posit the total object that I am led from what is given to what is not actually given; that I am given, together with the visible sides of the object, the nonvisible sides as well. It is, rather, a kind of practical synthesis: I can touch the lamp, and not only the side turned toward me but also the other side; I have only to extend my hand to hold it.

The classical analysis of perception reduces all our experience to the single level of what, for good reasons, is judged to be true. But when, on the contrary, I consider the whole setting [*l'entourage*] of my perception, it reveals another modality which is neither the ideal and necessary being of geometry nor the simple sensory event, the *"percipi,"* and this is precisely what remains to be studied now.

But these remarks on the setting [*entourage*] of what is perceived enable us better to see the perceived itself. I perceive before me a road or a house, and I perceive them as having a certain dimension: the road may be a country road or a national highway; the house may be a shanty or a manor. These identifications presuppose that I recognize the true size of the object, quite different from that which appears to me from the point at which I am standing. It is frequently said that I restore the true size on the basis of the apparent size by analysis and conjecture. This is inexact for the very convincing reason that the apparent size of which we are speaking is not perceived by me. It is a remarkable fact that the uninstructed have no awareness of perspective and that it took a long time and much reflection for men to become aware of a perspectival deformation of objects. Thus there is no deciphering, no mediate inference from the sign to what is signified, because the alleged signs are not given to me separately from what they signify.

In the same way it is not true that I deduce the true color of an object on the basis of the color of the setting or of the lighting, which most of the time is not perceived. At this hour, since daylight is still coming through the windows, we perceive the yellowness of the artificial light, and it alters the color of objects. But when daylight disappears this yellowish color will no longer be perceived, and we will see the objects more or less in their true colors. The true color thus is not deduced, taking account of the lighting, because it appears precisely when daylight disappears.

If these remarks are true, what is the result? And how should we understand this "I perceive" which we are attempting to grasp?

We observe at once that it is impossible, as has often been said, to decompose a perception, to make it into a collection of sensations, because in it the whole is prior to the parts—and this whole is not an ideal whole. The meaning which I ultimately discover is not of the conceptual order. If it were a concept, the question would be how I can recognize it in the sense data, and it would be necessary for me to interpose between the concept and the sense data certain intermediaries, and then other intermediaries between these intermediaries, and so on. It is necessary that meaning and signs, the form and matter of perception, be related from the beginning and that, as we say, the matter of perception be "pregnant with its form."

In other words, the synthesis which constitutes the unity of the perceived objects and which gives meaning to the perceptual data is not an intellectual synthesis. Let us say with Husserl that it is a "synthesis of transition" [*synthèse de transition*] [2]—I anticipate the unseen side of the lamp because I can touch it—or a "horizonal synthesis" [*synthèse d'horizon*]—the unseen side is given to me as "visible from another standpoint," at once given but only immanently. What prohibits me from treating my perception as an intellectual act is that an intellectual act would grasp the object either as possible or as necessary. But in perception it is "real"; it is given as the infinite sum of an indefinite series of perspectival views in each of which the object is given but in none of which is it given exhaustively. It is not acci-

2. The more usual term in Husserl is "passive synthesis," which designates the "syntheses" of perceptual consciousness as opposed to the "active syntheses" of imagination and categorial thought.—*Trans.*

dental for the object to be given to me in a "deformed" way, from the point of view [place] which I occupy. That is the price of its being "real." The perceptual synthesis thus must be accomplished by the subject, which can both delimit certain perspectival aspects in the object, the only ones actually given, and at the same time go beyond them. This subject, which takes a point of view, is my body as the field of perception and action [pratique]—in so far as my gestures have a certain reach and circumscribe as my domain the whole group of objects familiar to me. Perception is here understood as a reference to a whole which can be grasped, in principle, only through certain of its parts or aspects. The perceived thing is not an ideal unity in the possession of the intellect, like a geometrical notion, for example; it is rather a totality open to a horizon of an indefinite number of perspectival views which blend with one another according to a given style, which defines the object in question.

Perception is thus paradoxical. The perceived thing itself is paradoxical; it exists only in so far as someone can perceive it. I cannot even for an instant imagine an object in itself. As Berkeley said, if I attempt to imagine some place in the world which has never been seen, the very fact that I imagine it makes me present at that place. I thus cannot conceive a perceptible place in which I am not myself present. But even the places in which I find myself are never completely given to me; the things which I see are things for me only under the condition that they always recede beyond their immediately given aspects. Thus there is a paradox of immanence and transcendence in perception. Immanence, because the perceived object cannot be foreign to him who perceives; transcendence, because it always contains something more than what is actually given. And these two elements of perception are not, properly speaking, contradictory. For if we reflect on this notion of perspective, if we reproduce the perceptual experience in our thought, we see that the kind of evidence proper to the perceived, the appearance of "something," requires both this presence and this absence.

Finally, the world itself, which (to give a first, rough definition) is the totality of perceptible things and the thing of all things, must be understood not as an object in the sense the mathematician or the physicist give to this word—that is, a kind of unified law which would cover all the partial phenomena or as a fundamental relation verifiable in all—but as the universal style of all possible perceptions. We must make this notion of the world, which guides the whole transcendental deduction of Kant, though Kant does not tell us its provenance, more explicit. "If a world is to be possible," he says sometimes, as if he were thinking before the origin of the world, as if he were assisting at its genesis and could pose its *a priori* conditions. In fact, as Kant himself said profoundly, we can only think the world because we have already experienced it; it is through this experience that we have the idea of being, and it is through this experience that the words "rational" and "real" receive a meaning simultaneously.

If I now consider not the problem of knowing how it is that there are things for me or how it is that I have a unified, unique, and developing perceptual experience of them, but rather the problem of knowing how my experience is related to the experience which others have of the same objects, perception will again appear as the paradoxical phenomenon which renders being accessible to us.

If I consider my perceptions as simple sensations, they are private; they are mine alone. If I treat them as acts of the intellect, if perception is an inspection of the mind, and the perceived object an idea, then you and I are talking about the same world, and we have *the right* to communicate among ourselves because the world has become an ideal existence and is the same for all of us—just like the Pythagorean theorem. But neither of these two formulas accounts for our experience. If a friend and I are standing before a landscape, and if I attempt to show my friend something which I see and which he does not yet see, we cannot account for the situation by saying that I see something in my own world and that I attempt, by sending verbal messages, to give rise to an analogous perception in the world of my friend. There are not two numerically distinct worlds plus a mediating language which alone would bring us together. There is—and I know it very well if I become impatient with him—a kind of demand that what I see be seen by him also. And at the same time this communication is required by the very thing which I am looking at, by the reflections of sunlight upon it, by its color, by its sensible evidence. The thing imposes itself not as true for every intellect, but as real for every subject who is standing where I am.

I will never know how you see red, and you will never know how I see it; but this separation of consciousnesses is recognized only after a failure of communication, and our first movement is to believe in an undivided being between us. There is no reason to treat this primordial communication as an illusion, as the sensationalists do, because even then it would become inexplicable. And there is no reason to base it on our common participation in the same intellectual consciousness because this would suppress the undeniable plurality of consciousnesses. It is thus necessary that, in the perception of another, I find myself in relation with another "myself," who is, in principle, open to the same truths as I am, in relation to the same being that I am. And this perception is realized. From the depths of my subjectivity I see another subjectivity invested with equal rights appear, because the behavior of the other takes place within my perceptual field. I understand this behavior, the words of another; I espouse his thought because this other, born in the midst of my phenomena, appropriates them and treats them in accord with typical behaviors which I myself have experienced. Just as my body, as the system of all my holds on the world, founds the unity of the objects which I perceive, in the same way the body of the other—as the bearer of symbolic behaviors and of the behavior of true reality—tears itself away from being one of my phenomena, offers me the task of a true communication, and confers on my objects the new dimension of intersubjective being or, in other words, of objectivity. Such are, in a quick résumé, the elements of a description of the perceived world.

Some of our colleagues who were so kind as to send me their observations in writing grant me that all this is valid as a psychological inventory. But, they add, there remains the world of which we say "It is true"—that is to say, the world of knowledge, the verified world, the world of science. Psychological description concerns only a small section of our experience, and there is no reason, according to them, to give such descriptions any universal value. They do not touch being itself but only the psychological peculiarities of perception. These descriptions, they add, are all the less admissible as being in any way definitive because they are contradicted by the perceived world. How can we admit ultimate contradictions? Perceptual experience is contradictory because it is confused. It is necessary to think it. When we think it, its contradictions disappear under the light of the intellect. Finally, one correspondent tells me that we are invited to return to the perceived world as we experience it. That is to say that there is no need to reflect or to think and that perception knows better than we what it is doing. How can this disavowal of reflection be philosophy?

It is true that we arrive at contradictions when we describe the perceived world. And it is also true that if there were such a thing as a non-contradictory thought, it would exclude the world of perception as a simple appearance. But the question is precisely to know whether there is such a thing as logically coherent thought or thought in the pure state. This is the question Kant asked himself and the objection which I have just sketched is a pre-Kantian objection. One of Kant's discoveries, whose consequences we have not yet fully grasped, is that all our experience of the world is throughout a tissue of concepts which lead to irreducible contradictions if we attempt to take them in an absolute sense or transfer them into pure being, and that they nevertheless found the structure of all our phenomena, of everything which *is* for us. It would take too long to show (and besides it is well known) that Kantian philosophy itself failed to utilize this principle fully and that both its investigation of experience and its critique of dogmatism remained incomplete. I wish only to point out that the accusation of contradiction is not decisive, *if the acknowledged contradiction appears as the very condition of consciousness.* It is in this sense that Plato and Kant, to mention only them, accepted the contradiction of which Zeno and Hume wanted no part. There is a vain form of contradiction which consists in affirming two theses which exclude one another at the same time and under the same aspect. And there are philosophies which show contradictions present at the very heart of time and of all relationships. There is the sterile non-contradiction of formal logic and the justified contradictions of transcendental logic. The objection with which we are concerned would be admissible only if we could put a system of eternal truths in the place of the perceived world, freed from its contradictions.

We willingly admit that we cannot rest satisfied with the description of the perceived world as we have sketched it up to now and that it appears as a psychological curiosity if we leave aside the idea of the true world, the world as thought by the understanding. This leads us, therefore, to the second point which I propose to examine: what is the relation between intellectual consciousness and perceptual consciousness?

Before taking this up, let us say a word about the other objection which was addressed to us: you go back to the unreflected [*irréfléchi*]; therefore you renounce reflection. It is true that we discover the unreflected. But the unreflected we go back to is not that which is prior to philosophy or prior to reflection. It is the unreflected which is understood and conquered by reflection. Left to itself, perception forgets itself and is ignorant of its own accomplishments. Far from thinking that philosophy is a useless repetition of life I think, on the contrary, that without reflection life would probably dissipate itself in ignorance of itself or in chaos. But this does not mean that reflection should be carried away with itself or pretend to be ignorant of its origins. By fleeing difficulties it would only fail in its task.

Should we now generalize and say that what is true of perception is also true in the order of the intellect and that in a general way all our experience, all our knowledge, has the same fundamental structures, the same synthesis of transition, the same kind of horizons which we have found in perceptual experience?

No doubt the absolute truth or evidence of scientific knowledge would be opposed to this idea. But it seems to me that the acquisitions of the philosophy of the sciences confirm the primacy of perception. Does not the work of the French school at the beginning of this century, and the work of Brunschvicg, show that scientific knowledge cannot be closed in on itself, that it is always an approximate knowledge, and that it consists in clarifying a pre-scientific world the analysis of which will never be finished? Physico-mathematical relations take on a physical sense only to the extent that we at the same time represent to ourselves the sensible things to which these relations ultimately apply. Brunschvicg reproached positivism for its dogmatic illusion that the law is truer than the fact. The law, he adds, is conceived exclusively to make the fact intelligible. The perceived happening can never be reabsorbed in the complex of transparent relations which the intellect constructs because of the happening. But if this is the case, philosophy is not only consciousness of these relations; it is also consciousness of the obscure element and of the "non-relational foundation" on which these relations are based. Otherwise it would shirk its task of universal clarification. When I think the Pythagorean theorem and recognize it as true, it is clear that this truth is not for this moment only. Nevertheless later progress in knowledge will show that it is not yet a final, unconditioned evidence and that, if the Pythagorean theorem and the Euclidean system once appeared as final, unconditioned evidences, that is itself the mark of a certain cultural epoch. Later developments would not annul the Pythagorean theorem but would put it back in its place as a partial, and also an abstract, truth. Thus here also we do not have a timeless truth but rather the recovery of one time by another time, just as, on the level of perception, our certainty about perceiving a given thing does not guarantee that our experience will not be contradicted, or dispense us from a fuller experience of that thing. Naturally it is necessary to establish here a difference between ideal truth and perceived truth. I do not propose to undertake this immense task just now. I am only trying to show the organic tie, so to speak, between perception and intellection. Now it is incontestable that I dominate the stream of my conscious states and even that I am unaware of their temporal succession. At the moment when I am thinking or considering an idea, I am not divided into the instants of my life. But it is also incontestable that this domination of time, which is the work of thought, is always somewhat deceiving. Can I seriously say that I will always hold the ideas I do at present—and mean it? Do I not know that in six months, in a year, even if I use more or less the same formulas to express my thoughts, they will have changed their meaning slightly? Do I not know that there is a life of ideas, as there is a meaning of everything I experience, and that every one of my most convincing thoughts will need additions and then will be, not destroyed, but at least integrated into a new unity? This is the only conception of knowledge that is scientific and not mythological.

Thus perception and thought have this much in common—that both of them have a future horizon and a past horizon and that they appear to themselves as temporal, even though they do not move at the same speed nor in the same time. We must say that at each moment our ideas express not only the truth but also our capacity to attain it at that given moment. Skepticism begins if we conclude from this that our ideas are always false. But this can only happen with reference to some idol of absolute knowledge. We must say, on the contrary, that our ideas, however limited they may be at a given moment—since they always express our contact with being and with culture—are capable of being true provided we keep them open to the field of nature and culture which they must express. And this possibility is always open to us, just because we are temporal. The idea of going straight to the essence of things is an inconsistent idea if one thinks about it. What is given is a route, an experience which gradually clarifies itself, which gradually rectifies itself and proceeds by dialogue with itself and with others. Thus what we tear away from the dispersion of instants is not an already-made reason; it is, as has always been said, a natural light, our openness to *something*. What saves us is the possibility of a new development, and our power of making even what is false, true—by thinking through our errors and replacing them within the domain of truth.

But finally, it will be objected that I grasp myself in pure reflexion, completely outside perception, and that I grasp myself not now as a perceiving subject, tied by its body to a system of things, but as a thinking subject, radically free with respect to things and with respect to the body. How is such an experience of self, of the *cogito*, possible in our perspective, and what meaning does it have?

There is a first way of understanding the *cogito*: it consists in saying that when I grasp myself I am limited to noting, so to speak, a psychic fact, "I think." This is an instantaneous constatation, and under the condition that the experience has no duration I adhere immediately to what I think and consequently cannot doubt it. This is the *cogito* of the psychologists. It is of this instantaneous *cogito* that Descartes was thinking when he said that I am certain that I exist during the whole time that I am thinking of it. Such certitude is limited to my existence and to my pure and completely naked thought. As soon as I make it specific with any particular thought, I fail, because, as Descartes explains, every particular thought uses premises not actually given. Thus the first truth, understood in this way, is the only truth. Or rather it cannot even be formulated as truth; it is experienced in the instant and in silence. The *cogito* understood in this way—in the skeptical way—does not account for our idea of truth.

There is a second way of understanding the *cogito:* as the grasping not only of the fact that I think but also of the objects which this thought intends, and as evidence not only of a private existence but also of the things which it thinks, at least as it thinks them. In this perspective the *cogito* is neither more certain than the *cogitatum,* nor does it have a different kind of certainty. Both are possessed of ideal evidence. Descartes sometimes presented the *cogito* in this way—as, for example, in the *Regulae* when he placed one's own existence (*se esse*) among the most simple evidences. This supposes that the subject is perfectly transparent for itself, like an essence, and is incompatible with the idea of the hyperbolic doubt which even reaches to essences.

But there is a third meaning of the *cogito,* the only solid one: the act of doubting in which I put in question all possible objects of my experience. This act grasps itself in its own operation [*à l'oeuvre*] and thus cannot doubt itself. The very fact of doubting obturates doubt. The certitude I have of myself is here a veritable perception: I grasp myself, not as a constituting subject which is transparent to itself, and which constitutes the totality of every possible object of thought and experience, but as a particular thought, as a thought engaged with certain objects, as a thought in act; and it is in this sense that I am certain of myself. Thought is given to itself; I somehow find myself thinking and I become aware of it. In this sense I am certain that I am thinking this or that as well as being certain that I am simply thinking. Thus I can get outside the psychological *cogito*—without, however, taking myself to be a universal thinker. I am not simply a constituted happening; I am not a universal thinker [*naturant*].[3] I am a thought which recaptures itself as already possessing an ideal of truth (which it cannot at each moment wholly account for) and which is the horizon of its operations. This thought, which *feels* itself rather than *sees* itself, which searches after clarity rather than possesses it, and which creates truth rather than finds it, is described in a formerly celebrated text of Lagneau. Should we submit to life or create it, he asked. And he answered: "Once again this question does not pertain to the domain of the intellect; we are free and, in this sense, skepticism is true. But to answer negatively is to make the world and the self unintelligible; it is to decree chaos and above all to establish it in the self. But chaos is nothing. To be or not to be, the self and everything else, we must choose" (*Cours sur l'existence de dieu*). I find here, in an author who spent his whole life reflecting on Descartes, Spinoza, and Kant, the idea—sometimes considered barbarous—of a thought which remembers it began in time and then sovereignly recaptures itself and in which fact, reason, and freedom coincide.

3. The reference is to Spinoza's *natura naturans.*—Trans.

Finally, let us ask what happens, from such a point of view, to rationality and experience, whether there can be any absolute affirmation already implied in experience.

The fact that my experiences hold together and that I experience the concordance of my own experiences with those of others is in no way compromised by what we have just said. On the contrary, this fact is put in relief, against skepticism. Something appears to me, as to anyone else, and these phenomena, which set the boundaries of everything thinkable or conceivable for us, are certain as phenomena. There is meaning. But rationality is neither a total nor an immediate guarantee. It is somehow open, which is to say that it is menaced.

Doubtless this thesis is open to two types of criticism, one from the psychological side and the other from the philosophical side.

The very psychologists who have described the perceived world as I did above, the Gestalt psychologists, have never drawn the philosophical conclusions of their description. In that respect they remain within the classical framework. Ultimately they consider the structures of the perceived world as the simple result of certain physical and physiological processes which take place in the nervous system and completely determine the *gestalten* and the experience of the *gestalten*. The organism and consciousness itself are only functions of external physical variables. Ultimately the real world is the physical world as science conceives it, and it engenders our consciousness itself.

But the question is whether Gestalt theory, after the work it has done in calling attention to the phenomena of the perceived world, can fall back on the classical notion of reality and objectivity and incorporate the world of the *gestalten* within this classical conception of reality. Without doubt one of the most important acquisitions of this theory has been its overcoming of the classical alternatives between objective psychology and introspective psychology. Gestalt psychology went beyond this alternative by showing that the object of psychology is the structure of behavior, accessible both from within and from without. In his book on the chimpanzees, Köhler applied this idea and showed that in order to describe the behavior of a chimpanzee it is necessary, in characterizing this behavior, to bring in notions such as the "melodic line" of behavior. These are anthropomorphic notions, but they can be utilized objectively because it is possible to agree on interpreting "melodic" and "non-melodic" behaviors in terms of "good solutions" and "bad solutions." The science of psychology thus is not something constructed outside the human world; it is, in fact, a property of the human world to make the distinction between the true and the false, the objective and the fictional. When, later on, Gestalt psychology tried to explain itself—in spite of its own discoveries—in terms of a scientistic or positivistic ontology, it was at the price of an internal contradiction which we have to reject.

Coming back to the perceived world as we have described it above, and basing our conception of reality on the phenomena, we do not in any way sacrifice objectivity to the interior life, as Bergson has been accused of doing. As Gestalt psychology has shown, structure, *Gestalt*, meaning are no less visible in objectively observable behavior than in the experience of ourselves—provided, of course, that objectivity is not confused with what is measurable. Is one truly objective with respect to man when he thinks he can take him as an object which can be explained as an intersection of processes and causalities? Is it not more objective to attempt to constitute a true science of human life based on the description of typical behaviors? Is it objective to apply tests to man which deal only with abstract aptitudes, or to attempt to grasp the situation of man as he is present to the world and to others by means of still more tests?

Psychology as a science has nothing to fear from a return to the perceived world, nor from a philosophy which draws out the consequences of this return. Far from hurting psychology, this attitude, on the contrary, clarifies the philosophical meaning of its discoveries. For there are not two truths; there is not an inductive psychology and an intuitive philosophy. Psychological induction is never more than the methodological means of bringing to light a certain typical behavior, and if induction includes intuition, conversely intuition does not occur in empty space. It exercises itself on the facts, on the material, on the phenomena brought to light by scientific research. There are not two kinds of knowledge, but two different degrees of clarification of the same knowledge. Psychology and philosophy are nourished by the same phenomena; it is only that the problems become more formalized at the philosophical level.

But the philosophers might say here that we are giving psychology too big a place, that we are compromising rationality by founding it on the texture of experience, as it is manifested in perceptual experience. But either the demand for an absolute rationality is only a wish, a personal preference which should not be confused with philosophy, or this point of view, to the extent that it is well-founded, satisfies it as well as, or even better than, any other. When philosophers wish to place reason above the vicissitudes of history they cannot purely and simply forget what psychology, sociology, ethnography, history, and psychiatry have taught us about the conditioning of human behavior. It would be a very romantic way of showing one's love for reason to base its reign on the disavowal of acquired knowledge. What can be validly demanded is that man never be submitted to the fate of an external nature or history and stripped of his consciousness. Now my philosophy satisfies this demand. In speaking of the primacy of perception, I have never, of course, meant to say (this would be a return to the theses of empiricism) that science, reflection, and philosophy are only transformed sensations or that values are deferred and calculated pleasures. By these words, the "primacy of perception," we mean that the experience of perception is our presence at the moment when things, truths, values are constituted for us; that perception is a nascent *logos*; that it teaches us, outside all dogmatism, the true conditions of objectivity itself; that it summons us to the tasks of knowledge and action. It is not a question of reducing human knowledge to sensation, but of assisting at the birth of this knowledge, to make it as sensible as the sensible, to recover the consciousness of rationality. This experience of rationality is lost when we take it for granted as self-evident, but is, on the contrary, rediscovered when it is made to appear against the background of non-human nature.

The work [4] which was the occasion for this paper is still, in this respect, only a preliminary study, since it hardly speaks of culture or of history. On the basis of perception—taken as a privileged realm of experience, since the perceived object is by definition present and living—this book attempts to define a method for getting closer to present and living reality, and which must then be applied to the relation of man to man in language, in knowledge, in society and religion, as it was applied in this work to man's relation to perceptible reality and with respect to man's relation to others on the level of perceptual experience. We call this level of experience "primordial"— not to assert that everything else derives from it by transformations and evolution (we have expressly said that man perceives in a way different from any animal) but rather that it reveals to us the permanent data of the problem which culture attempts to resolve. If we have not tied the subject to the determinism of an external nature and have only replaced it in the bed of the perceptible, which it transforms without ever quitting it, much less will we submit the subject to some impersonal history. History is other people; it is the interrelationships we establish with them, outside of which the realm of the ideal appears as an alibi.

This leads us . . . to draw certain conclusions from what has preceded as concerns the realm of the practical. If we admit that our life is inherent to the perceived world and the human world, even while it re-creates it and contributes to its making, then morality cannot consist in the private adherence to a system of values. Principles are mystifica-

4. The *Phenomenology of Perception.—Trans.*

tions unless they are put into practice; it is necessary that they animate our relations with others. Thus we cannot remain indifferent to the aspect in which our acts appear to others, and the question is posed whether intention suffices as moral justification. It is clear that the approval of such or such a group proves nothing, since, in looking for it, we choose our own judges—which comes down to saying that we are not yet thinking for ourselves. It is the very demand of rationality which in poses on us the need to act in such a way that our action cannot be considered by others as an act of aggression but, on the contrary, as generously meeting the other in the very particularity of a given situation. Now from the very moment when we start bringing the consequences of our actions for others into morality (and how can we avoid doing so if the universality of the act is to be anything more than a word?), it appears possible that our relations with others are involved in immorality, if perchance our perspectives are irreconcilable—if, for instance, the legitimate interests of one nation are incompatible with those of another. Nothing guarantees us that morality is possible, as Kant said in a passage which has not yet been fully understood. But even less is there any fatal assurance that morality is impossible. We observe it in an experience which is the perception of others, and, by sketching here the dangerous consequences which this position entails, we are very much aware of its difficulties—some of which we might wish to avoid. Just as the perception of a thing opens me up to being, by realizing the paradoxical synthesis of an infinity of perceptual aspects, in the same way the perception of the other founds morality by realizing the paradox of an *alter ego*, of a common situation, by placing my perspectives and my incommunicable solitude in the visual field of another and of all the others. Here as everywhere else the primacy of perception—the realization, at the very heart of our most personal experience, of a fecund contradiction which submits this experience to the regard of others—is the remedy to skepticism and pessimism. If we admit that sensibility is enclosed within itself, and if we do not seek communication with the truth and with others except on the level of a disembodied reason, then there is not much to hope for. Nothing is more pessimistic or skeptical than the famous text in which Pascal, asking himself what it is to love, remarks that one does not love a woman for her beauty, which is perishable, or for her mind, which she can lose, and then suddenly concludes: "One never loves anybody; one loves only qualities." Pascal is proceeding like the skeptic who asks *if* the world exists, remarks that the table is only a sum of sensations, the chair another sum of sensations, and finally concludes: one never sees anything; one sees only sensations.

If, on the contrary, as the primacy of perception requires, we call what we perceive "the world," and what we love "the person," there is a type of doubt concerning man, and a type of spite, which become impossible. Certainly, the world which we thus find is not absolutely reassuring. We weigh the hardihood of the love which promises beyond what it knows, which claims to be eternal when a sickness, perhaps an accident, will destroy it . . . But it is *true*, at the moment of this promise, that our love extends beyond *qualities*, beyond the body, beyond time, even though we could not love without qualities, bodies, and time. In order to safeguard the ideal unity of love, Pascal breaks human life into fragments at will and reduces the person to a discontinuous series of states. The absolute which he looks for beyond our experience is implied in it. Just as I grasp time through my present and by being present, I perceive others through my individual life, in the tension of an experience which transcends itself.

There is thus no destruction of the absolute or of rationality here, only of the absolute and the rationality separated from experience. To tell the truth, Christianity consists in replacing the separated absolute by the absolute in men. Nietzsche's idea that God is dead is already contained in the Christian idea of the death of God. God ceases to be an external object in order to mingle in human life, and this life is not simply a return to a non-temporal conclusion. God needs human history. As Malebranche said, the world is unfinished. My viewpoint differs from the Christian viewpoint to the extent that the Christian believes in another side of things where the *"renversement du pour au contre"* takes place. In my view this "reversal" takes place before our eyes. And perhaps some Christians would agree that the other side of things must already be visible in the environment in which we live. By advancing this thesis of the primacy of perception, I have less the feeling that I am proposing something completely new than the feeling of drawing out the conclusions of the work of my predecessors.

. . . .

DISCUSSION

M. Bréhier. Your paper contains not only the exposition of your ideas but also a discussion of them. You have spoken on two different points: a theory of perception and a certain philosophy. . . . I will speak to the second point, which I find the more interesting.

On the first point you have made a number of remarks of great interest. You have shown that the problem of perception should not be posed in the manner in which it is usually posed, by first presupposing objects, then a man who enters this region of objects from without, and then the relations between this man and these objects. Merleau-Ponty recognizes neither these objects nor this man, and he restricts himself to perception. And I believe he has said some very interesting things on this point, with which I am in full agreement.

But there is in M. Merleau-Ponty a philosopher, and with this philosopher we can certainly find many points of disagreement. M. Merleau-Ponty changes and inverts the ordinary meaning of what we call philosophy.

Philosophy was born of the difficulties encountered in ordinary perception [*perception vulgaire*]. It was from ordinary perception and by getting away from it that men began to philosophize. The first philosophers and Plato, our common ancestor, philosophized in this way. Far from wanting to return to an immediate perception, to a lived perception, he took his point of departure in the insufficiencies of this lived perception in order to arrive at a conception of the intelligible world which was coherent, which satisfied reason, which supposed another faculty of knowing other than perception itself.

You take up this Platonic idealism and follow a specifically reverse direction. You attempt to reintegrate it in perception, and I believe that all your difficulties lie here. These are difficulties which you yourself have indicated.

The first is a relativism which you attempt not to excuse but to explain in a manner which would satisfy the demands of our scientific and intellectual life. But I believe your explanation is insufficient, and the question I would pose is this: is not your relativism purely and simply a Protagorism? When you speak of the perception of the other, this other does not even exist, according to you, except in relation to us and in his relations with us. This is not the other as I perceive him immediately; it certainly is not an ethical other; it is not this person who suffices to himself. It is someone I posit outside myself at the same time I posit objects. Now this is very serious; the other is posited by us in the world just like other things.

But even this is not the principal difficulty. It is a question of whether philosophy consists in engaging oneself in the world, in engaging oneself in things—not to the point of identifying oneself with them, but to the point of following all their sinuosities—or of whether philosophy does not consist precisely in following a route directly contrary to this engagement.

In my view philosophy always supposes an inversion of this kind. Suppose philosophers had been phenomenologists from antiquity. I ask you this question: would our science exist now? Could you have constructed your science if Anaximenes and Anaximander had not said: this perception, we do not believe in it; the true reality is air, or fire, or (as the Pythagoreans said) number. If instead of positing these realities they had already been phenomenologists, do you think they could have created philosophy?

M. Merleau-Ponty. This hypothesis is itself impossible. Phenomenology could never have come about before all the other philosophical efforts of the rationalist tradition, nor prior to the construction of science. It measures the distance between our experience and this science. How could it ignore it? How could it precede it? Second, there have not always been phenomenologists, but there have always been skeptics who have always been accorded a place in the history of philosophy. If there had been only the Greek skeptics, or only Montaigne, or only Hume, could science have progressed? It seems to me that your objection is even more valid with respect to them.

M. Bréhier. I do not think so. Montaigne criticized reason in a manner which helped science progress.

M. Merleau-Ponty. The will to apply reason to what is taken as irrational is a progress for reason.

M. Bréhier. You do not have the right to incorporate Montaigne and Hume in your viewpoint. They followed a route completely different from yours.

M. Merleau-Ponty. Hume is one of the authors Husserl read the most. For my part, I read Montaigne and Hume very sympathetically, though I find them too timid in the return to the positive after their skeptical criticisms. The whole question is to know whether by recognizing the difficulties in the exercise of reason one is working for or against reason. You have said that Plato tried to quit perception for ideas. One could also say that he placed the movement of life in the ideas, as they are in the world—and he did it by breaking through the logic of identity, by showing that ideas transform themselves into their contraries.

M. Bréhier. To combat the rationalists you have to attribute to them a notion of reason which they do not hold.

M. Merleau-Ponty. Then I am in agreement with them.

M. Bréhier. Then your position in fact forces you to agree with them.

I would say that in the very formulation of your doctrine you destroy it. If I am exaggerating a little, I ask your pardon. In order to formulate your doctrine of perception you are obliged to say that man perceives objects, and consequently you must speak of man and objects separately. There results a fatal contradiction, which you indicate under the name of the contradiction of immanence and transcendence.

But this contradiction comes from the fact that, once you formulate your doctrine, you necessarily posit an object exterior to man. Thus your doctrine, in order not to be contradictory, must remain unformulated, only lived. But is a doctrine which is only lived still a philosophical doctrine?

M. Merleau-Ponty. Assuredly a life is not a philosophy. I thought I had indicated in passing that description is not the return to immediate experience; one never returns to immediate experience. It is only a question of whether we are to try to understand it. I believe that to attempt to express immediate experience is not to betray reason but, on the contrary, to work toward its aggrandizement.

M. Bréhier. It is to betray immediate experience.

M. Merleau-Ponty. It is to begin the effort of expression and of what is expressed; it is to accept the condition of a beginning reflection. What is encouraging in this effort is that there is no pure and absolutely unexpressed life in man; the unreflected [*irréfléchi*] comes into existence for us only through reflection. To enter into these contradictions, as you have just said, seems to me to be a part of the critical inventory of our lives as philosophers.

M. Bréhier. I see your ideas as being better expressed in literature and in painting than in philosophy. Your philosophy results in a novel. This is not a defect, but I truly believe that it results in that immediate suggestion of realities which we associate with the writings of novelists. . . .

M. Merleau-Ponty. I would like to answer briefly one of M. Bréhier's earlier remarks—namely, that it is "serious" to posit the other in his relations with us and to posit him in the world. I think that you mean to say "ethically dangerous." It was never my intention to posit the other except as an ethical subject, and I am sure I have not excluded the other as an ethical subject.

M. Bréhier. It is a consequence of your theory.

M. Merleau-Ponty. It is a consequence which you draw.

M. Bréhier. Yes.

M. Merleau-Ponty. From the simple fact that I make of morality a problem, you conclude that I deny it. But the question is posed for all of us. How do we know there is someone there before us unless we look? What do we see, first of all, but corporeal appearances? How do these automata . . . become men for me? It is not the phenomenological method which creates this problem—though it does, in my view, allow us better to solve it When Brunschvicg said that the "I" is achieved by reciprocity and it is necessary that I become able to think the other as reciprocable with me, he meant that morality is not something given but something to be created. I do not see how anyone could posit the other without the self; it is an impossibility for my experience.

M. Bréhier. The other is "reciprocable to me" by reason of a universal norm. Where is your norm?

M. Merleau-Ponty. If it is permissible to answer one question by another, I would ask: where is yours? We are all situated in an experience of the self and of others which we attempt to dominate by thought, but without ever being able to flatter ourselves that we have completely achieved this. Even when I believe I am thinking universally, if the other refuses to agree with me, I experience this universality as only a private universality (as I am verifying once more at this moment). Apart from a pure heteronomy accepted by both sides (but I do not think you meant "norm" in the sense of "heteronomy") there is no given universality; there is only a presumptive universality. We are back at the old problem: how do we reach the universal? It is a problem which has always existed in philosophy, though it has never been posed in such a radical manner as it is today because two centuries after Descartes philosophers, in spite of their professions of atheism, are still thinking on the basis of Cartesian theology. Thus these problems seem to me more or less traditional. If I have given a different impression to those who have heard this paper, it is only a question of terminology.

M. Lenoir. . . . I was impressed with the resolutely realistic attitude which you have adopted. I find no fault with this. The aftermaths of all the great social upheavals have presented a similar phenomenon. In 1920 we saw the important Anglo-American movement of neorealism; a plethora of different philosophical systems arose in the same year in the United States. There was a similar development in an even more troubled epoch, at the time Victor Cousin dictated the laws of traditional philosophy and when he attempted to lay down the fundamental attitudes of mind which determine the main lines of the various philosophical systems: materialism, idealism, skepticism, mysticism. And here you give us, with your realism, a kind of materialism in reverse. But if you apply it to the problems of perception, it is vitiated, and I agree with M. Bréhier. Your analysis is somehow paralyzed by terminological difficulties. We use, in the realm of psychology, groups of associated words which have connotations that do not go together, that do not correspond to one another. Thus alongside the real problems which are suggested by this terminology there arise false problems or deviations from the true problems. But I think that the French tradition has attempted to overcome this danger of terminology. Auguste Comte himself indicated the way out. He attempted to get away from the tendency common to ideologists, "psychologists," and phrenologists. For this psychological orientation he substituted a fundamental notion of contemporary physics—energy. The notion of energy was his starting point. He showed how all the encyclopedic divisions which attempt to classify the human attitudes called behavior should be abandoned. He returned to the classical attitude, that of Descartes, who distinguished reflexion, meditation, and contemplation. Comte appealed only to secondary aspects. But he insisted on *synergie*, on the contrast between impression and impulsion—that is to say, between the aspects which come from without and those which come from within. You also have alluded to this.

The difficulties that arose for philosophy after Comte, which accepted the data of voluntarism and Renouvier, came from an attempt to effect an exchange analogous to the exchange in physics between the notion of matter and the notion of energy. Perception is dematerialized into true hallucinations in Taine, into the immediate data of consciousness in Bergson, into mystical experience in Lévy-Bruhl. However, William James attempted to materialize sensation by turning to the work of the artist. Perception, which has been so impoverished that it is now reduced to nothing but a motor schema of present existence can only recover its fullness and its meaning in esthetic activity.

M. Merleau-Ponty. I deliberately avoided the use of the word "realism," since this would involve us in all sorts of historical explanations of the kind you have gone into, and I see no advantage in using this term. It only prolongs the discussion without clarifying it. For my part, I would prefer to answer a concrete question rather than a question bearing on the interrelations of historical doctrines.

M. Lupasco. What I have to say concerns mathematical experience. Euclidean geometry, which is the geometry of the perceived world, has been shown to be only an ideal geometry, and the physical universe, whose geometry is riemannian, and whose internal structure is of a more and more abstract mathematical complexity, escapes more and more from the psychology of perception.

M. Merleau-Ponty. There is a misunderstanding, doubtless through my fault. I did not mean to say that mathematical thought was a reflection, or a double, of perceptual experience. I meant to say that mathematical thought has the same fundamental structures; it is not absolute. Even when we believe we are dealing with eternal truths, mathematical thought is still tied to history.

M. Lupasco. It is conceived independently; it has its own history. It is, rather, mathematics which commands and modifies perception, to the extent that it commands and modifies the physical world and even history. Generally speaking, I do not see what would become of the mathematical world in a universe in which everything is perception.

M. Bauer. Perhaps my language will appear naïve, but it seems to me impossible to base a theory of knowledge on perception. Perception is almost as far removed from the primitive data of our senses as science itself. It seems to me that there is a discontinuity between perception and scientific knowledge; the former is an instinctive and rudimentary scientific knowledge. When we perceive a table, or a lamp on this table, we already interpret our visual sensations to a large extent. We associate them with other possible sensations, tactile or visual—for example, of the underside of the table, its solidity, or of the other side of the lamp. We thus make a synthesis; we enunciate an invariable connection between certain actual sensations and other virtual sensations. Science does nothing more than extend and make this process of synthesis more and more precise.

From this point of view we can say that the most abstract sciences, geometry, and even arithmetic or algebra, are colored by sensations. It seems to me at any rate that when I affirm, as a physicist, that "the sky is blue because there are molecules of air which diffuse the light of the sun," the workings of my mind are about the same as when I say "I perceive a lamp" at the moment when I see a green shade covering a brightly lighted spot. Only, in this latter case, the sense of my affirmation is more easily understood and its experimental verification more immediate.

M. Merleau-Ponty. This answers M. Lupasco's question. I would only add that it is necessary to distinguish perception from the construction of a mathematical theory; it is necessary to create a theory of language and of presumptively "exact" science.

I did not mean to say that culture consists in perceiving. There is a whole cultural world which constitutes a second level above perceptual experience. Perception is rather the fundamental basis which cannot be ignored.

M. Salzi. . . . The primacy of perception can have three meanings, and I think M. Merleau-Ponty moves from one sense to the other.

The first would be that of the primacy of psychology. The primacy of perception would follow necessarily from the notion of consciousness in which it is comprised. I believe that this is already an error in psychology. When a small baby is hungry, its consciousness of hunger is the consciousness of a lack. At the beginning, in the psychology of the infant, there is no distinction between the consciousness of a lack and consciousness of an object or of a subject. There is no duality; there is consciousness of a lack without there being either object or subject. This is one objection to this conception of the primacy of perception.

The second meaning could be that perception, as intuition or the basic contact with the real, is the exclusive source of truth. But it seems to me that, no matter how brilliant present-day science may be, we cannot erase metaphysical intuition any more than we can do away with mystical intuition or, perhaps even less, psychological intuition.

The third meaning would involve saying that this is not a question of fact but of principle [*de droit*], that, whatever the development of the human intellect through history may have been, we know henceforth, through the triumphs of contemporary science—and M. Merleau-Ponty seems to incline in this direction—that all our hypotheses must be supported by contact with perceptual experience.

And here I would oppose this sense of the primacy of perception. For contemporary science has little by little removed its postulates and its implications from perception. It denounces the postulates and implications derived from perception as inexact and says they must be replaced by other postulates which have nothing to do with perception—thus, for instance, the discontinuity of the quantum of energy, or we could mention the recent analysis of infra-atomic particles. The perceptual space—this space and time which since the time of Kant have served as the basis of perception—disappears, and consequently the physicist no longer has any concern at all with perception. Thus the world of the scientists would seem to escape the fetters of perception to a greater and greater degree. . . .

M. Merleau-Ponty. I have never claimed that perception (for example, the seeing of colors or forms), in so far as it gives us access to the most immediate properties of objects, has a monopoly on truth. What I mean to say is that we find in perception a mode of access to the object which is rediscovered at every level, and in speaking of the perception of the other I insisted that the word "perception" includes the whole experience which gives the thing itself. Consequently I do not detract anything from the more complex forms of knowledge; I only show how they refer to this fundamental experience as the basic experience which they must render more determinate and explicit. Thus it has never entered my mind to do away with science, as you say. It is rather a question of understanding the scope and the meaning of science. It is the problem of Poincaré in his book *La Valeur de la science;* when he put this title on his work no one thought that he was denying science. To be more specific, do you think that natural science gives you a total explanation of man—I say "total"—or do you not think there is something more?

M. Salzi. Without any doubt. I have, therefore, misunderstood the sense of the "primacy of perception."

M. Merleau-Ponty. If we reflect on our objects of thought and science, they ultimately send us back to the perceived world, which is the terrain of their final application. However, I did not mean to say that the perceived world, in the sense of the world of colors and forms, is the totality of our universe. There is the ideal or cultural world. I have not diminished its original character; I have only tried to say that it is somehow created *à ras de terre*.

It seems to me that these objections could be made to any philosopher who recognizes that philosophy has an original role distinct from that of science. The scientists have often said to philosophers, "Your work is otiose; you reflect on science but you do not understand it at all. This disqualifies you." And it is certain that by asserting that there *is* philosophy we thereby take something away from the scientist; we take away his monopoly on truth. But this is the only way in which I would limit the role of science.

As to mystical experience, I do not do away with that either. It is only a question of knowing just what it proves. Is it the effective passage to the absolute, or is it only an illusion? I recall a course by Brunschvicg which was entitled *Les techniques du passage à l'absolu*. Brunschvicg studied the various methods, all of which he considered fallacious, by which men attempt to reach the absolute. When I ask myself whether mystical experience means exactly what it thinks it means, I am posing a question to myself which everyone should pose. If, in order to be fair with respect to the fact of mystical experience, it is necessary to grant in advance that it is what it claims to be, if every question is an offense, then we must give up the quest for truth altogether.

I have expressed myself poorly if I have given the impression that I meant to do away with everything. On the contrary, I find everything interesting and, in a certain way, *true*—on the sole condition that we take things as they are presented in our fully elucidated experience. M. Bréhier asked me just now, "Do you posit the other as an absolute value?" I answered, "Yes, in so far as a man can do so." But when I was in the army, I had to call for an artillery barrage or an air attack, and at that moment I was not recognizing an absolute value in the enemy soldiers who were the objects of these attacks. I can in such a case promise to hold generous feelings toward the enemy; I cannot promise not to harm him. When I say I love someone at this moment, can I be sure that in this love I have reached the substance of the person, a substance which will absolutely never change? Can I guarantee that what I know of this person and what makes me love her, will be verified throughout her whole life? Perception anticipates, goes ahead of itself. I would ask nothing better than to see more clearly, but it seems to me that no one sees more clearly. I can promise here and now to adopt a certain mode of behavior; I cannot promise my future feelings. Thus it is necessary to confide in the generosity of life—which enabled Montaigne to write in the last book of his *Essais: "J'ai plus tenu que promis ni dû."*

Mme Roire. Is there a scale of values in all these experiences, and what is it? For example, are mystical experiences or the mathematical sciences at the top? Is there a scale of values with respect to the primacy of perception? How are the other forms of experience to be situated?

M. Merleau-Ponty. Assuredly for me there is a scale. This does not mean, however, that what is at the bottom is to be suppressed. It seems to me, for instance, that if we make it our goal to reach the concrete, then in certain respects we must put art above science because it achieves an expression of the concrete man which science does not attempt. But the hierarchies of which you are speaking suppose a point of view; from one point of view you get one hierarchy and from another point of view you get another hierarchy. Our research must be concentric rather than hierarchized.

Mme Prenant. . . . First of all, in this scale of values which has just been mentioned, does M. Merleau-Ponty place a higher value on the sun of the astronomer or on the sun of the peasant? . . . Does he consider the scientific theory as absolutely opposed to perception? And yet does not what he has said of the asymptotic character of scientific truth in Brunschvicg establish a certain continuity between ordinary perception and scientific perception? Are these diverse theories of perception opposed to one another, and should not M. Bauer's question be repeated?

My second question is related to the first: . . . Do I not possess a way of thinking which shows me that the sun of the astronomer is superior to the sun of the peasant?

M. Merleau-Ponty. I am in complete agreement with this and for two reasons. Recall the famous phrase from Hegel: "The earth is not the physical center of the world, but it is the metaphysical center." The originality of man in the world is manifested by the fact that he has acquired the more exact knowledge of the world of science. It is strictly necessary that we teach everybody about the world and the sun of the astronomer. There is no question of discrediting science. Philosophical awareness is possible only on the basis of science. It is only when one has conceived the world of the natural sciences in all their rigor that one can see appear, by contrast, man in his freedom. What is more, having passed a certain point in its development, science itself ceases to hypostatize itself; it leads us back to the structures of the perceived world and somehow recovers them. For example, the convergence between the phenomenological notion of space and the notion of space in the theory of relativity has been pointed out. Philosophy has nothing to fear from a mature science, nor has science anything to fear from philosophy.

Mme Prenant. By the same token, history is a concrete study.

M. Merleau-Ponty. Certainly. For my part, I would not separate history from philosophy. That is what I meant to say when I said that we could not imagine philosophers being phenomenologists from the beginning.

Mme Prenant. One could say that geodesy is also a science of the concrete.

M. Merleau-Ponty. Why not? But human geography much more so. As to the asymptotic character of scientific truths, what I meant to say was that, for a long time and in some respects, science seems to have tried to give us an image of the universe as immobile. It seemed to lack any conception of processes. To that extent, we can consider it to have been incomplete and partial.

. . . .

M. Césari. I only wish to ask M. Merleau-Ponty for a simple clarification. He seems to affirm that there is a certain continuity between science and perception. We can admit this point of view, which is that of Brunschvicg and which could be that of M. Bachelard, to the extent that new experiences can bring about an evolution within the realm of ideas. But M. Merleau-Ponty has insisted in an exaggerated fashion on the instability of the realm of ideas. But that is a question of degree; what confuses me is something else. I do not see how the phenomenological study of perception can serve the progress of science in any way. It seems to me that there is a discontinuity between perception as you describe it—that is, lived perception—and the perception on which the scientist bases himself in order to construct certain theories. It seems to me that there is a contradiction in your arguments. You say, "The study of perception, carried out by psychologists without presuppositions, reveals that the perceived world is not a sum of objects in the sense in which the sciences understand this word." Perfect. We are in complete agreement. It is a fact that perception at the level of lived experience does not describe objects in the way science does. But this being the case, what purpose does it serve for us to appeal to this purely lived experience to construct scientific experience, which, as M. Bachelard has said, must get away from immediate experience? Science will not be constructed unless we abandon the sensations and perceptions of ordinary experience, unless we define facts as technical effects—like the Compton-effect, for example.

Under these conditions, I do not see how phenomenology can be of any use to science.

M. *Merleau-Ponty*. The first thing to be said is that I do not know whether the phenomenological attitude is of any use to the other sciences, but it certainly is of use to psychology.

M. *Césari*. I agree as to psychology, but to evaluate the role of reason in science itself is another matter. You have compared phenomenological experience with that of Brunschvicg, who speaks of a highly elaborated experience which has nothing to do with lived experience.

M. *Merleau-Ponty*. Lived experience is of immediate interest only to those who are interested in man. I have never hoped that my work would be of much interest to the physicist as physicist. But your complaint could as well be addressed to all works of philosophy.

M. *Césari*. I am not making a complaint. I consider your point of view very interesting as it concerns the psychology of perception, but in its relation to scientific thought, I do not see its relevance except, once again, for psychology.

There is a second question which I would like to pose. You said at one point in your paper that "matter is pregnant with its form," and at that point you follow Gestalt theory. And in this theory there is an explanation of the genesis of perception (isomorphism). You have, on the contrary, compared your point of view to that of Bergson as it is given at the beginning of *Matière et mémoire*. But I have been unable to understand whether, according to you, the problem of the relation of the stimulus to perception really poses itself, since it is a question which interests science, while the existential viewpoint obliges you to consider the man-world complex as indissoluble, as giving perception immediately. I separate myself from the world when I ask about the relation between sensation and perception.

Since in your paper you uphold the view that there is no discontinuity between the existential and the scientific viewpoints, at some point the question of the relation between the stimulus and perception will perhaps pose itself, no doubt in a paradoxical manner. Exactly what solution do you give for this problem? For Bergson it was a question of possible reactions of the body to the world.

M. *Merleau-Ponty*. I have said that the point of view of the scientist with respect to perception—a stimulus *en soi* which produces a perception—is, like all forms of naive realism, absolutely insufficient. Philosophically I do not believe that this image of perception is ultimately defensible. But it seems to me indispensable for science to continue its own proper study of perception. For the time comes when, precisely because we attempt to apply the procedures of scientific thought to perception, we see clearly why perception is not a phenomenon of the order of physical causality. We observe a response of the organism which "interprets" the stimuli and gives them a certain configuration. To me it seems impossible to hold that this configuration is produced by the stimuli. It comes from the organism and from the behavior of the organism in their presence.

It seems to me valuable, even for psychology and philosophy, that science attempt to apply its usual procedures even if, and precisely if, this attempt ends in failure.

M. Césari. Doubtless these explanations are satisfactory. The only question which remains is that of the relation between the motivating rationalism of science and the phenomenology of perception.

M. Merleau-Ponty. I refuse to recognize a dilemma here.

M. Hyppolite. I would say simply that I do not see the necessary connection between the two parts of your paper—between the description of perception, which presupposes no ontology, and the philosophical conclusions which you draw, which do presuppose an ontology, namely, an ontology of meaning. In the first part of your paper you show that perception has a meaning, and in the second part you arrive at the very being of this meaning, which constitutes the unity of man. And the two parts do not seem to me to be completely interdependent. Your description of perception does not necessarily involve the philosophical conclusions of the second part of your paper. Would you accept such a separation?

M. Merleau-Ponty. Obviously not. If I have spoken of two things it is because they have some relation to one another.

M. Hyppolite. Does the description of perception require the philosophical conclusion on "the being of meaning" which you have developed after it?

M. Merleau-Ponty. Yes. Only I have not, of course, said everything which it would be necessary to say on this subject. For example, I have not spoken of time or its role as foundation and basis.

M. Hyppolite. This problem of "the being of meaning," with the implied unity of the relative and the absolute, which is finality—this recovered unity leads me to a question which is perhaps more precise: it does not seem to me that you have made clear the drama which reflexion causes in the pre-reflexive life—that is to say, the new form of life which is created by the projection of an eternal norm by means of reflexion. The fact of reflexion, joining itself to the pre-reflexive life, leads to a going-beyond, to a transcendence—formal perhaps, illusory perhaps, but without which reflexion could not occur.

Mme Prenant. The Drama of the evil genius.

M. Hyppolite. Perhaps. Do you agree that this reflexion gives us a new sense of transcendence?

M. Merleau-Ponty. Certainly there is much to be added to what I have said. On the basis of what I have said, one might think that I hold that man lives only in the realm of the real. But we also live in the imaginary, also in the world of ideality. Thus it is necessary to develop a theory of imaginary existence and of ideal existence. I have already indicated in the course of this discussion that by placing perception at the center of consciousness I do not claim that consciousness is enclosed in the observation of a natural datum. I meant to say that even when we transform our lives in the creation of a culture—and reflexion is an acquisition of this culture—we do not suppress our ties to time and space; in fact, we utilize them. Reciprocally one could say that in a completely explicitated human perception we would find all the originalities of human life. Human perception is directed to the world; animal perception is directed to an environment, as Scheler said. The same creative capacity which is at work in imagination and in ideation is present, in germ, in the first human perception (and I have obviously been incomplete on this point). But the essential difference between my point of view and that of a philosophy of the understanding is that, in my view, even though consciousness is able to detach itself from things to see itself, human consciousness never possesses itself in complete detachment and does not recover itself at the level of culture except by recapitulating the expressive, discrete, and contingent operations by means of which philosophical questioning itself has become possible.

M. Hyppolite. My question does not only concern the incomplete character of your exposition. It is to know whether human reflexion, contrary to every other form of life, does not pose problems not only of this or that meaning but of meaning in general, and whether this introduction of a reflexion on "the very being of all meaning" does not imply a new problem and a new form of life.

M. Merleau-Ponty. I am in complete agreement with that.

M. Hyppolite. Still it does not seem to me that the solution you give is a satisfying one, because man is led to pose to himself the question of a "being of all meaning," the problem of an "absolute being of all meaning."

In other words, there is in human reflexion a kind of total reflexion.

M. Merleau-Ponty. In my paper, taking up a saying from Rimbaud,

I said that there is a center of consciousness by which "we are not in the world." But this absolute emptiness is observable only at the moment when it is filled by experience. We do not ever see it, so to speak, except marginally. It is perceptible only on the ground of the world. In short, you are simply saying that I have no religious philosophy. I think it is proper to man to think God, which is not the same thing as to say that God exists.

M. Hyppolite. You said that God was dead.

M. Merleau-Ponty. I said that to say God is dead, as the Nietzscheans do, or to speak of the death of God, like the Christians do, is to tie God to man, and that in this sense the Christians themselves are obliged to tie eternity to time.

M. Hyppolite. You attempted to do a kind of ontology of the problem, which I have the right to call ambiguous, when you spoke of the death of God.

M. Merleau-Ponty. One is always ambiguous when one tries to understand others. What is ambiguous is the human condition. But this discussion is becoming too rapid; it is necessary to go over all this.

M. Hyppolite. Therefore you are not engaged by your description of perception, and you admit it.

M. Merleau-Ponty. I do not admit it at all. In a sense perception is everything because there is not one of our ideas or one of our reflexions which does not carry a date, whose objective reality exhausts its formal reality, or which transcends time.

M. Beaufret. What I have to say will not add much to what Hyppolite has already said. I wish only to emphasize that many of the objections which have been addressed to Merleau-Ponty seem to me unjustified. I believe that they come down simply to objecting to his perspective itself, which is that of phenomenology. To say that Merleau-Ponty stops at a phenomenology without any means of going beyond it is to fail to understand that the phenomenon itself, in the phenomenological sense of the term, goes beyond the realm of the empirical. The phenomenon in this sense is not empirical but rather that which manifests itself really, that which we can really experience, in opposition to what would be only the construction of concepts. Phenomenology is not a falling back into phenomenalism but the maintenance of contact with "the thing itself." If phenomenology rejects "intellectualist" explanations of perception, it is not to open the door to the irrational but to close it to verbalism. Nothing appears to me less pernicious than the *Phenomenology of Perception*. The only reproach I would make to the author is not that he has gone "too far," but rather that he has not been sufficiently radical. The phenomenological descriptions which he uses in fact maintain the vocabulary of idealism. In this they are in accord with Husserlian descriptions. But the whole problem is precisely to know whether phenomenology, fully developed, does not require the abandonment of subjectivity and the vocabulary of subjective idealism as, beginning with Husserl, Heidegger has done.

M. Parodi. We may have to leave one another without treating the principal question—namely, to come to a precise understanding of your theory of perception. In general, what do you think of the classical doctrine of perception which you seem to reject? I would like to see the positive part of your thesis recalled before we end this session. If perception is only a construction composed of materials borrowed from memory and based on immediate sensations, how do you explain the process?

M. Merleau-Ponty. Naturally there is a development of perception; naturally it is not achieved all at once. What I have attempted to say here presupposes (perhaps too much) the reading of the book which I devoted to this question. On the other hand, it seemed neither possible nor desirable for me to repeat it here.

M. Parodi. Could you tell us what is your most important contribution on this question of fact? You began with very clear examples: we think we perceive things which we really only see in part, or more or less. What, according to you, is the essential element in this operation?

M. Merleau-Ponty. To perceive is to render oneself present to something through the body. All the while the thing keeps its place within the horizon of the world, and the structurization consists in putting each detail in the perceptual horizons which belong to it. But such formulas are just so many enigmas unless we relate them to the concrete developments which they summarize.

M. Parodi. I would be tempted to say that the body is much more essential for sensation than it is for perception.

M. Merleau-Ponty. Can they be distinguished?

. . . .

3 / Phenomenology and the Sciences of Man [1]

Translated by John Wild

INTRODUCTION

IN CONSIDERING THE RELATIONS between phenomenology and the sciences of man, I do not think that I am approaching a mere scholastic problem which would be raised only by certain theses or opinions of a special philosophical school. Since its beginning, phenomenology has been attempting to solve a problem which is not the problem of a sect but, perhaps, the problem of our time. Since 1900 it has concerned us all, and it still concerns us all today. Husserl's philosophical endeavor is basically directed toward the simultaneous solution of a crisis in philosophy, a crisis in the sciences of man, and a crisis in science as such which we have not yet passed through.

The crisis in science is attested by the many studies devoted to the value of science from 1900 to 1905 in France (Poincaré, Duhem, LeRoy, and others). It was to be expected that Husserl, coming to philosophy from scientific disciplines (he began as a mathematician and his first work was a *Philosophy of Arithmetic*), should take very seriously this questioning of dogmatism concerning the foundations of geometry and physics. His desire to work out a new foundation for the sciences certainly weighed heavily in his decision to pursue a radical investigation in philosophy.

The sciences of man (psychology, sociology, history) and philosophy also found themselves in crisis. To the extent that it was really advancing, research in these fields tended to show that all opinion, and in particular all philosophy, was the result of external psychological, social, and historical conditions working in combination. Psychology was tending toward "psychologism," as Husserl called it, soci-

1. "Les sciences de l'homme et la phénoménologie," from the series *Cours de Sorbonne* (Paris, 1961).

ology toward "sociologism," and history toward "historicism." But in the process they were undermining their own foundations. If, indeed, the guiding thoughts and principles of the mind at each moment are only the result of external causes which act upon it, then the reasons for my affirmation are not the true reasons for this affirmation. They are not so much reasons as causes working from the outside. Hence the postulates of the psychologist, the sociologist, and the historian are stricken with doubt by the results of their own researches.

So far as philosophy is concerned, under these conditions it loses any possible justification. How can one pretend as a philosopher that one is holding truths, even eternal truths, as long as it is clear that the different philosophies, when placed in the psychological, social, and historical frame where they belong, are only the expression of external causes? In order to practice philosophy, in order to distinguish between the true and the false, it is necessary for the philosopher to express not merely certain natural or historical conditions external to him but also a direct and internal contact of the mind with itself, an "intrinsic" truth which seems impossible so long as research in the field of the human sciences shows that at each moment this mind is externally conditioned.

The crisis of science in general, of the sciences of man, and of philosophy leads to an irrationalism. Reason itself appears to be the contingent product of certain external conditions. From the beginning of his career, Husserl recognized that the problem was to give a new account of how all three—philosophy, science, and the sciences of man—might be possible. It was necessary once again to think them through to their foundations. He saw that these different disciplines had entered into a state of permanent crisis which would never be overcome unless one could show, by a new account of their mutual relations and their methods of knowing, not only how each alone might be possible but how all three might exist together. It must be shown that science is possible, that the sciences of man are possible, and that philosophy also is possible. The conflict between systematic philosophy and the advancing knowledge of science must cease.

Husserl raised this problem at the beginning of the century, and he raised it again at the end of his life in 1936 in the last work he partially published: *Die Krisis der Europäischen Wissenschaften.*[2] This book is made up of lectures delivered at Belgrade during the last years of his life. The role of the philosopher is here defined in a very striking manner. The philosopher is, he says, "working in the service of hu-

2. "Die Krisis der Europäischen Wissenschaften und die transzendentale Phänomenologie; Eine Einleitung in die phänomenologische Philosophie," *Philosophia* I (Belgrade, 1936), pp. 77–176.

manity," meaning that the philosopher is professionally bound to the task of defining and clarifying the conditions which make humanity possible—that is, the participation of all men in a common truth.

The problem that we shall deal with is not a problem of the history of philosophy in a narrow sense. This would be a question of knowing just what phenomenologists have thought or think of psychology, and of just what psychologists have thought or think of Husserl, Scheler, and Heidegger. It would be necessary to present the views of phenomenologists on psychology exactly as they have expressed them and, on the other side, the reactions of the psychologist to these phenomenological theses exactly as found in their writings. Such an enterprise would lead to very confusing results, for there have perhaps never been writers who were further from understanding each other. Most of the time phenomenologists have not understood what might be basically convergent with their own inspiration in contemporary psychology. We shall soon find an example of this in Husserl's criticisms of Gestalt psychology. And on their side the psychologists have been very deficient in their understanding of the phenomenologists. For example, they almost constantly fall into the error of supposing that phenomenology wishes to lead them back to a psychology of introspection. Misunderstandings are so very frequent on both sides that we could never finish sorting them out.

We may grant that our question is indeed a historical question, but only on the condition that we understand by the "history of philosophy" a dialectical history. This means that we shall not develop the ideas of the phenomenologists merely according to the texts but according to their intentions. It is a question here not of an empirical history, which limits itself to the gathering of facts on the one hand and texts on the other, but rather of an "intentional history," as Husserl called it, which in a given assemblage of texts and works tries to discover their legitimate sense. We shall not restrain ourselves from explaining the phenomenological texts by considerations which are not found there in writing. It will even happen sometimes that certain discoveries of the psychologists will help us in interpreting them. Similarly psychology will not be interpreted merely from its express declarations. If one took a plebiscite among psychologists to find out what they think of phenomenologists, the result would be, without doubt, humiliating to the phenomenologists. But we shall seek to discover whether there is anything in the spontaneous development of psychology that is in convergence with the insights of phenomenology correctly understood. We shall not, therefore, restrict our attentions to psychologists who, rightly or wrongly, make some claim to phenomenological knowledge. Rather we shall consider the modern development of psychology and the conditions under which it has occurred. It is in the problems and difficulties it has encountered that we shall find both an influence of phenomenology and a harmony of two parallel investigations into common problems of the time.

In a broad sense our study will be historical. But the perspective on this history will be established by us and by the problems with which we are concerned. Our basic intention is, therefore, just as much systematic as it is historical. At the end, we shall attempt to reinterpret both the meaning of philosophical activity and the conditions underlying a psychology that is truly rigorous.

The history of philosophy can never be the simple transcription of what the philosophers have said or written. If this were the case, we would have to replace the historical manuals of philosophy with the complete works of all the philosophers. As a matter of fact, as soon as one approaches two texts and opposes to them a third, one begins to interpret and to distinguish what is really proper to the thought of Descartes, let us say, and, on the contrary, what is only accidental. Thus in Cartesianism, as it is defined by the texts, one begins to see an intention that the historian has taken the initiative in singling out, and this choice evidently depends on his own way of encountering the problems of philosophy. The history of philosophy cannot be separated from philosophy. There is, of course, a difference between reflection on texts and the purely arbitrary. But in interpreting these texts, we do not exceed the ordinary rights of the historian if we distinguish what our author has said from what we think he should have said. Let us now say only that the questions we pose to psychology and phenomenology are ours and that they have never been raised in the same words by the authors themselves.

[1] The Problem of the Sciences of Man According to Husserl

1. *The problem of psychology and the problems of Husserl*

LET US first of all ask how Husserl, the founder of phenomenology in the modern sense, understood the sciences of man and their relation to his own research. We need to consider this, of course, not only at the beginning of his thought and in his earlier works but in the development of his philosophy and especially during the last ten years of his life.[3] In commenting on the last works of Husserl we shall

3. The works of this period are now in course of publication by The Husserl Archives of Louvain under the direction of R. P. H. Van Breda.

indicate briefly how they are related to the investigations of Scheler and Heidegger, to which they are very near and yet from which they are at the same time very far.

Then we shall have to speak of the psychologists and sociologists who have expressly recognized their debt to phenomenology. Many are the psychologists who have done so—for example, Koffka, one of the three principal members of the school of Berlin, and Jaspers, who before becoming a philosopher published a general psychopathology. In this work he recognized expressly, by the very terms he used, the phenomenological origin of his conceptions. Binswanger, the Swiss psychologist and psychiatrist, explicitly states that his works have come forth under the simultaneous or successive influence of both Husserl and Heidegger.

Among us M. Minkowski has often spoken of the role played by Husserl and also by Heidegger in the formation of his thought. Last year at the Philosophical Institute he gave two lectures on phenomenology and existential analysis which have since been published in the journal *Evolution Psychiatrique*.

But we shall not limit ourselves to those authors who have explicitly recognized a debt to phenomenology. We also wish to deal with a diffuse influence that was not always intended by Husserl or recognized by those who experienced it. All that was done in Germany from 1915 to 1920 under the direct or indirect influence of phenomenology was by no means accomplished exclusively in the courses of Husserl.

This diffuse influence was transported to the United States by Koffka, Köhler, Wertheimer, and Goldstein, and the same current is found to be at work there in the revision of behaviorism carried out by American psychologists.

Psychoanalysis, though in many respects it represents a very different mode of thought, has felt these phenomenological tendencies in its recent development. Nothing in the writings of Freud reveals the least knowledge of, or the least sympathy with, the phenomenological literature. But the exigencies of his own problems led him to a dynamic conception of psychoanalysis and elicited from Freud himself a revision of the theoretical framework which he had first used. One can see the joining of these two currents in a psychologist like Lewin, who was strongly influenced by phenomenology.

There will not be sufficient time to complete what we propose to do even concerning psychology. We must pass over the development of sociology, history, and linguistics, though it would be possible and useful to attempt this—perhaps as the subject matter for another course of lectures.

The man who philosophizes believes wrongly that when he thinks and affirms he is only expressing the mute contact of his thought with his thought. He is wrong to proceed as if he were not linked with the surrounding circumstances, for as soon as one considers him from the outside, as the historian of philosophy already does, he appears to be conditioned by physiological, psychological, sociological, and historical causes. His thought appears therefore as a product with no intrinsic value, and what seems to him the pure adequation of his thought, appears to the external critic as a residual phenomenon or a mere result. From the standpoint of a psychologist, a sociologist, or a historian one could therefore conceive of a critique which would consist simply in relating the thought which is considered to its exterior conditioning. Instead of discussing the problems of philosophy by plunging into them, one would do much better to discredit philosophy in general by revealing the historical, social, and physiological conditions on which it depends.

But this process has the inconvenience of turning against the very person who employs it. If "psychologism" says to us that the philosopher and his thinking are only the marionettes either of psychological mechanisms or of an external history, one can always answer that the same holds true of *it*, and thus discredit this criticism. Thus if it is consistent, psychologism becomes a radical skepticism which is skeptical with respect to itself.

"Sociologism" is open to the same consequence. By showing that all our thinking is the expression of a social situation whose limitations prevent it from being *true*, one falls into the danger of proving too much, since sociologism also will bear no true meaning in itself. This can lead to political irrationalism and to political action without criteria. It was against these dangers, as we have seen, that Husserl decided to return to the task of the philosopher: to restore certitude and the distinction of the true from the false.

His originality at this point was that he did not oppose psychologism and historicism by simply reaffirming the contrary position which he himself calls "logicism." This attitude admits that beyond the chain of psychological and social causes there is a special sphere, the place of thought in the strict sense of the term, where the philosopher may get in touch with an intrinsic truth. Elevating the sphere of thought in this way brings forth the return of psychologism and sociologism as soon as one perceives that philosophical thinking actually is not without roots.

From the beginning to the end of his career, Husserl tried to discover a way between logicism and psychologism. By a truly radical reflection, which reveals the prejudices established in us by the external environment, he attempts to transform this automatic conditioning into a conscious conditioning. But he never denies that it exists and that it is constantly at work. He notes in a striking way that even philosophy descends into the flux of our experience and that it must itself flow on [*sich einströmen*]. Even the thought which pretends to ignore the temporal flux or to dominate it takes place in this flux and descends into it as soon as it is constituted. The philosopher, in so far as he is a philosopher, ought not to think like the external man, the psychophysical subject who is *in* time, *in* space, *in* society, as an object is in a container. From the mere fact that he desires not only to exist but to exist with an understanding of what he does, it follows that he must suspend the affirmations which are implied in the given facts of his life. But to suspend them is not to deny them and even less to deny the link which binds us to the physical, social, and cultural world. It is on the contrary to *see* this link, to become conscious of it. It is "the phenomenological reduction" alone which reveals this ceaseless and implicit affirmation, this "setting of the world" [*thèse du monde*] which is presupposed at every moment of our thought.

What is peculiar to the philosopher is certainly that he considers his own life, so far as it is individual, temporal, and conditioned, as one possible life among many others. But then, by taking account of what it is actually, he may grasp what it might be, considering his own empirical personality as only one possibility in a much larger universe which needs to be explored. But this effort never permanently disregards our links with the physical and human world. We consider these spontaneous theses *ohne mitzumachen*—that is, without ourselves carrying them out at the very same moment. But this is the condition of all thought which claims to be true, and at the end of his career Husserl admitted that the first result of reflection is to bring us back into the presence of the world as we lived it before our reflection began [*Lebenswelt*].

The phenomenological reduction of the link, which is indeed a schism established by life between our thought and our physical and social situation, never leads us in any way to negate time or to pass beyond it into a realm of pure logic or pure thought. One never gets beyond time. Husserl says only that there are many ways of living time. On the one hand, there is the passive way, in which one is inside time and submits to it—being in time [*Innerzeitigkeit*]. On the other hand, one can take over this time and live it through for oneself. But in either case one is temporal and never gets beyond time. Philosophy has been traditionally regarded as the science of eternal truths. If we are to be exact, we should, rather, follow Husserl in the last years of his life and call it the science of the all-temporal, that which holds throughout all time, instead of a truth which would absolutely escape from the temporal order. This is a deepening of temporality. There is no passing beyond it.

Logic is not wrong in considering the laws of our thinking as universally valid. But we need to ask why they are universal and to see how Husserl justifies this. Logicism maintains that when I am concerned with a recognized law and affirm it unconditionally, I am communicating through the center of my being with a pre-personal thought. It founds the universality of logic, therefore, on an absolute right that is derived from its capacity to express the internal structure of the world as it is for a universal thinker. Even in his earliest works, Husserl's procedure of justification is very different. In the first part of the *Logical Investigations* he says that the laws of our thought are for us laws of being, not because we communicate with a pre-personal thought but rather because they are for us absolutely coextensive with everything that we can affirm.

If we wished to suppose other laws of a superhuman thought, either divine or angelic, then in order to find any meaning in these new principles, we would have to bring them under ours, so that to us they would be as nothing. We cannot conceive of them truly as thinkers, except in so far as they conform to the laws of our thought. An angel who would think in accordance with laws radically different from those governing human thought and who would thus cast doubt on these—this angel cannot be thought by me. Hence the universality of thought is not founded on any communication with a universal thinker, the center of all spirits, but simply on the fact that my thinking belongs to me. In order to be sure that a certain thought is a rule for all men and for all being, it is sufficient if I find that it concerns something truly essential, something which cannot be separated from me even in thought.

It is relevant to note here that Husserl goes so far as to say that even God could not have an experience of the world which would not present itself in the manner of our experience as a series of always incomplete profiles.[4] This leads us, therefore, to a *phenomenological positivism* which refuses to found rationality, the agreement of minds, and universal logic on any right that is prior to fact. The universal value of our thinking has no justifiable foundation in anything independent of the facts. It is founded, rather, on a central and fundamental fact that I myself discover by reflection: the nonsense of anything that violates a principle of thought, such as the law of contradiction or other laws, for naturally the question remains open as to

---

4. The idea of God is used here, as Husserl said in another place, not to introduce a theological affirmation, but as a philosophical index to place the situation of man in better relief.

whether we may not arrive at a better formulation of the principles of true logic.

Husserl, therefore, never agreed with a certain philosophical tradition in holding that philosophy could be a system of definitive results never requiring reexamination with the advance of experience. For him philosophy is essentially progressive. As he says in his last years, it is an *infinite meditation;* and one of his better students, Eugen Fink, says that we are here involved in a "situation of dialogue." This means that as long as the philosopher remains within the realms of fact which limit his vision, he will never become a thinker who is universal in all respects. He is always situated and always individuated; this is why he is in need of dialogue. The surest way of breaking through these limits is to enter into communication with other situations—that is, other philosophers or other men. As Husserl stated in his last years, the last subjectivity, philosophical, ultimate, radical subjectivity, which philosophers call *transcendental,* is an *intersubjectivity.*

It is also stated in a passage of the *Nachwort* added to the *Ideas* that "philosophy is an idea." Husserl used the word "idea" here in the Kantian sense of a limiting concept to designate a thinking which we cannot properly think through, or totalize, which we envisage only on the horizon of our efforts as the limit of a certain number of thought operations which we are able to perform. "It is an idea which is realizable only in the style of a relative, provisional validity, and in a historical process without end, but which, under certain conditions, is also effectively realizable."

We see, therefore, that what Husserl opposed to the crisis resulting from psychologism and sociologism is not the mere reaffirmation of the old philosophical dogmatism of eternal truths. The philosophical task to which he devoted himself was, rather, the establishment of an integral philosophy which would be compatible with the development of all the different investigations on the conditioning of man. During the whole career of Husserl, therefore, the struggle is on two fronts. On the one hand it is a struggle against psychologism and historicism, in so far as they reduce the life of man to a mere result of external conditions acting on him and see the philosophizing person as entirely determined from the outside, lacking any contact with his own thought and therefore destined to skepticism. But on the other hand, it is also a struggle against logicism, in so far as this is attempting to arrange for us an access to the truth lacking any contact with contingent experience. Husserl is seeking to reaffirm rationality at the level of experience, without sacrificing the vast variety that it includes and accepting all the processes of conditioning which psychology, sociology, and history reveal. It is a question of finding a method which will enable us to think at the same time of the externality which is the principle of the sciences of man and of the internality which is the condition of philosophy, of the contingencies without which there is no situation as well as of the rational certainty without which there is no knowledge.

In short, this enterprise is fairly close to that of Hegel, as is suggested by Husserl's use of the word "phenomenology." In Hegel's sense this is a logic of content. Instead of a logical organization of the facts coming from a form that is superimposed upon them, the very content of these facts is supposed to order itself spontaneously in a way that is thinkable. A phenomenology, therefore, has a double purpose. It will gather together all the concrete experiences of man which are found in history—not only those of knowledge but also those of life and of civilization. But at the same time it must discover in this unrolling of facts a spontaneous order, a meaning, an intrinsic truth, an orientation of such a kind that the different events do not appear as a mere succession. For a conception of this kind one comes to the spirit only by "the spirit of the phenomenon"—that is, the visible spirit before us, not just the internal spirit which we grasp by reflection or by the *cogito*. This spirit is not only in us but spread far and wide in the events of history and in the human milieu. If it is true that Husserl sought by the study of phenomena to find the roots of reason in our experience, we should not be surprised that his phenomenology ended with the theory of a "reason hidden in history."

Only, with Hegel phenomenology is merely a preface to logic, so that, at least according to certain interpreters, it is only the introduction to a philosophy which belongs to another order. But if it finally turns out to be a logic which is ruling over the development of the phenomena, the philosopher is doing just what Hegel warns against in his introduction to *The Phenomenology of the Spirit*. "He is putting himself in the place of consciousness itself, in making up his experiences." With Husserl, on the other hand, it is logic itself which becomes phenomenological. That is, he will not wish to give any other foundation to the affirmations of logic than our actual experience of truth.

For a philosopher of this kind, who desires to be integral, there is no question—as many of us, and above all many psychologists, have believed—of sacrificing science and in particular the science of psychology. On the contrary, Husserl thinks that the reform of psychology for which he is striving will lead to a new development then being retarded, in the psychologism of his time, by an inadequacy of methodological conceptions. In the *Ideas* [5] he speaks of certain criticisms which implied that his investigations had been meant to replace psy-

5. *Ideen zu einer reinen und phänomenologischen Philosophie* (Halle, 1928), p. 2.

chological research. "I have protested against this conception," he says, "without any success, it seems." The explanations that "I have added have not been understood, and have been rejected without careful examination. Instead of answering the simple sense of my demonstration, this criticism of psychological methods has merely been dismissed. It never questioned the value of modern psychology. It never rejected the experimental work of eminent men. It pointed out certain radical weaknesses in method, in the literal sense of this word. In correcting them, psychology must be elevated, in my opinion, to a higher level of scientific certitude, and must vastly enlarge its field of work. I shall add a few words elsewhere on the way in which psychology has been very inadequately defended against these supposed attacks of mine."

Husserl, therefore, is not opposed to a scientific psychology. He simply believes that the existence and development of such a psychology raise certain philosophical problems, the solution of which are relevant to psychology itself if it is to advance. In the light of the situation at the time when Husserl was writing, the problem was this: there seemed to be a conflict between the needs of philosophy, considered as pure rational interiority, and the needs of a psychology considered as the science of the external determination of human conduct.

How, then, does Husserl face this difficulty? He must find a way of knowing which is neither deductive nor purely empirical. This knowledge must not be purely conceptual in detaching itself from facts. Nevertheless it must be philosophical, or at least it must not make the existence of a philosophizing subject impossible. It is essential that our life should not be reduced exclusively to psychological events and that in and through these events there should be revealed a meaning which is irreducible to these particularities. This emergence of truth in and through the psychological event is what Husserl called *Wesenschau,* the intuition of essences.

In defending Husserl against the false interpretations that are so common, we must emphasize the concrete and familiar nature of this *Wesenschau.* It is a grasping of universal meanings in and through my contingent experience, which is not at all, as Husserl sees it, a peculiar, mystical operation that transports us beyond empirical facts. Thanks to its dual character, at the same time universal and concrete, this *Wesenschau* is capable of renewing and of developing psychology. For anyone who considers them from the outside, the experiences we live through, our *Erlebnisse,* as Husserl calls them, can certainly be socially and physically determined. Nevertheless there is a way of taking them through which they acquire a meaning that is universal, intersubjective, and absolute. But in pursuing this way, I must not limit myself to living through the experience; I must grasp its sense, and this is the function of "eidetic intuition."

It is indeed a fact, a simple fact determined by external conditions, that I am going to such and such a concert today and that I am hearing the Ninth Symphony. But I am able to discover inside this experience, as I live it through, something which is independent of the factual conditions which have brought forth my decision. The Ninth Symphony is not enclosed within the time during which I am listening. It appears in the different performances of different orchestras. It is a cultural object which is brought forth under the baton of this director and through the playing of these violinists. But it cannot be reduced to any single performance that one gives of it. Hence if I succeed in bringing out of my experience all that it implies, in thematizing what I have lived through at this time, I come to something which is neither singular nor contingent—namely, the Ninth Symphony in its essence. This orientation of consciousness toward certain "intentional objects," which are open to an "eidetic" analysis, is what Husserl calls *intentionality*.

One can say that, by its antecedent conditions, my consciousness is bound to the contingent events which act on me. But in so far as it envisages certain terminations, in so far as it has a "teleology," in so far as it is concerned with certain cultural entities which are not divided by their different manifestations at different moments of my life or in different minds, it is open to a different kind of analysis. According to Husserl, the seeing of essences, or *Wesenschau*, is nothing but the clarification of the sense, or essence, toward which our consciousness is directed. He says in the *Ideas* that we should give neither a mystical nor even a Platonic meaning to the word *Wesenschau*. It does not involve the use of a super-sensible faculty absolutely strange to our experience and exercised only under exceptional conditions. *Wesenschau* is constant, he says, even in a life that conforms most closely to the natural attitude.

The insight into essences rests simply on the fact that in our experience we can distinguish *the fact that* we are living through something from *what it is* we are living through in this fact. It is by this vision that Husserl tries to find a way between psychologism and logicism and to bring forth a reform of psychology. In so far as the essence is to be grasped through a lived experience; it is concrete knowledge. But in so far as I grasp something through this experience which is more than a contingent fact, an intelligible structure that imposes itself on me whenever I think of the intentional object in question, I gain another kind of knowledge. I am then not enclosed in the particularity of my individual life, and I attain an insight which holds for all men.

I get beyond my singularity not in so far as my consciousness is merely a series of facts or events but in so far as these events have a sense. The intuition of essences is simply a regaining of this sense, which is not thematized in our spontaneous, unreflective experience.

[2] HUSSERL'S CONCEPTION OF AN EIDETIC PSYCHOLOGY

1. *The problem of eidetic psychology up to the* Ideas

IF ONE examines the *Philosophy of Arithmetic*, the first work of Husserl, one must take account of the fact that at this moment the author had just left mathematics for philosophy. Having found the logicist conceptions of mathematics insufficient, he now proposed to found arithmetical operations on psychological acts, and he defined phenomenology as "descriptive psychology." Later on he renounced this conception because it led to psychologism and interpreted basic notions of our thought—numbers, for example—as simple attributes of a psychological nature. In brief, he perceived at the beginning of his philosophical career that it was necessary to return to consciousness. One must look for the sense of mathematical concepts in the life of consciousness on which they rest.

But he did not understand this consciousness, to which he was returning as a philosopher, in the right way. He was opposing it to the world as one region to another. Later on he saw that this consciousness, on which the operations of logic are founded, is not merely a part of being but the source from which all being can receive its sense and its value of being for us. It is, in fact, the correlate of all being, whatever it may be. Mathematical being, for example, is an intentional correlate of consciousness, and so is the external world. Consciousness is, therefore, coextensive with all being of which we can gain any knowledge. Nothing can have the value of being for us if it does not offer its sense to consciousness. The notion of consciousness is now generalized. It is no longer one being among others. It is, rather, the theater of all being and of the transcendental positing of any object.

One is here confronted with a philosophy that seems close to idealism. The formulae of the *Philosophy of Arithmetic* were insufficient because they were too psychological. On the other hand, the later formulae were too Platonic, in the vague and historically controversial sense that one ordinarily gives to this word. It is always between the Scylla of psychologism and the Charybdis of logicism that Husserl steers his course. Let us now define the position he took at the moment when he published the *Ideas*. The famous reduction, which gives us access to phenomenology, is not a mere return to the psychological subject. But even less does it turn our thought away from existence toward essences which would transcend it. This reduction is the decision not to suppress but to place in suspense, or out of action, all the spontaneous affirmations in which I live, not to deny them but rather to understand them and to make them explicit.

By his theory of the "phenomenological reduction" Husserl broke absolutely with every remnant of psychologism in his thought as well as with every remnant of Platonism in his early works. The philosophical *I* is going to withdraw from every condition of fact, as well as from every way of perceiving and understanding them, in order to leave nothing unnoticed. And the task of philosophy will then be to explain, with a complete lucidity, how both the manifestations of the external world and the realizations of the incarnate self are possible. Every intentional object refers to consciousness but to a consciousness which is not the incarnate individual that I am as a man, living at a certain moment of time and in a certain position in space. When I carry out the phenomenological reduction, I do not bring back information concerning an external world to a self that is regarded as a part of being, nor do I substitute an internal for an external perception. I attempt rather to reveal and to make explicit in me that pure source of all the meanings which constitute the world around me and my empirical self.

At this stage of his thinking what, then, was Husserl's view of the situation of psychology in relation to phenomenology?

Psychology, he said, is a science of fact. It is the science of man in the world, facing different situations and responding to them by different types of behavior. Hence it is certainly not to be confused with transcendental, phenomenological philosophy, which, as we have just explained, is a universal reflection that attempts to make explicit and to clarify conceptually all the intentional objects that my consciousness can envisage.

But precisely because it has its own proper region, psychology is not in the position of philosophy. The thesis of psychologism is precisely this: that psychology can take the place of philosophy. But this is impossible because psychology, together with common sense and the different sciences, shares in those convictions concerning being which need to be clarified by philosophy. All of us live in the natural attitude—that is, in the conviction that we are a part of the world and subject to its action on us, which we passively receive from the outside. Psychology accepts this realistic postulate from common sense, and sets up its problems from this point of view. The psychologist tries to see how man works out his responses to certain situations and stimuli, and to discover the laws which rigorously bind together such and such a group of stimuli with such and such a reaction. As Husserl saw it, this is perfectly legitimate, but it simply does not take the place of philosophy. We must not give an ontological value—that is, an ultimate weight—to this way of thinking, for it is naive and unreflective.

If we actually reflect on our situation, we will find that the subject, thus situated in the world and submitting to its influences, is at the same time he who thinks the world. No world whatsoever is conceivable that is not thought by someone. Hence while it is true that the empirical subject is a part of the world, it is also true that the world is no more than an intentional object for the transcendental subject. Husserl defended this Copernican revolution, as Kant called it, which defined philosophy by its opposition to psychology up to the very end.

He consistently maintained that even a psychology which, like Gestalt psychology, recognizes that consciousness is unified and autonomous, that it is not made up of elements like an external thing, and that it is, rather, a whole whose parts have no separable existence is radically incapable of replacing philosophy. For even though the Gestaltists conceive of consciousness as a totality which cannot be dissolved into its elements, they nevertheless conceive of it as a natural totality existing in things. My consciousness, they would say is a form more integrated than this lamp, but it is nevertheless only a form. As Husserl sees it, the very fact that one uses the same term "Gestalt" to designate the unity of consciousness and that of the lamp justifies the conclusion that Gestalt psychology naturalizes consciousness. It defines consciousness as other objects can be defined, and does not see that it is the subject for every possible object.

In his philosophical rigor, Husserl excludes both Gestalt psychology and that of nineteenth-century atomism and placed them almost on the same level. Notice what he writes about this in his postscript to the *Ideas*: "Both atomistic psychology and Gestalt psychology remain in the same sense basically psychological naturalisms which, from their use of the expression 'internal sense,' can also be called sensualisms. There is no difference here, in principle, between 'atomistically' accumulating psychic data like grains of sand and considering them as parts of totalities held together by some empirical or *a priori* necessity, but nevertheless made up of such parts. There is no essential difference between saying with the associationists, 'Consciousness is a sum of sensations and images,' and with the Gestaltists, 'consciousness is a totality in which the elements have only an inseparable existence.' " So long as one does not radically reform the notion of totality so as to think of consciousness as a totality with no equivalent at all among the things of nature, one is still trapped in naturalism and psychologism.

Husserl maintained this up to the very end. He never thought that psychology would be able to take the place of philosophy, even a highly refined psychology having nothing to do with any atomism or with any reduction to elements of any kind. But he held something even more than this. Not only will psychology never take the place of philosophy, but as psychology it necessarily involves a deformation of consciousness.

As a matter of fact, it shares in the natural attitude which indeed enables it to consider man, but only as a part of the world. When a psychologist speaks of consciousness, the mode of being he attributes to it does not differ radically from that of things. Consciousness is an object to be studied, and the psychologist sees it among other things as an event in this system of the world. To arrive at a conception which will do justice to the radical originality of consciousness, we need an analysis of a very different type, which will find in our experience the meaning, or the essence, of every possible *psyche*. We will never really find out what consciousness is unless we grasp this internal meaning in ourselves and gain an eidetic intuition of it.

Consciousness is accessible only to intentional analysis and not to mere factual observation. The psychologist always tends to make consciousness into just such an object of observation. But all the factual truths to which psychology has access can be applied to the concrete subject only after a philosophical correction. Psychology, like physics and the other sciences of nature, uses the method of induction, which starts from facts and then assembles them. But it is very evident that this induction will remain blind if we do not know in some other way, and indeed from the inside of consciousness itself, what this induction is dealing with.

In order to understand truly what has been discovered about man, we must, therefore, combine induction with the reflective knowledge that we can obtain from ourselves as conscious subjects. This is what Husserl called *eidetic psychology*—that is, a reflective effort by which we clarify the fundamental notions which psychology uses constantly, through a contact with our own experience. According to Husserl, empirical psychology must be preceded by an eidetic psychology. The knowledge of facts belongs to psychology. But the definition of the notions which will enable us to understand these facts belongs to phenomenology.

We may take certain concepts, like image and perception, from common usage and then apply them without careful attention in interpreting psychological facts. But in so far as we have not given a coherent and adequate sense to these notions by reflecting on our experiences and perceptions, we will not know what they mean and what the facts concerning image and perception really show.

In general, Husserl thinks neither that psychology will be replaced by philosophy nor that philosophy will be replaced by psychology. It is essential that each should maintain its autonomy. To psychology is allotted the investigation of facts, and the relations of these facts. But the ultimate meaning of these facts and relations will be worked out only by an eidetic phenomenology which focuses the essence of perception, of image, and of consciousness itself.

2. *An illustration from the earlier works of Sartre*

THE FIRST works of Sartre on imagination and emotion illustrate very well Husserl's conception as it was presented in the middle period of his career.

At the end of his essay on the imagination, Sartre shows that in so far as we have not reflected on what an image is, all the experimental investigations that we can make remain a dead letter. Of course they give us results that are ultimately quantitative in character. But we do not know what these results mean or what it is that has been measured. For example, one sees under what conditions the image is presented. One finds that in our conscious life it corresponds to states of low tension and that it appears almost instantaneously without definite contours. One speaks of clear images, and shows that they are not, as is often believed, complete pictures of the objects they represent but only schematic outlines. One shows again that the image is never altogether self-sufficient in our conscious life and that it serves only to resume a certain project of thought or to carry symbolic references to certain objects.

All this is true. But it does not enable us to understand what the image is, how it enters into relation with a thought that uses it, and what the predominance of imaginary life means for a given subject. As long as we regard the image as a little frozen picture in consciousness, it is impossible for us to understand how this image-thing can enter into any real relation with active thought. It remains simply a sensible thing, veiled or suppressed or less complete. This conception of the image, which has no scientific value, introduces fixed elements into psychological analysis which do not belong there but which are derived rather from prescientific common sense. The same thing can also happen in a phenomenological clarification. One often does not understand what it is to imagine something and what purpose this may serve. What is the sense of imagining attitudes and behavior? What does an act of imagining mean in the life of man?

To answer these questions we need an analysis which would show us that, in principle, the image is not something observable, though it pretends to be—that it is, in short, essentially deceptive. We all believe that images are observable like the things we sense. But when we try to observe them, we find that this is impossible and that, as Alain says, we cannot count the columns of the Pantheon in our images of it. The image is, therefore, a claim to the presence of the imagined object, which is unfounded. It is an absence of the object which tries to pass as its presence. It calls up an object, as one speaks of calling up a spirit. The thinking self is referring to such and such a real object existing in the world, with the pretense of making it appear here and now just where I am. As Sartre says, there are not two Peters, one who is real and in West Africa and another Peter in my consciousness. In reality, there is my reference to the real Peter, with the pretense that I am making him appear here in my mental equipment. This kind of incorporation of something absent in present data is carried out naturally with the aid of certain perceptual elements which serve as analogues of the absent object. This is sufficient to show that in reality the image is not a content in my consciousness but rather an operation of my whole consciousness. To perceive oneself as imagining is to set up a certain kind of relation with the absent thing.

Understood in this way, the image can be compared to a whole series of other phenomena. For example, one can compare the awareness of a mental image of the Pantheon with an awareness of certain photographic images. Thus there is no essential difference between my awareness of the absent Pantheon and that which I have of a photograph under my eyes. When the object is totally absent without a representative, I make use of certain elements in my present perception which are analogous. To imagine is always to make something absent appear in the present, to give a magical quasi presence to an object that is not there. On this basis one may then investigate how the subject achieves this incantation of an absent visage in the present data of his perceptions. One will see that he must impress them with a physiognomy or a structure of some kind that he then projects actively by his motor-affective attitude. Such an eidetic analysis of the image will make possible experimental approaches which are no longer blind, because they will know something of what they are talking about and will understand the connection of the image with our motor-affective life.

In the same way, before we have worked out an eidetic psychology of emotion and before we have asked ourselves what it is to be emotionally moved, we may raise the problem of emotion in a very confused way, because we see it through a number of prejudices and prenotions which artificially separate the facts. Common sense, for example, will say of emotion that it involves two separate orders of fact, "corporeal manifestations" on the one hand and "representations" on the other. The question was raised in this way at the time of William James. One school then maintained that emotion must be understood from the standpoint of representations, while another defended the standpoint of corporeal facts.

Hence psychology held that a great victory had been won on the day when James reversed the traditional order in saying "I am sorry because I weep" instead of "I weep because I am sorry." Psychology still indulged in this type of speculation even after the coming of phenomenology and proposals to work out meaningful clarifications of emotion. But this does not involve any opposing of concepts to facts. It is a question, rather, of replacing habitual concepts, to which we pay no careful attention, by concepts which are consciously clarified and are therefore far less likely to remove us from experience as it is lived.

In connection with emotion, eidetic reflection will ask: after all, what is it to be moved; what is the meaning of emotion? Can one conceive of a consciousness which is incapable of emotion, and if not, why not? One will understand emotion as a total act of consciousness, as a mode of our relation to the entire world, and one will seek to determine its sense.

In earlier times psychology noted vaguely that emotion was both a "psychic" and a "physical" state and sought to determine which was the cause of the other. Phenomenology will remain neutral before this issue, and without assuming that emotion is either psychical or physical it will simply ask what emotion means and toward what it is tending.

Many psychologists have sketched out research of this kind. It will be a constant thesis of the following lectures that one does not have to be specially tutored by Husserl to discover psychological developments that are moving in a phenomenological direction. Janet, for example, raised the question of emotion in a very new way when he tried to find out what was the meaning of a given emotion. In a passage in *From Anxiety to Ecstasy* [6] he brought up the case of a young girl who came to consult him but refused to answer his questions. She ended by falling into a nervous crisis which naturally made it impossible for her to do

6. *De l'angoisse à l'extase* . . . (Paris, 1926–28).

this. The emotion, the nervous breakdown, and the anger had a sense. They were a way of avoiding the interrogatory situation which the girl had instinctively accepted in coming to see Janet but which she had really decided not to undertake.

In the same way Freud considered emotion as an action or realization which is symbolic. In one of his formulae, clearly showing the relation between his whole enterprise and that of the phenomenologists, he also maintained that "psychic facts have a sense" which must be deciphered. He tried to place them in the total life of the subject, the dynamics of his behavior, and thus to show what they mean.

According to Sartre, for example, emotion is the modification of our relation to the world when we abandon an ordered way of acting which takes account of causality, and change over to an immediate, magical, and fictitious transformation of the situation. Thus a man in a fit of anger will stop trying to untie the knot of a string or a shoelace and will suddenly tear it apart, which does not resolve the problem of the knot but simply suppresses it. An orderly way of relating to the object and the world is replaced by an irrational way in which everything happens as if the unconditional will of the subject were able to reach its result by merely projecting itself into the object without any employment of means. This is an example of what Husserl calls an eidetic analysis. One gathers together the lived facts involving emotion and tries to subsume them under one essential meaning in order to find the same conduct in all of them.[7]

Thus we may say, in using a formula of Husserl, that the relation of psychology to phenomenology is analogous to that of physics to geometry. In relation to methodological questions, psychology refers to phenomenology. For example, to know what an emotion is and how to approach it by way of the body or the spirit, or in a neutral phenomenological way, we need a clarification of the internal meaning of the phenomenon, which phenomenology can furnish. This does not mean that the work of the phenomenologist replaces that of the psychologist, any more than that of the geometer replaces that of the physicist. Geometry and mathematics in general were necessary preconditions for the development of a physics. But this does not mean that they can take its place.

In another passage Husserl says that the relation between empirical and eidetic psychology is the same as that between sociology and statistics. This means that statistics is necessary to sociology but does not coincide with it. We must get into contact with the social phenome-

7. This kind of investigation of essence is at the same time an analysis of existence in the modern sense of the word, or at least leads toward this, since the essence of an experience is always a certain modality of our relation to the world.

non, and understand it in its own proper frame, in order to find a social meaning in statistical facts. In the same way it is necessary to get into contact with the psyche by phenomenological reflection in order to understand the results of the empirical investigations of psychology.

In conclusion, Husserl believed that he saw in the psychological investigations of his time many uncertainties which are connected with the desire to use scientific techniques. Psychology rightly seeks to gain a factual knowledge which one obtains only through contact with a number of different instances of the phenomenon studied, not previously imaginable by us and therefore to be found only in experience. But the psychologist believes that it is sufficient merely to note down these facts in order to understand them. The result is that he examines them in a state of relative blindness and that in interpreting them he uses confused concepts taken from our pre-scientific experience.

From time to time, for example, the psychologist uses the concept of man, if only to mark off animal from human psychology. But what, more exactly, is the meaning of this notion of man? Since it is drawn from our common sense, perhaps it needs to be revised. Perhaps it is too broad, so that certain beings we commonly call men do not really merit the name in terms of a strict analysis. In any case, this needs to be examined. Or perhaps, on the contrary, our notion of man is too narrow. If we were to examine the chimpanzee more carefully, we might discover that there is no justifiable reason for excluding him from the class of animals known as men. Our present concept of man is not at all scientific. It is vague, confused, and in need of psychological clarification.

Phenomenological analysis is a clarifying effort of this kind. It is seeking to identify with rigor, and to link together in an intelligible way, the attitudes and traits that may justifiably be called human. One may say that "psychology will of course be able to define man, but only at the end of its inquiry." Still, this is not certain, since the investigation will be concerned with facts. Will it reveal merely certain characteristics which belong to the collection of individuals that one ordinarily calls "man," or will it show that these characteristics do not belong to all or that they also belong to other individuals not usually called human? Such a factual investigation will never enable us to decide whether the collection of traits obtained in this way deserves to constitute a definition. Are they essential or only accidental? Sooner or later this investigation of the essence with which an eidetic psychology is concerned should be undertaken. But it will never come to anything so long as the traits accepted for empirical investigation are chosen only because of their frequent occurrence and have no power to reveal the essence that must be understood.

3. Difficulties involved in a subordination of psychology: the interconnections of psychology and phenomenology

To THIS conception of an eidetic psychology two kinds of objection can be made and, as a matter of fact, have been made. The first we can easily discard since it rests on a misunderstanding. The second objection goes much further. It was seen by Husserl himself, and led him to alter his ideas and to develop his doctrines beyond the stage of the *Ideas*.

The first objection maintains that an eidetic psychology would be merely a return to introspection and would therefore lead to all the difficulties from which psychology attempted to escape when it decided to become a science.

On this point no confusion is possible. For Husserl the discovery of the essence, or the meaning, of a process certainly involves a power of reflection, the ability to find the sense of what is lived through by oneself or by another. At the period of the *Ideas* he thought that reflective consciousness can arrive at an evidence concerning itself which is absolutely final and that in it what appears and what is are not distinct. In this sense Husserl held that consciousness, or *cogito*, is incomparable with external things. These external things appear in successive experiences through different perspectives, or *Abschattungen*. If consciousness were eternal to itself there would be no certitude nor science concerning it. In this sense, it is true to say that for Husserl, as for all the Cartesians, the existence of consciousness is inseparable from the consciousness of existing and that consequently the consciousness I need to know is the subject that I am. It is also clear, finally, that Husserl wishes to use this proximity of myself to myself, and more generally of man to man, in defining the *cogito* and reflection. In order that knowledge may be possible, I must not be cut off from myself and from the other.

But this does not mean that the internal relation of myself to myself and to the other is already scientific knowledge and that reflective psychology is introspective. This introspection is supposed to consist in the presence of data internal to the subject, which he observes and which are revealed to him by the mere fact that they are "in him." This is an internal perception, the noting of an event with which I coincide. But reflection is not at all the noting of a fact. It is, rather, an attempt to understand. It is not the passive attitude of a subject who watches himself live but rather the active effort of a subject who grasps the meaning of his experience. Husserl was so far from making internal perception into a principle that he granted a greater certitude, in certain respects, to external perception than to internal observation.

Reflection on the meaning or the essence of what we live through is neutral to the distinction between internal and external experience.

It is rather a question of explaining what these phrases mean. In particular, nothing prevents my phenomenological reflection from having a bearing, for example, on another person, since I perceive him and his modes of behavior. Nothing prevents the clarification of the intentions or meanings or ways of acting from referring not only to my own conduct but to that of another whom I witness. Nothing prevents me from explaining the meaning of the lived experience of another person, in so far as I have access to it, by perception. According to Husserl, "Pure internal psychology, the authentic psychology of intentionality, is, in the last analysis, a psychology of pure intersubjectivity." This pure internal psychology is not restricted to the subject in himself. It grasps just as well the relations of different subjects to each other —i.e., intersubjectivity.

Internal observation is related to the empirical self. But Husserlian reflection is related to a transcendental subject which is pre-personal, and neutral with respect to the distinction between the empirical self and the other. In fact, in *The Cartesian Meditations,* he uses the notion of conduct, *Gebaren,* to introduce his discussion of the perceiving of another. Behavioristic psychology, therefore, offers no difficulties for an eidetic method. Eidetic insight applies just as well to the experience of another, because my experience and his are interrelated in my dealings with him (by "intentional transgression," as *The Cartesian Meditations* say). In a very early article of 1910 Husserl also said that the intersubjective determination of individual psychisms is possible.

Of this first objection, then, let us retain only the notions which Husserl left unclarified, at the time of the *Ideas,* concerning the relation between radical reflection—founded on the fact that I am no stranger to myself (Heidegger would say that I am not hidden from myself)— and that other awareness of myself which is not immediate and is capable of error as well as truth. This leads us now to the second objection, which is more interesting, since it penetrates to the heart of the matter. It will lead us to complete what we have said up to this point, just as it led Husserl himself to deepen his thought. Is it not true that an eidetic psychology, reflectively determining the basic categories of psychic life by reflecting on my experience of myself and the other, reduces psychology, in the narrower sense, to a very restricted role? Is it not, then, limited to a mere study of details?

In his earlier works Husserl went so far as to say at certain points that the relation of psychology to philosophy is almost that of content to form. It is philosophy that knows what space is. It is from psychology, on the other hand, that I gain some information concerning the perception of space through certain visual and tactual contents of experience. If one clings to formulae of this kind, everything essential seems to be furnished by phenomenology, or philosophic insight. Nothing more is left to psychology than to study certain empirical curiosities within the frames that are furnished by phenomenology.

In other texts Husserl wrote as if psychology ought to concern itself with causal relations, laws of fact through which the phenomena actually belonging to the province of philosophy are manifested. Psychology studies a consciousness which is introduced into the body and naturalized. It should concern itself only with those conditions of existence, or of the temporal order, in which certain aspects of the phenomenon, or essence, appear. But the description and comprehension of the phenomenon itself fall to phenomenology. Since the order of essences has its own certainties, these transcendental relations can never be denied by the order of psychological genesis which is concerned only with a special application. Is this really all that Husserl thought about the question? After all, the notion of *Wesenschau* was developed to found an activity of consciousness which would be concrete as well as philosophical, both linked to my experience as well as capable of universality. Does the conception of noetic insight, such as Husserl had developed it up to this point, correspond to these two conditions?

This question was not resolved in a satisfactory manner at the period of the *Ideas*, the work on which I have been so far commenting. But in the later works we can see a further effort to resolve it.

At the beginning of his career Husserl considered all questions concerning psychological genesis as secondary. They could in no case prevail against the philosophical problems concerning essence. But as his thought matured, he gave a meaning to genesis which was very different and much more positive—to such a degree, indeed, that in the *Cartesian Meditations* he speaks of a genetic phenomenology.

If in Husserl's view the knowledge of facts is impossible without some insight into essence and is always helped by this, it follows that all sound knowledge of facts must include, at least implicitly, some insight into essences, and that Husserl must admit, as he does in effect, that those psychologists who have been preoccupied with facts have nevertheless been able to find out something concerning essences. The division of labor between eidetic and empirical psychology turns out to be extremely difficult, since as soon as one engages in even the most experimental type of psychological research, in so far as he says anything sound and true, some insight into essence is implied by his work.

Husserl himself pointed out an analogy between what has happened in physics and what has happened in psychology. The physicists who created physics, in the modern sense of the word, had an insight into what a physical thing is. Galileo, for example, of whom Husserl often spoke, was certainly not a phenomenologist. He was not even a philosopher in any strict sense of the word. Nevertheless when he decided to study falling bodies, a certain intuition of what a physical body is was implied in this experimental investigation. Spatial determination, for example, was regarded as altogether fundamental. And when, after Galileo, other physicists added to our knowledge of nature, one can say that each of them contributed to the development of *an eidetic of physical things.* Husserl was not interested in making the knowledge of essences an exclusive privilege of phenomenologists. These are implied in all experimental research, and they appear there whether one is looking for them or not and whether one wants them or not.

But more needs to be said. It is not only true that a knowledge of facts always implies a knowledge of essences, but in addition to the factual link between the two psychologies, we are going to see that there is a much closer connection. In order to make this more precise, let us turn for a moment to the nature of the *Wesenschau.* We must remember that for Husserl this has the nature of a finding (constatation). He often speaks of an "eidetic constatation." We must also remember that he never envisaged an *a priori,* in the sense of a deductive psychology. He says in the *Ideas* that there is no "mathematics of phenomena," no "geometry of the lived." [8] Why not? Because eidetic, or phenomenological, psychology, in distinction from mathematics, is a science which is essentially descriptive. The multiplicities with which geometry is concerned are "mathematical multiplicities," which can be exhaustively defined—that is, by a system of axioms. But in phenomenology there is no question of defining the objects of psychology by any system of axioms which would enable us to construct these different psychical realities.

This is because the essences we may discover, when we force ourselves to think about lived experience, are not, in Husserl's terms, "exact essences" capable of an univocal determination. They are, rather, "morphological essences," which are inexact by nature. Husserl says in the *Ideas* that if one were to dream of a phenomenological psychology which would be deductive, he would fall into the same sort of difficulty as a geometer who, for example, might dream of giving a rigorous geometrical definition of terms such as "jagged," "notched like a lentil," or "like a sunshade." [9]

There is no geometric definition of these forms, and it is equally

8. *Idées directrices pour une phénoménologie,* trans. Ricoeur (Paris), p. 39.
9. *Ibid.,* p. 236.

impossible to give any constructive definition of the different realities with which psychology is concerned. It is through experience alone that they can be known, and not otherwise. From the very beginning, therefore, it has been necessary to maintain a close relation between eidetic intuition and that which we do, in fact, experience.

Husserl often says that to see an essence one must begin by having a perception, which serves as the base, or point of departure, for a *Wesenschau* but not as the source of its validity. The relation between perception and *Wesenschau* is one of founding [*Fundierung*]; perception, that is, serves as the ground, or pedestal, on which an insight into essence is formed. Thus insight into essence is an intellectual taking over, a making explicit and clarifying of something concretely experienced, and a recognition that it comes after something else, from which it starts, is essential to its nature. It also knows itself to be retrospective. The idea that it succeeds a more direct contact with the thing itself is enclosed within its very meaning.

One sees already in Husserl the idea of a double envelopment. It is true that reflective thought, which determines the meaning or essence, ends by possessing its object and enveloping it. But it is also true that essential insight always understands the concrete perception of experience as something here and now which precedes and therefore envelops it. In Husserl's words, the essence presupposes "an important part of intuition" bearing on the individual. It presupposes that an individual has appeared and that one has had a view of it. It also presupposes the *Sichtlichkeit,* the visibility of this individual. Or, to put it in another way, it is no insight into an essence if one's reflection cannot turn to a corresponding individual, if one cannot work out "a sense of examples" to illustrate his insight.

What, then, exactly is the relation between this sense of examples and what is called induction? It is in working out an answer to this question that we may be able to understand the relation between phenomenological and empirical, or inductive, psychology.

We must here recall the profound remarks of Husserl on induction in general. These were basically opposed to the theory of induction which held sway at the end of the nineteenth century, essentially that of Mill. According to this theory induction is a process by which, in considering a group of facts, we discover a common character and set it apart by abstraction, regarding it as essential to the group of facts from which we started. Or again, induction is an operation which enables us to find the cause of a phenomenon among its various antecedents, by discarding those which are neither constant nor unconditioned. According to Husserl, induction is not, and never has been, this. His remarks here anticipate those of Brunschwicg in his *l'Expérience humaine et la causalité physique.*

Let us return to the example of Galileo and the fundamental induction which, we may say, created modern physics. How does Galileo proceed? Does he consider different examples of falling bodies and then, by a method of agreement, following the theory of John Stuart Mill, abstract what is common to these examples? As a matter of fact, he proceeds in a totally different manner. The conception of the fall of bodies which guides his experiment is not found in the facts. He forms it actively; he constructs it. He freely conceives the pure case of a freely falling body, of which there is no given example in our human experience. Then, having constructed this idea, he verifies it by showing how the confused empirical facts, which never represent the free fall in its pure state, can then be understood through the introduction of additional conditions (friction, resistance, etc. . . .), which explain the difference between the facts and the pure concept. On the basis of the free fall, therefore, one constructs the fall of a body on an inclined plane.

Husserl says in the first volume of the *Logical Investigations* that the physicists proceed by *"idealisierende Fiktionen cum fundamento in re"*—that is, by idealizing fictions which are nevertheless founded on the facts. Let it be, he says, the law of Newton. Basically it makes no assertion about the existence of gravitating masses. It is another one of those idealizing fictions by which one purely conceives of what a gravitating mass would be. Then one determines what properties it would have, on the supposition that it exists. According to Husserl, Newton's law says nothing at all about existence. It refers only to what would belong to a gravitating mass as such.[10]

The method actually used by physicists, therefore, is not the chimerical induction of Mill, which is never practiced in the sciences. It is rather *a reading of the essence.* Through certain impure and imperfect phenomena, such as the fall of a body on an inclined plane, I read off the free fall of the body, which is theoretically conceived, or forged, by the intellect. That which gives its probable value to the induction and which finally shows that it is truly founded on things is not the number of facts invoked to justify it. No! It is rather the intrinsic clarity which these ideas shed on the phenomena we seek to understand. Just as Brunschwicg will show, in his *l'Expérience humaine et la causalité physique,* that one experiment will suffice to establish a law—that Davy, for example, established the existence of potassium by only one experiment of electrolysis—so Husserl maintained that induction is

10. "Prolegomena zur reinen Logik," *Logische Untersuchungen,* I, p. 150.

not founded on the collection of a vast number of cases. It is, rather, a process of intellectual analysis whose verification consists in the total, or at least sufficient, clarity which the group of concepts worked out in this way bring to the given phenomena. Thus laws are not basically live realities which would have a *force* and could rule over the facts. One should say, rather, in the language of Malebranche, that they are a light and not a force.

Let us now compare induction, understood in this way, with the phenomenological *Wesenschau*. This intuition of essences, like induction, as we have seen, is based on facts. The difference is that *Wesenschau* is based on the *imaginary "free variation" of certain facts*. In order to grasp an essence, we consider a concrete experience, and then we make it change in our thought, trying to imagine it as effectively modified in all respects. *That which remains invariable* through these changes is the essence of the phenomena in question.

For example, if we are seeking to form an idea of, or to understand the essence of, a spatial figure, such as this lamp, we must first perceive it. Then we will imagine all the aspects contained in this figure as changed. That which cannot be varied without the object itself disappearing is the essence. Suppose that we wish to form the idea of melody. We recall a tune which we have learned to sing, and suppose that all the notes and all the relations between the notes are changed. That which remains invariable and without which there would be no more melody is the essence we are seeking. In the same way, if we are trying to conceive the essence of a "social process," we will represent to ourselves a social process in which we have participated or concerning which we have some historical understanding. That which does not vary through all conceivable variations will be the essence. Even when one thinks in terms of the pure essence, one always thinks of the visible—the fact. But in the case of *Wesenschau*, the individual fact is neither grasped nor assumed as a reality, which is shown by the fact that we subject it to an imaginary variation.

We are thus led to the following conclusion: If eidetic psychology is a reading of the invariable structure of our experience based on examples, the empirical psychology which uses induction is also a reading of the essential structure of a multiplicity of cases. But the cases here are real and not imaginary. After closer examination, the only difference which we find between inductive procedure—so far as it is justifiable and moves toward what is truly essential—and the procedure of eidetic psychology is that the latter applies imaginary variation to its examples, while the former refers to effective variations in considering the different cases that are *actually realized*.

If we reflect further, we may see that the relation between the two is even closer. For when you make an induction on the basis of facts which are very large in number, you do not examine every possible, individual case. For example, when you establish the law of a physical phenomenon, you are not going to verify the law by every possible value of each variable. You will limit yourself to a finite number of experiments, and you will then single out one relation that you consider to be always true, even for the intermediate values between those that you have verified. This is called "interpolating," and it requires the use of that free variation of which Husserl spoke—at least in the intervals between the values effectively verified. In a certain number of decisive experiments you perceive certain relations, and you imagine the rest in function of these relations which are actually perceived in a finite number of cases. You link together the different examples effectively perceived by an imaginary variation which will lead from one to the other.

Let us now turn to an example from psychology, not physics: the important and interesting notion, now widely used, of behavioral lability or instability. How does one arrive at a notion of this sort? One says that a type of behavior is labile either when it is reproduced without any change under very different conditions—that is, when it is not flexible—or when it changes or disappears in a way that is wholly unpredictable. One calls an attitude labile both when it is too rigid and when it is not rigid enough. In using this notion, one therefore identifies the two extreme cases—excessive fixity on the one hand and too frequent change on the other. How is this possible? How does one arrive inductively at such a psychological notion? It is certainly not by any comparison of the given characters of psychological facts. One could compare the relevant psychological facts as much as one wishes without finding anything held in common. What is there in common between a stereotyped mode of conduct and one that is ever ready to disappear? Nothing, certainly, that is given with the facts. The notion of lability is constructed.

Goldstein introduced it with reference to what he called centered or non-centered behavior. The common element in extremely automatic behavior, on the one hand, and ephemeral behavior, on the other, is that neither of them is centered in the whole conduct of the individual. The lack of centering is the meaning held in common by modes of behavior which are absolutely episodic and others which are invariable and monotonous. In both of them we see that the connection between the situation and the response is wholly external, so that the situation does not guide the response. The construction of a concept of this kind is very close to Husserl's *Wesenschau*. This is doubtless why he says so often that everyone performs the *Wesenschau*. "The intuition of essences does not involve any more difficulties or 'mystical' secrets than perception." [11]

This *Wesenschau* is not the exclusive possession of the phenomenologists. As a matter of fact, Husserl says in the *Ideas* [12] that "everyone is constantly seeing ideas or essences and that everyone uses them in the operations of thought, in spite of the widespread opposition put forth in the name of points of view in the theory of knowledge." The empiricist theory of induction is one of these points of view (in the pejorative sense of this phrase), a vague opinion without rigor, which prevents us from seeing ourselves when we practice the *Wesenschau*, especially in making inductions.

In presenting the matter as I have, I am pushing Husserl further than he wished to go himself. He never expressly recognized the fundamental homogeneity of these two modes of knowledge, the inductive and the essential. He never admitted that in the last analysis they were indiscernible and simply differed in degree. Nevertheless his notion of an experienced essence, or an eidetic experience, contains in germ the consequence that I have just drawn from it. But it is a question here not so much of a consequence as of an inevitable dialectic of the concept of essence. It follows on principle from Husserl's point of departure and from what he proposed to do—namely, to show that this knowledge of essences is altogether experiential, that it does not involve any kind of supersensible faculty, and that in the last analysis the essence is just as contingent as the fact. It also follows inversely, from Husserl's point of departure and from the problem we have formulated in the preceding lectures, that any knowledge of fact always involves an *a priori* understanding of essence.

Instead of clearly recognizing the homogeneity of the two modes of knowledge, Husserl was content to insist, as he did very often, on the parallelism between psychology and phenomenology. "As a matter of principle," he said, psychology in its whole development is parallel to phenomenology. Of course, one might just as well say that phenomenology is always parallel to psychology and that every significant proposition of empirical psychology anticipates a phenomenological truth. As a matter of fact, Husserl did say that "every empirical discovery as well as every eidetic discovery made on the one side must correspond to a parallel discovery on the other." [13] This means that for every assertion

11. "Die Philosophie als strenge Wissenschaft," *Logos* I (1910), pp. 289 ff.
12. *Op. cit.*, p. 74.
13. *Nachwort zu meinen Ideen.*

of experimental psychology a corresponding eidetic assertion can be found.

We are here very far from the idea of an eidetic psychology which by reflection alone would give us the principles of any possible psychological process and which would pass from the particular case of a real mental activity to that of other men as well. We are far from the idea of a philosophical psychology which would determine not the real but the whole range of the possibly human. It is human reality which now emerges as *the locus of the Wesenschau.* It is in becoming conscious of myself as I am that I am able to see essences, and in this context the real and the possible are not distinct.

Husserl even comes to say that "intentional psychology already carries the transcendent within itself." [14] This really means that there cannot be any basic discord between the point of view of psychology and that of phenomenology. It is always the same subject, man, that is being approached in one way or the other. Our image of man may be acquired with all the presuppositions of an empirical psychology, which takes him as situated within the chains of worldly causality. But this empirical psychology, if it really pays attention to what it is describing, will always end by making room for a different perspective which sees man not as a mere part of the world but as the bearer of reflection. Thus the interpenetration of psychology and phenomenology—their reciprocal envelopment—is clearly indicated in these texts as well as in those I have previously cited.

Certain formulae of Sartre, therefore, in the last chapter of his small book on *Imagination,* where he tries to define the thought of Husserl, definitely stand in need of correction. Sartre writes here as if phenomenological, or eidetic, psychology ought to come *first* and ought to rule over all the fundamental questions. Then after we have learned something about all possible psychic processes in general, experience may show us the actual facts. But in the basic intention of Husserl, the relation of these two approaches is not merely one of simple succession, as if one could see essences without any factual experience or could come to the facts without implying, in his very approach, a certain vision of essence. Sartre writes: "After one has determined the various conditions that a psychic state must necessarily possess if it is to be an image, then only may we pass from the certain to the probable, and ask of experience what it can teach us about the images which are actually present in a contemporary human consciousness." What is perhaps the most important aspect of Husserl's whole project is lacking in this statement.

14. Méditations Cartésiennes (Paris, 1931), p. 126.

As a matter of fact, Sartre himself does not follow the rule that he here lays down. Although he presents empirical psychology as the servant of phenomenology, he says, nevertheless, that he embarks on the study of emotion "without waiting for the phenomenology of emotion to be completed." [15] This means that basically experimental studies, like those of Janet, Lewin, and the psychoanalysts, must already reveal to us, at least in a confused way, the essence of that with which they are concerned. However it may be with his formulations, Sartre actually understands the relation between psychology and phenomenology in the way which I have just now tried to explain.

When he departs from this, he is led to artificial distinctions. For example, his book, *l'Imaginaire*, follows this simple plan: Part I, "The Certain"; Part II, "The Probable." In the first part he gives a phenomenological analysis of the essence of the image. In the second, he turns to the data of experience with the understanding that what has been acquired in the first part is unshakable and certain, while what is now coming is only probable. But when one reads the work carefully, one finds that certain results of the first part are actually called in question in the second. At the beginning of his book, for example, Sartre shows that the image is defined by its deception and by the fact that it is unobservable and empty. When I try to imagine the Pantheon, I believe that I see it. But if I try to count the pillars, I find that I cannot do so, which means that basically I do not see anything at all. The initial phenomenological analysis determines the essence of the image as a false presence, as a nothing which tries to present itself as a something.

But in the second part of the book this fundamental definition of the image is placed in question when the author analyzes certain states where a clear distinction between the perceived and the imaginary cannot be made. If the image were nothing but what was first said— empty and absent—we would never confuse it with a perception, and illusions would be hard to understand. Thus in so far as Sartre raises the question of illusions in the second part, he necessarily suggests the possibility of a situation anterior to the clear distinction between perception and imagination which was made at the start. He does this, and with good reason. But this means that it is impossible to understand the image by an examination of the pure possibility of an image in general and by a definition which we would then merely apply to the analogous empirical examples.

These remarks have a certain importance because they will enable us to reply to a certain objection often made against phenomenologists —namely, that they represent a new type of scholasticism. This means

15. *Esquisse d'une théorie des émotions* (Paris, 1939).

that phenomenological research remains purely verbal. In this view, eidetic intuition would consist in reflecting on the meaning of certain words in use, like the word "image" or the word "emotion," and then in developing this meaning with the firm conviction of reaching the things themselves. This complaint is not well founded if one refers to what Husserl actually intended. But there are certain formulae of Max Scheler which merit this reproach. For example, Scheler says that the intuition of essences is absolutely indubitable for a rather simple reason: because, by definition, experience can never contradict such an intuition. If experience should show me an image which does not correspond to what I have determined to be the essence, then of course, by definition, this is not an image. In the same way I may lay down a certain idea of social process. Then if I find a so-called social process in everyday history or in the past, which does not possess the essential characteristics I have focused, I have the right to say that it is not a social process. Here we are certainly close to scholasticism. If one had followed this principle in practice, the whole of phenomenology would be an instrument for developing the definitions of words.

But Husserl never thought in this way, and he was fully aware of the danger. Since his early article on "Die Philosophie als strenge Wissenschaft," [16] he maintained that there was nothing in common between intuition, as he understood it, and a scholastic process which "pretends to draw a real knowledge of things from the analytic judgment that one can make on the meanings of words." Husserl was, therefore, well aware of the danger of self-deception in proceeding by "eidetic intuition." It is possible for me to believe that I am seeing an essence when, in fact, it is not an essence at all but merely a concept rooted in language, a prejudice whose apparent coherence reduces merely to the fact that I have become used to it through habit. The best way of guarding against this danger would be to admit that, though a knowledge of facts is never sufficient for grasping an essence and though the construction of "idealizing fictions" is always necessary, I can never be sure that my vision of an essence is anything more than a prejudice rooted in language—if it does not enable me to hold together all the facts which are known and which may be brought into relation with it. Failing this, it may not be an essence at all but only a prejudice. I believe that the logic of things ought to have led Husserl to admit a very close relation between induction, as he understood it, and *Wesenschau* and consequently a final homogeneity among the different psychologies, whether they be inductive or phenomenological. I have already said that Husserl never explicitly stated this. But at least he was well aware of the necessity of defending phe-

16. *Op. cit.*, p. 305.

nomenology against verbalism. Also, after he renounced the dogmatic solution of an "apodictic evidence" which would enable us from the very start to transcend language, he was obliged, as we shall see, to reconsider the imaginary "variation" of anthropological experience as the way toward eidetic intuition.

Husserl consistently rejected the different psychologies which developed in his time, including Gestalt psychology, which had been created by writers familiar with his teaching and influenced by him. In his *Nachwort zu meinen Ideen,* Husserl declared that it makes no difference in principle whether one conceives of consciousness as a totality or as a sum of psychic atoms, since even this totality of the Gestaltists is just another thing and therefore not a consciousness.

In his *Principles of Gestalt Psychology,* Koffka replied to this criticism in an interesting way. "A theory like mine," he said, "seems to imply an extreme psychologism, the idea that all logical relations and subsistents can be explained by existing relations in the domain of psychology or physiology." Gestalt theory admits that all structures of consciousness finally depend on physiological processes of the same form ("isomorphic") as their causal foundation. This would seem to imply a position of extreme psychologism, since the whole order of meanings would seem to rest on the order of natural events. But Koffka is saying here that in a psychology like his there is a new way of describing consciousness which avoids the opposed difficulties of both psychologism and logicism. The description of "psychic process" in terms of structure should give basic satisfaction to philosophy in vindicating the order of meanings.

Koffka developed this idea in the following words: "This conception [of psychologism], which had gained ground at the end of the last century, was violently attacked by some of our best philosophers, and in particular by Edmund Husserl, who claimed to have refuted it once and for all. But Husserl's argument rests on the explicit or implicit assumption that every psychological theory reduces psychological relations to external relations of pure fact. Husserl, and also other philosophers, have certainly refuted a psychologism of this kind. But this refutation does not affect our psychologism, if, indeed, this term truly applies to our conception, for according to it, psychological and physiological processes, or rather, psycho-physical processes, are organized by relations that are wholly intrinsic. This means that according to our view, psychology and logic, existence and subsistence, and in certain respects even reality and truth, do not belong to two domains or two universes of discourse so basically different that no intelligible relation can exist between them. Here lies the opportunity for psychology to play the integrating role which we have assigned to it at the beginning of our work." [17]

These remarks of Koffka go farther. Husserl's constant objection to Gestalt theory, as to all psychology, is that it fails to understand the radical and absolute originality of consciousness, which it reduces either to psychological atoms, as the older psychologists did, or to "total" structures which are nevertheless dependent on the natural order of events. But following certain suggestions of Husserl which we have cited above, we may give the following reply: If the notion of Gestalt helps us to understand many facts and is fruitful in the empirical order, it must have some phenomenological truth and must have something to contribute to phenomenology. We do not have to take over the physiological hypotheses of the Gestaltists, their cerebral explanations of conscious structures. We should directly consider what they say of consciousness and of the patterns of conduct. We may then see that they are calling our attention at this level, not to events that are completely external to each other, but to an internal organization which makes the notions of value and meaning come to life. This is enough to show that the Gestalt theory is not merely a new variety of psychologism. It is rather a way of showing that conscious phenomena are both temporal (for they happen in time and occur at a definite moment) and yet at the same time internally significant, so that they can support a certain kind of knowledge and truth.

In other words, I believe that to give weight to his eidetic intuition and to distinguish it sharply from verbal concepts, Husserl was really seeking, largely unknown to himself, a notion like that of the Gestaltists—the notion of an order of meaning which does not result from the application of spiritual activity to an external matter. It is, rather, a spontaneous organization beyond the distinction between activity and passivity, of which the visible patterns of experience are the symbol. In Gestalt psychology everything bears a meaning. There is no psychic phenomenon which is not oriented toward a certain significance. It is really a psychology founded on the idea of intentionality. But this sense, which inhabits all psychic phenomena, is not produced by a pure activity of the spirit. It is, rather, an earthy and aboriginal sense, which constitutes itself by an organization of the so-called elements.

This, perhaps, might have been the occasion for Husserl to recognize a certain truth in the "integrating psychology" of Koffka. By entering into the region of facts and clarifying some of them, it has at the same time glimpsed certain essential, philosophical truths without

17. Koffka, *Principles of Gestalt Psychology* (London, 1935), pp. 570–71.

knowing or willing this—just as Galileo, who had no intention of working out an eidetic of the *res extensa,* actually did, in his experimental work, lay the foundations for this eidetic.

[3] THE SCIENCES OF MAN ACCORDING TO HUSSERL

IN HUSSERL'S THINKING concerning linguistics and history, we observe a development of the way in which he focused the problem, which is quite similar to what happened to his conception of psychology and which, in fact, sheds light upon the latter. In what follows, our aim will not be to repeat everything that Husserl said about linguistics and history but rather to apply his thoughts on these subjects to the clarification of psychology.

1. *Linguistics*

AT THE beginning of his studies, like the grammarians of the seventeenth and eighteenth centuries, he proposed to phenomenology the task of establishing a universal grammar by an apprehension of the essence of language. Just as we need an eidetic psychology which will determine the essences of the different regions of psychic activity, so also we need an eidetic of language which will enumerate and describe those "forms of meaning" without which no language is possible. The grammarian will never be able really to engage in the study of languages without going through this eidetic. We speak German, Husserl says, and when we embark on the study of a foreign language, we tend to understand this language from a German point of view. We conceive of its grammar and its categories in relation to those of the German language.

But if we wish to gain a truly adequate understanding of a foreign mode of speech, we must not proceed in this way. First of all, we must perform a reduction on all the presuppositions of our native tongue, in order to isolate the fundamental articulations of language itself, without which no language is possible. It is only on the basis of this universal grammar that we will be able to think through the different languages in their specificity, by reconstructing their inner patterns. We must study, Husserl says, such basic forms as categorical propositions with their primitive specifications, complex conjunctive and disjunctive propositions, and the ways of expressing universality, particularity, and singularity. It is only by keeping these fundamental operations in view that we will be able to ask how the German language, the Chinese, etc., express "the" proposition of existence, "the" categorical proposition, "the" hypothetical premise, "the" plural, and "the" different modalities of the possible.

Husserl goes on to say: "We cannot evade the question as to whether the grammarian will be content with his own personal and prescientific views, or with the confused empirical representations provided by a particular historical grammar, like Latin, of the forms of signification. Is he following such feeble guides? Or does he have in view the pure system of linguistic patterns in a scientifically determined and theoretically coherent form—that is to say, in the form of our theory of patterns of signification?" [18]

The eidetic of language should therefore be established at the very beginning. The empirical study of language should come afterward, directing itself to the relevant facts, clarifying them, and then reconstructing them in the light of the essences already determined.

At the beginning of his career, Husserl thought that we could bypass our mother tongue in reflecting on language as such, thus penetrating to the essences which belong necessarily to any possible language. After this, we might then understand our own peculiar ways of speaking as special cases of this universal language. This mode of approach is interesting, because it involves a dogmatic conception of the *Wesenschau*. With respect to such a conception the following question at once arises: Do we have at our disposal the means of detaching ourselves from the historical roots of the language we speak, so that we can penetrate directly to the essence of language in general?

To arrive at this universal, rational grammar, is it sufficient merely to reflect on the language which we already speak and possess, or is it essential that we should first make contact with other languages? Is language an instrument that we may directly objectivize and dominate by the *Wesenschau*, which will give us a reliable knowledge of its necessary and universal structure? Or is it not true, rather, that we gain access to the universal structure of language only by first learning other languages and by coexisting with them?

Can we order the universal functions of language in a table of canonical forms that any language must possess to be a language? Or is it not true, rather, that we gain access to what different languages have in common only by grasping something of their total power of expression, without being able to make certain forms of one correspond to forms of the other, without seeing them all in the light of one single, universal language?

This question is exactly parallel to the one which we raised in our

18. "Der Unterschied der selbstständigen und unselbstständigen Bedeutungen und die Idee der reinen Grammatik," *Logische Untersuchungen*, II, 4, p. 339.

consideration of psychology. When Husserl laid it down that all empirical research must be preceded by an eidetic intuition of what an image is, what a perception is or in general by the apprehension of a pure essence, we raised the question of whether we could arrive at such conceptions without recourse to the facts. And since Husserl himself conceived of his eidetic intuition as an *experience,* a constatation, we then raised further questions concerning the relation between this contact with the facts, which is realized in science, and the sovereign insight which enables us to grasp essences through the facts in which they are incarnate.

At the beginning of his investigations, Husserl seems to absorb all facts into a universe of thought which determines every psychological possibility, as it should be determined, before any serious reference to empirical psychology. But here, as elsewhere, Husserl was not able, and finally did not wish, to defend a *dualism* between the experimental (scientific) knowledge of facts and philosophical reflection.

As his thought developed, his conception of the relation between language and reflection changed profoundly. At the beginning, there is a way of thought which detaches itself from concrete language and constructs a table of all linguistic possibilities. But as he advanced, our reflection on language appeared to him less and less an operation by which we may bypass concrete languages to arrive at a pure, universal essence, of which each empirical mode of speech is only a possible instance. This reflection becomes less and less a sovereign thinking, owing nothing to the facts. The a priori of language (what one finds by reflecting on it) is less and less a "general and rational grammar."

In an issue of the *Revue Internationale de Philosophie,* [19] H. J. Pos showed that, according to the last conceptions of Husserl, reflecting on language no longer means to depart from it in order to arrive at a thought which will completely envelop and possess it. To reflect on language is, rather, to recover an experience which is anterior to the objectivizing of language and certainly anterior to the scientific observation of it. In this experience the subject, who speaks and writes, passes beyond language only by exercising it and by taking it over.

According to Pos, there is a fundamental difference between the philosopher, or the phenomenologist, who reflects on language and the scholar who knows language objectively, according to the documents which are there before him. The phenomenologist tries to recover an awareness of what a speaking subject really is. He is certainly not in the attitude of a learned observer who is confronting something external to him. This observer, for example, may be considering the state of

19. *Phénoménologie de linguistique* (Bruxelles, 1939).

the French language at the time when I am speaking and may be showing how this is explained by some preceding state. He is thus relating the present to the past. But the speaking subject is not concerned with the past. Most of those who are presently speaking French know nothing of etymology or of the linguistic past which has made possible the language they are speaking. And the linguists themselves admit that this is explained not by its historical origins but rather by actual usage. The speaking subject is turned toward the future. Language for him is above all a means of expression and of communicating to others his intentions, which are also turned toward the future.

The observer also has a strong tendency to analyze into a series of processes which he regards as relatively independent of one another. He will show how such and such a French turn of phrase goes back to a certain origin and how other parts of the French system go back to other origins. He may even show, as a result of such analysis, how the unity of a given language breaks down. Thus there is no precise moment in history when Latin ceases and French begins. There is no such moment at which one can reasonably say: here is the frontier between Latin and French. There is no rigorous procedure which will enable us to determine the exact beginning of a linguistic reality. It has no precise spatial and temporal limits.

Similarly if we look within a given language, we find different dialects which are compatible with its unity but whose limits are extremely vague. If one defines *Provençal* by a certain number of words, turns of phrase, forms of expression, etc., there is no moment when all these are in use equally and at once, no determinate place where *Provençal* as a whole is perfectly realized. Between the regions where it is dominant and those where it does not prevail there are always zones of transition.

This led Vendryes [20] to say that a language can never be identified as a reality. It is, rather, "an ideal which never succeeds in being realized." We may say that it is in the air *between* the speaking subjects but never fully realized in any of them. From the point of view of the observer, therefore, there is reason for doubting the reality of different languages. And as we have seen, Vendryes conceded some truth to the idea that there is only one single language, since there is no way of finding the precise limit where one passes to another.

But for the subject who is actually speaking, who is no longer an *observer* confronting language as an *object*, his language is undoubtedly a distinct reality. There are regions where he can make himself understood and others where he cannot. For him it means

20. Joseph Vendryes, *Le langage; introduction linguistique à l'histoire* (Paris, 1921).

something to be speaking French. The circumstances may be more or less precise, more or less rigorous, more or less complex, depending on the culture of the speaker. But for him there is always a moment, a boundary, beyond which he no longer understands and is no longer understood.

These two points of view are different. And according to Pos, the most distinctive idea in Husserl's thought about language at the end of his life is that the chief task of linguistic philosophy, or phenomenology, is to regain an awareness of the speaking subject. He moved far from the old text of the *Logical Investigations,* to which I have just referred. There is no longer any question of making us leap beyond language into a universe of thought in which it would be included as a particular sector. Reflection on language now consists not in returning to a transcendental subject, disengaged from all actual linguistic situations, but to a speaking subject who has no access to any truth nor to any thought with a claim to universality except through the practice of his language in a definite linguistic situation.

Husserl's change of mind on this point is linked with the maturing of his whole philosophy. In our thinking we do not find in particular phenomena, such as language, a consciousness which can dispose in an explicit fashion of all that is necessary to constitute itself. We must, rather, become aware of this paradox—that we never free ourselves from the particular except by taking over a situation that is all at once, and inseparably, both limitation and access to the universal. There is no longer any question of constructing a logic of language, a universal grammar, but rather of finding a *logos* already incorporated in the word. Husserl was saying of language what he also said of other sectors of his philosophy, that the most profound reflection consists in rediscovering a basic faith, or opinion [*Urglaube, Urdoxa*]—that is, a reason which is already incorporated in sensible phenomena. It seemed to him that to reflect on language is to clarify the activity of the speaking subject, to find a reason already incorporated in these means of expression, this language which I know because I am it.

This is why, in his last unedited writings,[21] Husserl found a much deeper significance in the problem of language. In *Formal and Transcendental Logic,* published during his lifetime, he already expressly indicated that to speak is not at all *to translate a thought into words.* It is rather *to see a certain object* by the word. "The intention of signifying (*Meinung*) is not found outside the words or at their side. It is rather the case that, in speaking, I constantly achieve an internal fusion of the intention with the words. This intention, we may say, animates the

---

21. Many of these have now been published by the Husserl Archives at Louvain under the direction of R. P. H. Van Breda.

words, and as a result all the words, and indeed each word, incarnate an intention; and once incarnated, they bear this in themselves as their meaning." [22]

The relation of language to thought is here comparable to that of the body to consciousness, a problem with which Husserl was always preoccupied. At the beginning of his career, he insisted on the fact that this relation was purely external. When I reflect on consciousness, I find it pure. But when I think about man—that is, consciousness linked to a body—I must perform what he called an "apperception." This means that I must seize this consciousness not as it truly is in itself but only as it is causally linked to a certain object which I call "the body." Thus according to this first conception, my relation to another person consists only in conceiving, or "apperceiving," back of the body-object a thinker who is not mixed with this body and is not altered by being joined to it. But as Husserl's thought matured—for example, in the *Cartesian Meditations*, written much later—his conception of the relation of one person to another and of consciousness to the body, became much more profound.

In the *Cartesian Meditations* the experience of the other is like something taught me by the spontaneity of my body. It is as if my body learns what my consciousness cannot, for this body takes the actions of the other into account, realizes a sort of coupling with them, or an "intentional transgression," without which I would never gain the notion of the other as other. Thus the body is not only an object to which my consciousness finds itself externally linked. For me it is the only way of knowing that there are other animated bodies, which also means that its own link with my consciousness is more internal and essential.

The same is true of language. Consciousness of language is no longer the separated foundation of a language, which is secondary to it and derived. To know what language is, it is necessary first of all to speak. It no longer suffices to reflect on the languages lying before us in historical documents of the past. It is necessary to take them over, to live with them, to speak them. It is only by making contact with this speaking subject that I can get a sense of what other languages are and can move around in them.

This explains why it is that finally, in the unpublished texts of Husserl—that on *The Origin of Geometry*,[23] for example—he admitted that the problem of language is fundamental, if one wishes to gain any true clarity on the existence of ideas and cultural objects in the actual world. We must recognize that what we call "ideas" are carried into the

22. *Formale und Transzendentale Logik* (Halle, 1929), p. 20.
23. Published by the *Revue Internationale de Philosophie*, 1939.

world of existence by their instruments of expression—books, museums, musical scores, writings. If we wish to understand how the phenomenon of "ideal existence" is possible for a number of subjects, who do not live at the same time, to participate in the same ideas, we must first understand how the thoughts of one single subject are incorporated in the cultural instruments which convey them outside and make them accessible to others. "I do not wish to elaborate here on the problem of the origin of language in its ideal existence, as founded on external expression and on the public document, although I am perfectly clear that a radical clarification of the mode of being of ideal complexes finds here its last condition." [24]

We are far from the initial position of the *Logical Investigations,* where the existence of a given, particular language was founded on ideal existence, a universal grammar, the essence of language. Here the possibility of an ideal existence and of communication between particular subjects is finally founded on the act of speaking as it is realized in writing or in the spoken word. There is no longer any question of starting with a universal language which would furnish the invariable plan of any possible mode of speech, and of then proceeding to the analysis of particular languages. It is exactly the reverse. The language which is present, actual, and effective becomes the model for understanding other possible modes of speech. It is in our experience of the speaking subject that we must find the germ of universality which will enable us to understand other languages.

There is no doubt, I believe, that Husserl was here approaching certain insights of contemporary linguistics, especially that of Saussure. This return to the speaking subject, which Husserl called the phenomenology of language, is required not only for philosophic thought but for linguistics itself, as Saussure conceived of it. To deal with given languages objectively is not enough. We must study the subject who is actually speaking. To the linguistic of language we must add the linguistic of the word. This convergence of the thought of Husserl and Saussure is relevant to what I was saying above concerning the relation between psychology and phenomenology—namely, that there is agreement, not opposition, between the immanent development of the sciences of man and that of phenomenology. This agreement promises us a solution of problems concerning the relation between these sciences and philosophy. As his thinking developed, Husserl was led to link more and more what he had at first sharply separated—the possible and the actual, essence and existence. This movement corresponds to the evolution of the human sciences, in so far as they are tending to free themselves from those scientistic and positivistic postu-

24. *Ibid.,* p. 210.

lates which perhaps favored their beginnings but which are now re-
tarding their further development.

2. *History*

HERE AGAIN, at the beginning Husserl affirmed the neces-
sity of an eidetic of history, an *a priori* science which would determine
the real meaning of a number of concepts historians use blindly and
without careful examination. One cannot learn what a "social process"
or a "religion" is simply by doing empirical history and by being a
historian. It is certainly clear that, in so far as these historians have
not clarified the sense of the words they are using, they themselves
do not know what it is they are talking about. If it aims to show that
historical work must define the categories, or essences, implied in it,
this remark is sound.

Take, for example, Durkheim's famous investigation of totemism
in his *Formes élémentaires de la vie religieuse*. He asked himself how
one should understand the phenomenon of the sacred as it is found in
Australian totemism. Having shown that, in the tribes considered, the
experience of the sacred occurs at moments devoted to totemic celebra-
tions and at annual reunions when social bonds are strongest, he
thought he could draw the conclusion that in general the sacred is an
expression of the social. Since the sacred is an essential element in
religion, he also concluded that religion in general is the social.

It is of course true that definitions are free and that Durkheim had
the right to call the social, and the sacred, religious. But in giving the
title *Elementary Forms of the Religious Life* to his book, he implied
something more. He meant to say that the phenomena studied by him
(Australian totemism) are *elementary*—that is, they reveal the elements, or the essence, of religion in such a way that every particular
religion must be considered as a variation on this theme. With respect
to a postulate of this kind, the demands of Husserl seem to be justified.
Even if this study of the sacred in Australian totemism were itself
incontestable, the question of whether the sacred is the "elementary,"
or essential, religious phenomenon would still be left open. There are
many religious phenomena which are more rich and more varied
than Australian totemism. Must we believe that they are mere super-
structures based on the sacred as it is experienced by these tribes? This
cannot be postulated, and it is precisely the object of Husserl's questions to obtain such a clarification. What is a religion, or what is the
essence of religion? If it really is the sacred, then Durkheim may draw
his universal conclusion. But if the sacred is only a lateral, or derived,
phenomenon, always present but never having the same sense in differ-

ent religions, then Durkheim's investigations do not authorize the general conclusion he wished to draw from them.

There is, therefore, something well founded in this idea of Husserl that contact with the facts is not enough to determine, for example, whether we ought to distinguish between "religion as an idea and religion as a cultural form." History shows cultural forms to which we give the name "religion," but from the variety, confusion, and incoherence of these phenomena, as they are given, should we conclude that they can still be analyzed? Or should we wait for another possible experience that would be not only religious but also pure religion? This question cannot be answered by a mere examination of the facts. It requires reflection on the essence of religion, as well as a phenomenology of history. In the same way history shows us that Egyptian art is such and such, that Greek art is this and that. But on this basis one cannot come to any legitimate conclusion concerning the universal forms of all possible art. We must begin by reflecting on what art is, on what it can be—which is again a determination of essence. History also shows us a number of juridical systems. But according to Husserl the investigation of relevant historical facts in which just law is manifested remains "confused," unless one has determined what just law is, in principle, by a reflection that is not of the empirical order.

Husserl first said, in brief, that history is unable to judge an idea. It is true that there are historians who write as if the ideas are being judged by the facts. The reciting of events or the analysis of institutions seems by itself to show that a certain ideal pattern, such as religion or monarchy, either is or is not coherent, either depends or does not depend on a chance coincidence. But in reality, Husserl said, the history which sets up values and judges, arrives at these values not in the facts but in an ideal sphere. It involves a latent phenomenology which is not expressed and which is, therefore, probably incorrect. In his first conception the hierarchy is very clear. There is a reflection on historical possibilities which is autonomous and independent of any knowledge of historical facts.

The conception of historicity which Husserl constructed at the beginning of his career resulted directly from this principle. He found among his contemporaries certain philosophers who were concerned to remain in close touch with the present. They accepted the *Weltanschauung* conception of Dilthey. According to them, philosophy is not a type of knowledge which develops with absolute certainty outside time. At each moment it should be, rather, a conscious grasp of what is sound in the scientific results already acquired as well as a synthesis of these, which must be provisional, approximative, and only probable. In his article "Philosophie als strenge Wissenschaft" [25] Husserl took a stand against the position of these philosophers. He did this in a manner which was decisive but also carefully shaded.

He began by declaring that Dilthey and the *Weltanschauung* philosophy were certainly responding to a *legitimate need*—that of deciding in a single lifetime to live in the light of reflection and to arrive in this way at effective, practical conclusions. This philosophy, he said, has a firm grasp of the truth that we have an end in the finite, since our lives are limited and we have to govern them. It would be nonsense to deny these responsibilities. In a unique life there must be a method of constant approximation rather than practical, apodictic certainties. Morality would lose its meaning if it were emptied of its essential finitude. Moral man must arrive at judgments and, in any case, at acts which imply judgments. Similarly it is necessary for him to orient himself in the world and at each moment to have a conception of the world, even though scientific philosophy, which is certain and rigorous, is not yet fully developed.

Only, Husserl adds, this practical necessity of answering problems of existence is not a sufficient justification for the conception of philosophy as a *Weltanschauung* that is merely probable. A truly rigorous philosophy would give an answer to the problems of the time. It would construct the idea of our time, and would think this time through just as well as, or even better than, the others. As a consequence, precisely in being *philosophia perennis,* it would be the philosophy of the present. If under the pretext that this philosophy is not yet on hand, one turns from it and abandons it for the sake of a *Weltanschauung,* one weakens true philosophy and postpones the solution of the problems posed. Therefore we should not look to wisdom but to philosophy, not to a mere view of the world (*Weltanschauung*) but to the science of the world (*Weltwissenschaft*). So Husserl decided against these philosophers of *Weltanschauung,* who are able to struggle but never to gain a decisive solution. According to him, they "place their end in the finite. They wish to have their system, and then enough time to live in accordance with it." [26]

Husserl, therefore, recognized that the problems posed by the present are legitimate, and he never said that philosophy ought to abandon them. But he thought that it could not arrive at these problems of life except by the way of an absolute knowledge. If *de jure* philosophical research is not remote from the present, at least *de facto* it is, and since it requires much time and all our human powers, it should become in

25. *Op. cit.*
26. "Die Philosophie als strenge Wissenschaft," p. 338.

itself a way of existing and not a mere preparation for life, as it was for Dilthey. Thus Husserl never denied that the philosopher experiences the need of thinking through and of judging his time, in so far as he has to live an individual life. But he did not want to sacrifice the least element of philosophical rigor to present exigencies. Hence he conceded, as a consequence he had not wished but had to accept, that philosophers should not have any deeply motivated opinion on present affairs, if at this price they could contribute to the founding of a truly rigorous philosophy which eventually would be a total philosophy and, therefore, also a philosophy of the present.

We must here remember that even at the beginning Husserl never chose eternity as against time. He never said that philosophical existence was absolute. He said only that, since philosophy demands an unlimited effort, if we wish it to be truly rigorous and truly a philosophy, we must sell neither it nor our powers to our time. As a matter of fact, Husserl knew that philosophy had eaten up the whole of his life, and he never complained. But he never thought that philosophy was the whole of life.

Afterward he perceived that philosophical activity cannot be defined as reflection concerned with essences, as opposed to practical activity concerned with existence. In order to see things more clearly than he had been able to see them in the past, what was of primary importance now seemed to him to be historicity. When one reflects and thinks things through to the very end, one will not necessarily arrive at eternal truths. By the purest thought one will, rather, discover an intelligible becoming of ideas, a "generation of meaning" [Sinngenesis]. In the last analysis, cultural realities are of such a nature that we cannot reflect on them without discovering in the sense of these notions a "sedimented history." It may be the theorem of Pythagoras; it may be the more modern conceptions of geometry in the nineteenth century. When we reflect on these ideas it may seem to us, at our first view, that we have arrived at invariable elements, always the same in all thinking for all men who have lived or ever will live.

But after regarding them more carefully, we perceive that Euclidean geometry includes ideas, of course, but ideas that have a date. Nineteenth-century geometry takes them over but defines them otherwise and finally considers Euclidean space as a special case of one that is more general. This means that in spite of its apparent lucidity and its air of eternity, Euclidean space was not self-evident. Until the time of the non-Euclidean geometries, it was not entirely penetrated by the spirit but included a certain coefficient of contingency. It was, after all, a cultural formation which included finite and "naïve" elements linked to a certain temporal state of knowledge. Hence while it did not have to be destroyed or discounted by what came after, it had to be at least completed, elaborated, and sublimated by later geometric conceptions. Thus when we reflect even on geometric notions, we discover a historical becoming. As Plato said long ago, we discover that the ideas are not at rest.

If this is true, where, then—if we may speak in this way—is the place of philosophy? It is evidently not in the event; nor is it in the eternal. It is in a history which is not the sum of these events placed end to end, since they force each other out of existence. But this history is thinkable, comprehensible. It offers us an order, a sense to which I do not have to submit but which I can place in perspective. Husserl called this an "intentional history." Others have called it "dialectic." This is why we find terms in the later writings of Husserl that he would not have thought of employing at the beginning, such as "the European sciences." He came to see an essential value in the historical development of European philosophy and science which must be continued. Certain notions cannot be attained except by a series of successive steps and by a sedimentation of meaning which makes it impossible for the new sense to appear before its time and apart from certain factual conditions. Of course, this knowledge is universal, and there is no question of restricting it to those who have brought it forth or of limiting it to European forms of existence. In order to surmount the crisis it is going through, it must be rendered universal in fact, as it is in right. Certainly nothing was more foreign to Husserl than a European chauvinism. For him European knowledge would maintain its value only by becoming capable of understanding what is not itself.

What is new in the later writings is that to think philosophically, to be a philosopher, is no longer to leap from existence to essence, to depart from facticity in order to join the idea. To think philosophically, to be a philosopher—in relation to the past, for example—is to understand this past through the internal link between it and us. Comprehension thus becomes a coexistence in history, which extends not only to our contemporaries but also to Plato, to what is back of us, and to what is before us and far distant. Philosophy is the taking over of cultural operations begun before our time and pursued in many different ways, which we now "reanimate" and "reactivate" from the standpoint of our present. Philosophy lives from this power of *interesting* ourselves in everything that has been and is attempted in the order of knowledge and of life, and of finding a sharable sense in it, as if all things were present to us through our present. The true place of philosophy is not time, in the sense of discontinuous time, nor is it the eternal. It is rather the "living present" (*lebendige Gegenwart*)—that is, the present in which the whole past, everything foreign, and the whole of the thinkable future are reanimated.

So far as historical investigations are concerned, we can now see that at the end of his life Husserl came to have a very different idea of them from that which he had at the beginning. He now saw in histori- cal and ethnographic facts a value, a significance, a power of teaching that he had not seen before.

He admitted from the beginning that history can teach something to the philosopher; it can lead him to the objective spirit [*Gemein- geist*].[27] He had already indicated that a historian who criticizes a phenomenon—like "Christianity" or "monarchy," for example—show- ing that these are nothing but names given to series of incoherent facts lacking any essential unity, is already beginning a work of reflection and doing philosophy without knowing it. All criticism, he said, is the inverse side of a positive affirmation. Consequently, every historical criticism involves a systematic intuition which must be brought into the light. Hence he was prepared to grant, at this early stage of his career, that there was a confused intuition of essence in concrete historical research. Later on he conceded more explicitly that contact with historical or ethnological facts is not only suggestive but even indispensable for any true apprehension of the possible.

It is important to note the extraordinary interest aroused in Husserl by his reading of Lévy-Bruhl's *Primitive Mythology* (*Mythologie primi- tive*), which seems rather remote from his ordinary concerns. What interested him here was the contact with an alien culture, or the impulse given by this contact to what we may call his philosophical imagination. Before this, Husserl had maintained that a mere imagina- tive variation of the facts would enable us to conceive of every possible experience we might have. In a letter to Lévy-Bruhl which has been preserved, he seems to admit that the facts go beyond what we imagine and that this point bears a real significance. It is as if the imagination, left to itself, is unable to represent the possibilities of existence which are realized in different cultures. "It is a task of the highest importance, which may be actually achieved, to feel our way into a humanity whose life is enclosed in a vital, social tradition and to understand it in this unified social life. This is the basis of the world which is no mere representation (*Weltvorstellung*) but rather the world that actually is for it [*sondern die für sie wirklich seiende Welt ist*]."

Husserl was struck by the contact which Lévy-Bruhl had estab- lished, through his book, with the actual experience of primitive man. Having made this contact with the author's aid, he now saw that it is

27. *Ibid.*, p. 328.

perhaps not possible for us, who live in certain historical traditions, to conceive of the historical possibility of these primitive men by a mere variation of our imagination. For these primitives are non-historical [*Geschichtlos*]. There are certain "stagnant" societies, as they are sometimes called, in which our conception of history is simply absent. Life for them is only a present which is constantly renewed and simply succeeds itself. How is it possible for a German, born in the nineteenth century in a milieu [*Umwelt*] which is not fixed but in a world which has a national past to be realized and a future partly realized, to know this by mere imagination? If one is born into a culture which is structured by historical time, by an ancient past that has now arrived and a future becoming past, how will he represent "a life that is only a flowing present" [*strömende Gegenwart*]?

He will have to reconstitute the lived experience and the actual milieu of the primitive man. The merit of Lévy-Bruhl's work is that it revived this milieu, the environment of the primitive man. Civilizations like ours grant that men of the past had a future in view and that all these futures have come to a present in which they are sedimented. We now have the impression that we also are oriented toward a future which will take over what is good as well as what is bad in our present and, through this, in the life of our predecessors, perhaps giving them a sense which they did not have before or, on the contrary, remaining faithful to them. Whether we consider our lives as a rupture with the past or as a continuation of it, there is always an internal relation between that which has been, that which is, and that which will be. This is precisely that historicity [*Geschichtlichkeit*] which does not exist in stagnant, or frozen, societies.

We must have an experience which is organized in such a way as to express the whole environment [*Umwelt*] of these primitive men. There must be a joining of effort between anthropology as a mere inventory of actual facts and phenomenology as a mere thinking through of possible societies. It is essential that this abstract phenomenology should come into contact with the facts, that it should work out, as Lévy-Bruhl did, a way of animating and of organizing these facts which might convey them to the reader as they are lived by those who are actually caught up in this context.

With respect to this intentional analysis of different cultural formations, "historical relativism has its incontestable justification as an anthropological fact" [*der historische Relativismus sein zweifelloser Recht behält—als anthropologische Tatsache*]. But while anthropology, together with the other positive sciences, may have the first word in the gaining of scientific knowledge, it does not have the last. Historical relativism is now no longer dominated at one stroke by a mode of thought which would have all the keys of history and would be in a position to classify all possible histories before any factual inquiry. On the contrary, the thinker who wishes to dominate history in this way must learn from the facts and must enter into them.

In order to grasp the essential structures of a human community, one must himself take into account, and relive, the whole milieu [*Umwelt*] of this society. Historical knowledge is a coexistence with the meanings of a people and not merely the solitary reflection of a historian. The eidetic of history cannot dispense with factual investigation. In the eyes of Husserl, philosophy, as a coherent thought which leads to a classification of facts according to their value and truth, continues to have its final importance. But it must begin by understanding the lived experiences.

At this point phenomenology, in Husserl's sense, rejoins phenomenology in the Hegelian sense, which consists in following man through his experiences without substituting oneself for him but rather in working through them in such a way as to reveal their sense. The term *phenomenology* ends by bringing out into the open everything that is implicitly contained at the start. It was not by accident that Husserl made this choice.

CONCLUSION
FROM HUSSERL TO HIS SUCCESSORS

THE DEVELOPMENT OF Husserl's thought, which I have tried to trace, is not a mere change of mind, a hesitation, or a zigzag. His problem, as defined in the first lecture, was to find a way between psychology and philosophy—a mode of thinking, in short, which would be neither eternal and without root in the present nor a mere event destined to be replaced by another event tomorrow, and consequently deprived of any intrinsic value. Husserl began like all philosophers; that is, he tried to achieve a radical reflection. He tried to reflect on this power of thought which he was, and this radical reflection finally discovered, behind itself, the unreflected as the condition of its possibility, without which it would have no sense.

Reflection is historicity—on the one hand the possession of myself and on the other my insertion into a history. These two elements are not antagonistic to each other. In so far as thought matures, they become correlative. It belongs to the nature of my reflection to gain possession of myself and in consequence to free myself from determination by external conditions. But in reflecting in this way, and just because I am doing it with the purpose of escaping external temporality, I at once discover a temporality and a historicity that I am. My reflection is taken over from preceding reflections and from a movement of existence which offers itself to me. But, Husserl said, it always involves a certain degree of naïveté. It never lifts itself out of time.

For example, the relation between philosophy and the history of philosophy is reciprocal. The philosopher understands the history of philosophy by his own thoughts, and yet at the same time he understands himself in relation to the history of philosophy to which he has access as a spectacle. In short, he understands himself by the history of philosophy, and he understands this history by himself. "A relative clarification of the one side sheds some light on the other, which in its turn reflects back on the first," Husserl says in the last volume he prepared for publication. There is no doubt that he would have said of history in general just what he said here of the history of philosophy. As a result, we can say that the problem with which we were concerned at the beginning—must we be for fact or for essence, for time or eternity, for the positive science of man or philosophy?—was bypassed in the later thought of Husserl. Here he no longer considers essence as separated from fact, eternity from time, or philosophic thought from history.

It is at first rather surprising to find that in this effort to link philosophy with time and history, Husserl went much further than his successors, Max Scheler and Heidegger. They tried much more quickly than he to incorporate irrational elements, in the traditional sense of this phrase, into philosophy. They attempted to work out an analysis not only of consciousness, the privileged domain for Husserl, but of what Scheler called "the logic of the heart" and what Heidegger called "being in the world." One would therefore expect that they would be more ready to bring philosophy down into the sphere of "facticity," as Heidegger referred to it. But in fact, when they seek to define philosophical knowledge, we find them adopting dogmatic formulae which remind us of certain earlier statements of Husserl. They seem to see no difficulties in assuming an unconditional philosophic intuition.

For example, when Scheler defines intuition of essence in his famous book on *Ethics*, he says that we may know an essence without the slightest intervention of physical, physiological, psychological, or historical factors arising from our individuality. He maintains that, in seeing the "unities of ideal meaning," there is no need to pay any attention to these factors of particularity. They have no influence on our vision of what we take to be an essence which is, in fact, truly an essence. Husserl would have replied that an affirmation of this kind is "naïve." If I were to consider ten years afterward what had been for me ten years before an insight into essence, I would perceive that I had not been in the presence of the *things themselves* and that a number of momentary factors, such as my ruling prejudices and my particular way of existing, had entered into this so-called evidence.

In *Formal and Transcendental Logic* Husserl makes it clear that every insight into essence includes "a certain degree of naïveté"—that is to say, unconsciousness. He seemed to be much more conscious, much more rigorous than Scheler, and his effort to link essence with existence is finally much more mindful of the truth than Scheler's uncritical affirmation. Scheler expresses the curious juxtaposition of a philosophy which on the one hand seeks "alogical essences" and on the other hand conceives of itself as having an unconditioned power of arriving at the truth.

This comment also applies to Heidegger, who devotes himself to the description of being in the world. One might expect, therefore, that the philosopher who finds himself thrown into the world might also find some difficulty in arriving at an adequate state of knowledge. But Heidegger defines the attitude of the philosopher without recognizing any restriction on the absolute power of philosophical thought. For example, at the beginning of *Sein und Zeit*,[28] he said that the task of philosophy is to explore the natural concept of the world, independently of science, by the primordial experience we have of it. To determine the structure of this natural world, he adds, it is not at all necessary to have any recourse to ethnology or to psychology. These disciplines presuppose a philosophical knowledge of the natural world, and one can never find the principle which will enable us to order psychological or ethnographical facts by making inductions from these facts. In order to do this, the spirit itself must first possess the principle.

We have already found this antithesis of philosophy and psychology and this same reassertion of the priority of philosophy in Husserl. But we have seen how, as his thought matured, this relation of priority gave way to one of interdependence and reciprocity. In the point which concerns us, Scheler and Heidegger remained fixed in their thesis of a pure and simple opposition between philosophy and the sciences of man or, as Heidegger put it, between the ontological and the ontic. For Husserl, as we have seen, this opposition was only a point of departure, which later became a problem and finally a hidden connection between the two kinds of research. Husserl, who defined philosophy as the suspension of our affirmation of the world, recognized the actual being of the philosopher in the world much more clearly than Heidegger, who devoted himself to the study of being in the world.

It will not be possible for us here to reflect at length on this paradox.

28. 3rd edition (Halle, 1931), p. 45.

If we were to subject it to a close examination, we would perhaps find nothing unexpected in it. A certain form of immediate dogmatism, or rationalism, is not only reconcilable but deeply allied with irrationalism. The most effective defenders of reason in practice and even in theory are not those who abstractly make the strongest claims for it. And inversely it is quite in order that a philosopher like Husserl, who was particularly sensitive on the subject of rationality, should be more capable, precisely to this degree, of recognizing the link between reason and existence. This is because, for him, rationality is no phantom. He bears it within himself and practices it.

But let us now return to our problem. Phenomenologists, above all Husserl, have always felt that psychology was concerned with a very distinctive type of knowledge. It is not inductive in the sense which this word carries with empiricists. But neither is it reflective in the traditional philosophical sense—that is, a return to the *a priori* which would determine the form of all human experience. One may say indeed that psychological knowledge is reflection but that it is at the same time an experience. According to the phenomenologist (Husserl), it is a "material *a priori*." Psychological reflection is a "constatation" (a finding). Its task is to discover the meaning of behavior through an effective contact with my own behavior and that of others. Phenomenological psychology is therefore a search for the essence, or meaning, but not apart from the facts. Finally this essence is accessible only in and through the individual situation in which it appears. When pushed to the limit, eidetic psychology becomes analytic-existential.

Let us now turn to the psychologists. With reference to them I propose to show that, while the phenomenologists have been working out their reflections in the ways I have just indicated, the psychologists have also been led to redefine psychological knowledge in an analogous manner. This has been due in part to the direct influence of phenomenologies, in part to a diffuse influence of which they were not conscious, and above all to the pressure of the concrete problems with which they had to deal. I propose to show in the following lectures that psychology, as we have seen it developing during the last twenty-five or thirty years, is certainly not inductive in the empiricist sense of the term. But, of course, neither is it *a priori* in the sense of a reflexion which owes nothing to the contact of the psychologist himself with the facts and with the situation he is trying to clarify. Psychology is tending, rather, to rely on a disciplined reading of the phenomena which arise both in me and outside of me and on a resulting grasp of the meaning of human behavior. If this agreement is confirmed, it should enable us to relate philosophy to psychology in such a way as to make the existence of the one compatible with that of the other.

4 / The Child's Relations with Others[1]

Translated by William Cobb

Introduction

By way of introduction I should like to indicate to you, in this lecture and the next, what place this year's subject occupies within the study of child psychology in general.

1. "Les relations avec autrui chez l'enfant," from the series *Cours de Sorbonne* (Paris, 1960).

The subject of child psychology is of more than casual interest in any philosophical attempt at understanding individual and intersubjective existence. Freud showed that childhood is important, and in some respects decisive, for the character of adult life that follows it. This raises a serious question of principle for any account wishing both to describe the specific motivations and general nature of adult life and to acknowledge the continuity of that life with childhood. Granted that the child's early development has a profound influence on adult life, how, in principle, is that influence possible?

If, as has often been done, we begin with a naturalistic view of the child, in which the acquisition of such things as reflectivity, an ideal image of oneself, values, responsibility, etc., is explained in terms of a process essentially causal in nature, then consistency and continuity demand that we maintain this naturalism in accounting for the phenomena of adult life as well. The demonstrated failure of such theories to account for the phenomena of adult existence in turn forces us to abandon naturalism and mechanism in child psychology—unless we want to hold that to grow to maturity is to pass from one ontological order to another.

If, on the other hand, the child's growth is explained in terms of a cognitive grasp of the world that is held to be the condition for any concrete involvement in the world—if immediacy is denied the child merely in order to make theoretically plausible his passage to reflectivity—such a view overlooks important facts of adult as well as child existence. Psychologists have often spoken of learning in the child as though relations with self, world, and others originate in contemplative knowledge. Yet ordinary experience shows that, in imitating others, in learning to walk, in becoming familiar with an environment, what occurs cannot be explained by the notion that there is first an intellectual act of "knowing" rules, maps, or words and then a move to use them. Intellectualism of this kind is, therefore, an unsatisfactory alternative to naturalism in explaining the nature of childhood existence as well as its influence on adult life.

Merleau-Ponty has elsewhere criticized these two modes of explanation in at-

You can easily see the relation between this year's proposed subject and the subject we dealt with last year. Last year we attempted a study of certain aspects of the child's relations with nature—for example, the child's perception. These included the child's knowledge of external natural facts, also his representation of external facts (e.g., in drawing), the way his imagination makes use of perceptual experiences, his organization of these experiences into causal relations, and, finally, what has sometimes been called the child's conception of the world— that is, the group of ideas (if such they can be called) that would permit the child to have a view of the world.

The last paragraph brings us to the question of intelligence in the child, and you can see that, regardless of the diversity of questions we raised last year, they all involved not the relation between the child and other living beings but rather the child's relations to nature.

This year, on the contrary, in discussing the child's relations with others, we will be concerned with his relations with his parents, his brothers and sisters, other children, and even, if there is time, with his school environment, his social class, and, in general, his relation to culture, to the civilization to which he belongs. It is quite likely that we will not be able to treat these last questions this year, since to do so would take us too far and we have enough to occupy ourselves in the child's relations to parents, brothers and sisters, and other humans.

It might seem as though the question we shall treat this year is *more special* than last year's question. It might seem that last year we studied the "infrastructure" of the child's understanding, the collection of processes that enable him to feel, perceive, and understand; whereas this year we are interested in a fairly narrow sector of this perception and understanding—the perception and understanding of others. It might seem that last year we were concerned with the psychology of understanding in the child, while this year we will concern ourselves with the much more limited subject of affectivity.

This, however, is not the relation between the two kinds of question. I do not at all believe that the question of relations with others is a

---

tempting a description of adult existence. In "The Child's Relations with Others" his task is less critical than descriptive, less occupied with the refutation of theories which would reduce existence to either Nature or Thought than with finding terms for a positive description of the origin of intersubjective relations. Throughout the essay he endeavors to describe these relations in a language that avoids either of the reductions mentioned above.

The essay itself is a fragment of a larger lecture course in child psychology. Its rather abrupt ending suggests that the inquiry was extended in further lectures. No other texts on the subject by Merleau-Ponty are available, however, and for reasons indicated above it was decided to publish this essay in English as it stands.

I am grateful to Michèle Jacquemain and Robert V. Stone for checking the translation and making many improvements.—*Trans.*

secondary and more particular problem, more strictly confined to affectivity than the problem with which we occupied ourselves last year.

The very results of last year's study prevent us from treating the problem of relations with others as secondary and subordinate.

In speaking of the child's perception or of causal relations as grasped by the child, what struck us was the fact that, in the case of the child's perception, it is not a matter of a simple reflection of external phenomena within the child or of a simple sorting of data resulting from the activity of the senses. It seemed to us to be a question of an actual "informing" [*Gestaltung*] of experience in the child. For example, in the case of causal relations, which have traditionally been thought to have been learned by an intellectual operation in the child, we have seen instead, with Michotte, that such relations are anchored in the child's very perception of external events and that perception in the child is not a simple reflection nor the result of a process of sorting data. Rather, it is a more profound operation whereby the child organizes his experience of external events—an operation which thus is properly neither a logical nor a predicative activity.

When we considered the child's imagination, it appeared likewise that we could not assimilate what is called the *image* in the child to a kind of degraded, weakened copy of preceding perceptions. What is called *imagination* is an emotional conduct. Consequently here again we found ourselves, as it were, *beneath* the relation of the knowing subject to the known object. We had to do with a primordial operation by which the child organizes the imaginary, just as he organizes the perceived.

When we examined the child's drawing, one of the faults we found with the famous book by Luquet was precisely this: The child's drawing is considered by Luquet to be an abortive adult drawing, and the development of the child, viewed through the stages of his drawing, appears as a series of frustrations of the attempt to represent the world as the adult does (at least the white, "civilized," Western adult)—that is, according to the laws of classical geometrical perspective. We tried to show, on the contrary, that the child's processes of expression could not be understood as simple breakdowns on the road to "visual realism" and that, instead, these processes testified to the presence in the child of a relation with things [2] and with the sensible very different from the one that is expressed in the perspective projection of drawing in the classic style.

Finally, it appeared to us, following certain indications of Wallon, that there is perhaps no place for the question of the child's conception of the world. In order to be able to speak of a conception of the world,

2. In the text *"droves"* appears to be a misprint for *"choses."*—*Trans.*

the child would actually have to totalize his experience under general concepts. But, as Wallon remarked, an entire sector of this experience is fragmentary [*lacunaire*] for the child; it contains what Wallon called "ultra things," i.e., entities of which the child has no direct experience, which are at the horizon of his perception—like the sun, the moon, etc. These entities remain for the child in a state of relative indetermination; he has, strictly speaking, no conception of them. With respect to nearby objects, the child often has a conception that is very close to that of the adult (Huang). The concepts of animism and of artificialism, employed a bit recklessly, are adult ways of expressing the child's confusion in the face of "ultra things"; they are the expedients sometimes used by the child in replying to the adult's questions and perhaps do not arise in his own experience.

All this, I believe, converged on the following idea: What classical academic psychology calls "functions of cognition"—intelligence, perception, imagination, etc.—when more closely examined, lead us back to an activity that is prior to cognition properly so called, a function of organizing experiences that imposes on certain totalities the configuration and the kind of equilibrium that are possible under the corporeal and social conditions of the child himself.

In another course, moreover, we examined the problem of the acquisition of language, and there again we reached the same kind of conclusion: The acquisition of language appeared to us to be the acquisition of an open system of expression. That is, such a system is capable of expressing, not some finite number of cognitions or ideas, but rather an indeterminate number of cognitions or ideas to come. The system that is speech is learned by the child, not at all by a genuine intellectual operation (as though by means of intelligence the child understood the principles of speech, its morphology, and its syntax). Rather, what is involved is a kind of *habituation*, a use of language as a tool or instrument. The employment of language, which is an effect and also one of the most active stimuli of intellectual development, does not appear to be founded on the exercise of pure intelligence but instead on a more obscure operation—namely, the child's assimilation of the linguistic system of his environment in a way that is comparable to the acquisition of any habit whatever: the learning of a structure of conduct.

These results lead us to think that between the functions of understanding we studied last year and affectivity itself there must be an altogether different relation than that of the simple subordination of the latter to the former.

However, I would like to show this more directly by means of two examples. First, recent studies have tended to show that even external perception of sense qualities and space—at first glance the most disin-terested, least affective of all the functions—is profoundly modified by the personality and by the interpersonal relationships in which the child lives. The second example has to do with the learning of lan-guage. Certain authors show that there is a very close and profound relation between the development of language and the configuration of the human environment in which the child develops.

1. *Psychological rigidity*

ON THE FIRST POINT, I have in mind the interesting work of Else Frenkel-Brunswik, described in an article entitled "Intolerance of Ambiguity as an Emotional and Perceptual Personality Variable." [3] This work is connected with a whole series of earlier studies. In particular, it recalls the work of the German psychologist Erich Jaensch, who twenty-five years ago was well known for his research on eidetic imagery [4] and who has since turned to research on perception designed to show a close relation between the way a person perceives objects and the general characteristics of his personality and, in particular, of his relations with others. Ambiguous perceptions (the same drawing of a cube seen now from one standpoint, now from another) would be more frequent in "liberal" subjects (meaning subjects who are likely to recognize several aspects of things even if, on first glance, these differ-ent aspects are not easily reconciled with one another). Actually the research by Jaensch is in this sense very hasty and bold. Mrs. Frenkel-Brunswik, on the contrary, endeavored to carry out a rigorous experi-mental study. She bases her approach firmly on the principle of projective techniques. Rorschach constructed his test on the idea that the subject's perception is entirely altered by his personality, since he relied on the subject's manner of perceiving certain visual data in order to deduce from it certain personality traits.

Mrs. Frenkel-Brunswik chose a precise personality trait in order to study its correlation with certain types of perception. She called this trait "psychological rigidity," and we are going to define it shortly. The author endeavored to study the correlation between this trait and cer-tain modes of perception by means of an experimental method. A study was made by the University of California on 1500 schoolchildren between the ages of 11 and 16. Of these children she chose 120 who represented the extreme limiting-case of psychological rigidity. She submitted them to interviews, clinical examinations, and tests. The parents of these children were visited, and one third of them were

3. *Journal of Personality*, vol. 18 (September, 1949), pp. 108–43.
4. Cf. Erich Jaensch, *Eidetic Imagery and Typological Methods of Investigation*, trans. Oscar Oeser (New York, 1930).—*Trans.*

submitted to exact perceptual experiments of a kind designed to show the link between the type of perception and the personal and interpersonal factors I spoke of earlier.

The personality variable chosen for these experiments, "psychological rigidity," is a notion that originated in psychoanalysis, although it is far from being an orthodox Freudian conception. It means the attitude of the subject who replies to any question with black-and-white answers; who gives replies that are curt and lacking in any shading; who also is generally ill disposed, when examining an object or a person, to recognize in them any clashing traits; and who continually tries, in his remarks, to arrive at a simple, categorical, and summary view.

In the eyes of the author this "psychological rigidity" is by no means the sign of an actual psychological force, as people who know the subject sometimes believe. It is only a mask. Beneath this rigidity one could easily enough find real chaos or at least a deeply divided personality. Psychological rigidity, according to Mrs. Frenkel-Brunswik, is what the Freudians call a "reaction formation"; that is, a façade interposed by the subject between his psychological reality and others who are there to examine him. The principle of this formation is well known: If the individual is very aggressive he conceals his aggression under an acquired veil of politeness, and often the most apparently polite people are, at bottom, the most aggressive. The author brings to light the "reactional" character of rigidity. Rigid subjects are in reality, when more closely examined, likely to be profoundly divided in their personality dynamics. If they are questioned about their families, in general they reply with categorical affirmations. Either the family is perfection itself—one could not wish for a better—or it is horrible. In any case there are never any nuances. More often than not, such persons are traditionalists. They declare that their families—and their parents in particular—are perfect. For them their parents represent an absolute. What allows us to say that beneath this rigidity there is no psychological force or genuine conviction is this: First, when these subjects analyze and describe their parents, they always confine themselves to mentioning the inessential, external traits, as though they are afraid to enter into a more detailed analysis and to recognize imperfections in the persons around them. Second, each time one tries to catch them unawares and obtain responses whose real significance escapes them they are generally negative toward their parents. Instead of being asked directly what they think of their parents, they are asked, for example, to make a list of the people they would take along if they had to live for several years on a desert island. It is significant that many of them who are absolutely in favor of the family regularly exclude their parents from the list. Third, when they are given the Thematic Apperception Test, one notices that their descriptions of their parents emphasize their coercive, punitive aspects. These different indications, when joined with the evidence from clinical experiments, permit us to say that their wholesale affirmation of the merits of the family is, rather, a mask behind which a fairly lively aggression may be found. When aggression against the parent figures becomes too urgent and agonizing, these subjects superimpose a phenomenon of reaction to that aggression. They systematically avoid lifting the mask; hence their refusal to admit shading into the picture of their parents. If they begin to admit any shading at all, they will admit too much.

In a more general way, not only with their parents but with regard to all moral and social problems as well, these subjects proceed by dichotomizing—the dichotomy of authority and obedience. The child must be absolutely obedient, or else the very principle of authority is called in question. Another example is the dilemma of cleanliness and dirtiness. The mania for cleanliness (a familiar trait) can make certain women into passionate house cleaners and fanatic polishers of furniture, etc. All this has its roots in the rigidity of the child. Thus we have the dualism of good and evil, virtue and vice, and even that of masculinity and femininity. Of course, nobody denies that each of these differences is considered to be an *absolute* difference, founded in nature, excluding any appearance of transition, degree, or change. Mrs. Frenkel-Brunswik thinks that these subjects have acquired this attitude in their initial relations with the family, inasmuch as these relations are also their first relations to values and to the world. The parents are the means by which they first communicate with the world. The families in question are usually authoritarian; they are the ones in which the child is strictly "trained," the "frustrating" families in which the child feels insecure and in danger.

Psychological rigidity can be found occasionally in all subjects, but it is only in an especially authoritarian environment that it becomes a constant conduct, of which the child cannot rid himself. In this kind of authoritarian atmosphere the child divides the parent figure in half. On the one hand there is the kindly image of his parents that is willingly avowed, and on the other there is the image he is struggling against. As Melanie Klein has said, two images (the "good mother" and the "bad mother"), instead of being united in relation to the same person, are arranged by the child with the former prominent and the latter completely concealed from himself. When questioned, the child overtly recognizes only the favorable image, and this is what, according to Melanie Klein, defines ambivalence. Ambivalence consists in having two alternative images of the same object, the same person, without making any effort to connect them or to notice that in reality they relate to the same object and the same person.

Melanie Klein has established a profound distinction between ambivalence of this kind and ambiguity. As opposed to ambivalence, ambiguity is an adult phenomenon, a phenomenon of maturity, which has nothing pathological about it. It consists in admitting that the same being who is good and generous can also be annoying and imperfect. Ambiguity is ambivalence that one dares to look at face to face. What is lacking in rigid subjects is this capacity to confront squarely the contradictions that exist in their attitudes toward others.

The families in which these children are found are authoritarian, as we have said, and they are equally the "socially marginal" families (here we are extending the social aspect of this phenomenon). There also exists a social marginalism in France. The *nouveau riche* is marginal in the sense that he is placed in a category in which he does not feel himself thoroughly integrated. It is the same with the "newly poor." This latter category is much more important in the United States because of its national minorities.

When conjoined with social conditions, rigidity has social consequences. Unaware of his double attitude, refusing even to recognize in himself the image of "bad parents," the rigid child tends to project outside himself the part of himself he does not want to be. The aggression he wants to be rid of is projected outside by a process of externalization that in certain cases is evident beyond any doubt.

According to the best observers, the legends in America and French Africa concerning the sexuality of Negroes display a mechanism of this type. Subjects project onto the Negro (considered to represent a "natural" sexuality that is stronger and more violent than their own) something of themselves that they would like not to have. The same mechanism is called into play with the Jews; the construction of the Jewish character often proceeds by a division of this kind. The anti-Semite throws off onto the Jew the part of himself he does not want and is most ashamed of, as others do with the Negro. This is true also of other minorities. The minority is all the more hateful for representing the behavior whose germs the subject carries within himself and will not admit are his own. Simone de Beauvoir has analyzed a mechanism of the same kind in the phenomenon of the "battle of the sexes." [5] From age ten on, this phenomenon appears in schools where boys and girls are reared together. If the boys and girls are asked the reasons for this social dichotomization (for this is what it already is), one is forced to admit something like this: Each attributes to the other the character-

5. Simone de Beauvoir, *The Second Sex*, trans. and ed. H. M. Parshley (New York, 1952).—*Trans.*

istics of his humanity that he does not want. For example, men who, by virtue of the established myths as well as certain tendencies of their own physiological constitutions, do not want to be weak and sensitive and want to be self-sufficient, decisive, and energetic, project on women exactly those personality traits they do not themselves want to have. Women, who are accomplices in this masquerade, from their side project on men the personality traits they wish to be rid of or are unable to assume. There is thus a mutual disparagement which is at the same time the basis of a pact concluded between the two sexes. The very women who proclaim their hatred of men also admit that it is, after all, men's business to make decisions, pay taxes, carry the bags to the station, and hold positions, etc. In reality it is scarcely necessary to say that even men are frivolous and capable of being mistaken; by the same token, women are as decisive as men and as capable of being in business or a profession. But by a sort of tacit agreement men and women are at the same time accomplices and enemies, and thus they continue to live side by side, in a love that is hate, a hate that is love.

It remains for us to see how the type of personality and of interpersonal relations designated by the term "psychological rigidity" express themselves in the anonymous functions of external perception. Let us now turn to the experiments designed to make evident the relation between psychological rigidity, as a mode of relation to self and others, and perception in its own right.

A study was made of 1500 schoolchildren between eleven and sixteen years old, and, in particular, of 120 of them who were remarkably "rigid." These subjects showed very strong racial and social prejudices—prejudices which, you recall from what we have already said, bear witness to a sort of interior schism between what the subjects admit and recognize in themselves and what they do not admit, do not recognize, and are unwilling to see in themselves. The latter traits are projected on external subjects who play the role of scapegoat; while, on the contrary, the subject appears in his own eyes as immune to the defects he finds in external groups.

The experimenters asked a certain number of questions designed to reveal psychological rigidity. Here are some examples of the test questions. Subjects were asked to evaluate the following phrase: "People can be divided into two categories—the weak and the strong." Or again, "Teachers should tell their students what to do, rather than trying to find out what the students want." This last sentence served to test for the authoritarian tendencies of the subjects. Again, "Girls should learn only about household matters." Another test sentence (this test was given in the United States) was "We should deport all refugees and give their jobs to veterans." Finally, "There is only one way to do something properly." Psychologically rigid subjects agreed immediately with this last proposition.

After these tests for "rigidity," experiments were made to show the characteristic ways in which the subjects perceive. Psychologically rigid subjects could be expected to show, in the same way, a sort of perceptual rigidity. It would be hard for them to modify their attitude and to adopt a new account of new aspects of a problem. They would have a tendency to refer any new experience of a different type that might be presented to them back to already familiar experiences. For example, they were shown films in which the images gradually changed, e.g., the image of a dog transformed little by little into a cat. Members of the strongly prejudiced group held more firmly, in general, to their antecedent mode of perception and saw no appreciable change in the figure which was presented to them, even when the changes were already objectively noticeable.

In more general terms, such a subject rebels against all aspects of the phenomenon of transition. Even if, in effect, he is not immediately acquiescent to the changes in the stimuli that are presented to him, he might at least notice that something has changed. Without altering his perception of the whole he might, all the same, recognize that the figure is in the process of disorganization. But this recognition of the phenomenon of transition is exactly what is repugnant to him.

In sum, the subjects who carry within themselves extremely strong conflicts are precisely those who reject, in their views of external things, the admission that there are particular situations that are ambiguous, full of conflicts, and mixed in value. This occurs in such a way that one can say that a very strong emotional ambivalence shows up, at the level of understanding or perception, as a very weak ambiguity in the things perceived or in the subject's ideas of them. The more emotionally ambivalent the subject, the less it suits him that there should be any ambiguity in things and in his view of things. Emotional ambivalence is what demands the denial of intellectual ambiguity. In subjects whose intellectual ambiguity is strong it often happens that the emotional foundation is much more stable than in other subjects.

Another series of experiments was designed to measure the speed with which a subject adapts to a new type of problem. The subject was trained to solve a certain number of elementary tasks that implied a certain method of solution. He was then presented with other problems that were apparently of the same form but in reality could be solved much more easily by another method. Only, in order to find the other method, the subject must be supple and capable of responding to the situation in a way appropriate to its new content. One finds in the same way that psychologically rigid subjects in general react against this modification of their techniques.

Here we must interject two remarks that are indispensable for an understanding of the exact scope of these investigations.

1. Mrs. Frenkel-Brunswik does not say that psychological rigidity, or rigidity in psycho-social relations, necessarily appears in an unequivocal manner in the domain of perception. The relation established by the author between affective life and intersubjectivity, on the one hand, and the functions of understanding or of perception, on the other, is much more subtle and fluid. There is always a relation between these two domains, but it is not always that of a single relation of analogy. There are subjects who, although psychologically rigid, *compensate* for that rigidity by great flexibility in the perceptual domain. The two phenomena always occur together, but they may be united in several different ways. Sometimes the same structure is met with in both domains—psychological rigidity appearing as perceptual rigidity—and sometimes, in other cases, the perceptual phenomenon compensates for (rather than simply resembles) the affective phenomenon. What is important in both cases, however, is that the two phenomena always comprise a single whole.

2. In outlining a social psychology of social and political opinions,[6] Mrs. Frenkel-Brunswik does not propose that psychology *alone* is in a position to solve political problems. There are, in her view, subjects who are without social prejudices of any kind, who are perfectly "liberal" in the sense that they admit that all men are brothers, that one cannot concentrate all the characteristics of evil in Negroes, Jews, or any other minority and yet who, for all that, are rigid subjects because they refuse to see among men even the most striking differences of *situation*—differences which pertain to the collectivity in which they have lived and received their initial training. There is an abstract or rigid liberalism which consists in thinking that all men are *identical*. There are also liberals who are truly liberal, in the sense that they conceive very well that there can be differences of historical situation among men and different cultural environments. This does not prevent them from treating each man (in so far as his situation permits him to be a man) like any other. But the fundamental identity of men does not close their eyes to the cultural differences which may develop and which must be understood in action, if they do not want to arrive at results that are sometimes contrary to the ones they aimed for.

6. Cf. Else Frenkel-Brunswik and R. N. Sanford, "Some Personality Factors in Anti-Semitism," *Journal of Personality*, vol. 20 (1945), pp. 271–91. Merleau-Ponty cites at this point a partial French translation of this article under the title "La personnalité antisémite," which appeared in *Les Temps Modernes*, no. 60 (October, 1950).—*Trans.*

Racist opinions, on the other hand, are necessarily linked to psychological rigidity, since they rest on a myth and can thus be explained only by a psychological mechanism. But most political opinions, unlike these, are not reducible to psychological factors. Not every political question can be cut short with a psychological analysis. What betrays psychological rigidity is not the adoption of this or that conception of the state or of history; it is the *manner* in which one adopts this thesis and tries to justify it. Similarly, what characterizes a psychologically mature subject for Mrs. Frenkel-Brunswik is not that he does or does not have ambiguities; it is the *way in which he treats his ambiguities*. If he hides them from himself, if he flees them, if he does not confront them, he is psychologically rigid. If, on the contrary, he faces them squarely, he has arrived at maturity. Everyone is ambiguous in one way or another; it is just that there are subjects who refuse to take into account, to "interiorize," their ambiguities. This is ambivalence properly so called. Other subjects consent to see problems that arise on account of the discordant traits that are to be found in each and every individual.

To appreciate thoroughly the nature of anti-Semitism or prejudice against Negroes, it is not enough merely to be a psychologist, any more than an appreciation of this or that political doctrine necessarily requires a psychological study of those who adopt it. Psychology describes conducts; it cannot inform us about the internal content of the theses to which they address themselves. It can only describe attitudes.

My aim, as well as the aim of the author whose work I have been utilizing, has not been to show that the cognitive functions, like perception, are *explained* by the social structure in which the individual finds himself and in which he has the task of adjusting his perception to his environment and vice versa. The question of causality is not resolved by these investigations. They merely establish a correlation between the manner of perceiving and that of structuring the social world. But this correlation can be understood in two ways. On the one hand, we might decide that it is because the subject perceives in a rigid fashion (on account of his constitutional make-up) that he is predisposed in social matters to a dichotomization of things and to the prejudices I have already mentioned. On the other hand, one might decide that it is because the subject has organized his relations with others and with the social world in this or that way that he is brought to perceive them in the same way. The establishment of a correlation does not allow us to resolve this issue.

What must be understood, moreover, is that the question of a causal sequence of the two phenomena is *meaningless*. For it to be meaningful would require that the two phenomena be capable of standing in isolation. But this is never the case. In fact, from the time of his birth the child who will have prejudices has been molded by his environment, and in that respect has undergone a certain exercise of parental authority. Consequently there is no moment at which you could grasp, in a pure state, his way of perceiving, completely apart from the social conditioning that influences him. Inversely, you can never say that the way in which the child structures [met en forme] his social environment is unrelated to the hereditary or constitutional dispositions of his nervous system. He himself is the one who structures his surroundings, after all. It is as though there is in the child a sort of elasticity that sometimes makes him react to the influences of his surroundings by finding his own solutions to the problems they pose. And so the internal characteristics of the subject always intervene in his way of establishing his relations with what is outside him. It is never simply the outside which molds him; it is he himself who takes a position in the face of the external conditions. If, therefore, we refuse to answer yes or no to the problem of causality, it is not simply because we lack necessary information; rather, it is for reasons of principle. It is because, in fact and in principle, it is impossible to establish a cleavage between what will be "natural" in the individual and what will be acquired from his social upbringing. In reality the two orders are not distinct; they are part and parcel of a single global phenomenon.

Consequently our aim has not been to connect the functions of intellect to the subject's relation to society, as they depended on it in an unequivocal way, but to bring to light the profound relation of the two phenomenal orders that are part of a single global project of the individual—a global project in which are established his relations with the neutral perceptual fields that can be given in his experience, as well as his relations with his human and social surroundings.

2. Affectivity and language

I PASS to the second fact that appeared to me to be worthy of mention by way of introduction to this course: the relation that can be established between the development of intelligence (in particular, the acquisition of language) and the configuration of the individual's affective environment.

I call your attention to a short article by François Rostand entitled "Grammaire et affectivité." [7] Rostand begins by remarking that from the start there is a correlation between the age at which the child is most dependent on his parents (i.e., about two years) and the age at

7. Revue Française de Psychanalyse, vol. 14 (April–June, 1950), pp. 299–310.

which he begins to learn language. There is a period when the child is "sensitive" with regard to language, when he is capable of learning to speak. It has been shown that if the child up to two years of age does not have a linguistic model to imitate, if he does not find himself in an environment in which people are speaking, he will never speak as do those who have learned language during the period in question. This is the case with those children who are called "savages," who have been raised by animals or far from contact with speaking subjects. In no case have these subjects ever learned to speak with the linguistic perfection that is found among ordinary subjects. Deaf children whose retraining has been delayed and who consequently have not learned to speak during the "sensitive" period never speak their language in exactly the same way as do those who can hear. One can show, in fact, that in their syntax or their morphology there exist, after retraining, some very odd peculiarities: for example, the absence or rarity of the passive voice in verbs. This allows us to presume that there will be a profound link between the acquisition of language (which would seem to be a strictly intellectual operation) and the child's place in the family environment. It is this relation that Rostand seeks to define exactly.

It is a commonplace that the child's acquisition of language is also correlated with his relation to his mother. Children who have been suddenly and forcibly separated from their mothers always show signs of a linguistic regression. At bottom, it is not only the word "mama" that is the child's first; it is the entire language which is, so to speak, maternal.

The acquisition of language might be a phenomenon of the same kind as the relation to the mother. Just as the maternal relation is (as the psychoanalysts say) a relation of *identification,* in which the subject projects on his mother what he himself experiences and assimilates the attitudes of his mother, so one could say that the acquisition of language is itself a phenomenon of identification. To learn to speak is to learn to play a series of *roles,* to assume a series of conducts or linguistic gestures.

Rostand mentions an observation made by Dr. Dolto-Marette in a case of jealousy in a child. The younger of two children shows jealousy when his new brother is born. During the first days of the newborn child's life, he identifies with it, carrying himself as though he himself were the newborn baby. There is a striking regression in language as well as in character. In the following days one notices in him a change of attitude. The subject identifies himself with his older brother and overcomes his jealousy; he adopts all the characteristics of the eldest, including an attitude toward the new baby that is identical to what, until now, had been his older brother's attitude toward him. Thanks to a fortunate circumstance his jealousy is overcome. By chance, just as the baby is born, a fourth child comes to stay in the family. This fourth child is bigger than all three brothers in the family. The presence of a child who is older than the eldest brother robs the latter of his status as the "absolute eldest." The eldest is now no longer "absolutely big," since there are others who are bigger than he is. The fourth child aids in the middle brother's transition and assimilation of the role of the eldest.

It is in this way that a case of neurotic stuttering is cured and a marked linguistic progress realized from day to day. The subject acquires the use of the simple past tense, the imperfect, the simple future, and the future with the verb *to go* ("I am *going to* leave"). Coming back to this observation, Rostand interprets it in the following fashion: The jealousy that invades the subject when he confirms the arrival of a new brother is essentially a refusal to change his situation. The newcomer is an intruder and is going to confiscate to his own advantage the place in the family that was held until now by our jealous subject. It is in the phase of the "surpassing" of jealousy that one notices the appearance of a link between the affective phenomenon and the linguistic phenomenon: jealousy is overcome thanks to the constitution of a scheme of past-present-future. In effect, jealousy in this subject consists in a rigid attachment to his present—that is, to the situation of the "latest born" which was hitherto his own. He considered the present to be absolute. Now, on the contrary, one can say that from the moment when he consents to be no longer the latest born, to become in relation to the new baby what his elder brother had until then been in relation to him, he replaces his attitude of "my place has been taken" with another, whose schema might be somewhat like this: "I *have been* the youngest, but I *am* the youngest no longer, and I *will become* the biggest." One sees that there is a solidarity between the acquisition of this temporal structure, which gives a meaning to the corresponding linguistic instruments, and the situation of a jealousy that is overcome. For the subject the situation of jealousy is the occasion both for re-structuring his relations with the others he lives with and at the same time for acquiring new dimensions of existence (past, present, and future) with a supple play among them.

Speaking Piaget's language, one might say that the whole problem of overcoming jealousy is a problem of "de-centering." Until now the subject has been centered on himself, centered on the situation of the latest born that he has occupied. In order to accept the birth of a new child, he must de-center himself. But the de-centering involved here is not, as it was for Piaget, a primarily intellectual operation, a phenomenon of pure knowledge. It is a matter of a lived de-centering, aroused by the situation of the child inside the family constellation.

One might even say that what the child learns, in solving the problem of jealousy, is to relativize his notions. He must relativize the notions of the youngest and the eldest: he is no longer *the* youngest; it is the new child who assumes this role. He thus must come to distinguish the absolute "youngest" from the relative "youngest" which he now becomes. And in the same way he must learn to become the eldest in relation to the newborn child, whereas until now the notion of "eldest" had only an absolute meaning.

In Piaget's language, the child must learn to think in terms of reciprocity. Rostand himself cites Piaget's terms. But these terms take on a new meaning from the fact that training in reciprocity, relativity, and de-centering occurs here not by intellectual acts of "grouping" but by operations within the vital order, by the manner in which the child restores [*réétablit*] his relations with others.

To this preliminary observation Rostand adds the following personal one: He noticed in a little girl of thirty-five months an interesting linguistic phenomenon that followed a frightening emotional experience (an encounter, while walking alone, with a big dog). Two months later this experience seemed to bear fruit. There was an abrupt acquisition of certain modes of expression (in particular, the imperfect tense of verbs) which until then the child had not used.

This step occurred at the birth of a younger brother. What we have to understand is the exact relation between this linguistic phenomenon, the birth of the younger brother, and the emotional experience of two months earlier.

The child had come across a dog who was nursing its young. At the time she encountered the dog, she knew already from her parents that she was going to have a little brother or sister in about two months. Meeting the dog which was nursing its litter was not an indifferent experience for the child; it was a visible symbol of something analogous that was about to happen in her own world. The pattern about to be realized two months later in the child's environment (parents, little girl, little brother) was already prefigured by the pattern (big dog; me, the little girl; the little dogs). The sight of the dogs was of paramount significance by virtue of its relation to the situation in which the child was about to find herself.

In order for her to accept the birth of a younger brother, what was basically necessary was a change of attitude. Whereas the little girl had been, until then, the object of all attention and of all caresses, she now had to accept the fact that some of this attention and these caresses would be transferred to another, and to associate herself with this attitude. She had to pass from an ingratiating [*captative*] attitude (i.e., one in which the child receives without giving) to a selfless [*oblative*], quasi-maternal attitude toward the child about to be born. It was necessary for her to accept a relative abandonment, to turn and confront a life that would henceforth be *her* life, that would no longer be supported, as it had been until then, by the exclusive attention of her parents. In short, the girl had to adopt an active attitude, whereas until then her attitude had been passive.

The linguistic phenomenon that emerges at this same time can be understood in this perspective. I said earlier that the imperfect tense appeared in the child's language after the birth of her brother. More important, however, was the emergence of four verbs in the future tense; there was also a great increase in the use of "me" and "I." If the future is a time of aggressiveness, a time when projects are envisioned, when one takes a stand in the face of what is to come and, instead of allowing it to come, moves actively toward it—then how was it made possible by the new situation of the little girl? The answer is that this was precisely the attitude demanded of the child by the birth of her brother. The acquisition of "me" and "I" presented no problems; it indicated that the subject adopted a more personal attitude and lived to a relatively greater degree by herself. Finally, the acquisition of the imperfect tense at the birth of her little brother indicated that the child was becoming capable of understanding that the present changes into the past. The imperfect is a former present which, moreover, is still referred to as present, unlike the past definite.[8] The imperfect is "still there." The acquisition of the imperfect thus presupposes a concrete grasp of the movement from present to past which the child, on her part, was just in the process of achieving in her relations with her family. The fact is, all the verbs she used in the imperfect after the birth of her brother had to do with the baby. The baby *is* what the elder sister *used to be* in the world of the family.

To be sure, emotion plays a role only to the extent that it gives the subject the occasion to re-structure her relations with her human environment, and not at all simply as emotion. If the problem had not been resolved, if the subject had shown herself incapable of overcoming her jealousy or her uneasiness, nothing good would have come from the experience. Inversely, there can be cases in which the subject progresses in language without apparent emotion. In such cases, however, linguistic progress always has an interrupted character; the acquisition of the modes of expression always represents a sort of crisis, in which a whole realm of expression is annexed in a single stroke.

In sum, the intellectual elaboration of our experience of the world is constantly supported by the affective elaboration of our inter-human

8. The difference in question here is that between, e.g., "I was going" (imperfect) and "I went" (past definite).—*Trans.*

relations. The use of certain linguistic tools is mastered in the play of forces that constitute the subject's relations to his human surroundings. The linguistic usage achieved by the child depends strictly on the "position" (in psychoanalytic terms) that is taken by the child at every moment in the play of forces in his family and his human environment.

Here again it is not a question of a causal analysis. There is no question of saying that the linguistic progress is *explained* by the affective progress, in the sense in which expansion is explained by heat. One might reply that the affective progress itself is also a function of the intellectual progress and that the entire intellectual development makes possible a certain affective progress. And this would also be true.

What we are seeking here is not a causal explanation, any more than before. My effort is to show the solidarity and unity of the two phenomena, not to reduce the one to the other, as is traditionally done by both empiricist and intellectualist psychologists. The child's experience of the constellation of his own family does more than impress on him certain relations between one human being and another. At the same time that the child is assuming and forming his family relations, an entire form of thinking arises in him. It is a whole usage of language as well as a way of perceiving the world.

[1] THE PROBLEM OF THE CHILD'S PERCEPTION OF OTHERS: THE THEORETICAL PROBLEM

BEFORE STUDYING the different relations established between the child and his parents, his peers, other children, brothers, sisters, or strangers, before undertaking a description and analysis of these different relations, a question of principle arises: How and under what conditions does the child come into contact with others? What is the nature of the child's relations with others? How are such relations possible from the day of birth on?

Classical psychology approached this problem only with great difficulty. One might say that it was among the stumbling blocks of classical psychology because it is admittedly incapable of being solved if one confines oneself to the theoretical ideas that were elaborated by academic psychology.

How does such a problem arise for classical psychology? Given the presuppositions with which that psychology works, given the prejudices it adopted from the start without any kind of criticism, the relation with others becomes incomprehensible for it. What, in fact, is the psyche [*psychisme*]—mine or the other's—for classical psychology? All psychologists of the classical period are in tacit agreement on this point: the psyche, or the psychic, is *what is given to only one person*. It seems, in effect, that one might admit without further examination or discussion that what constitutes the psyche in me or in others is something incommunicable. I alone am able to grasp my psyche—for example, my sensations of green or of red. You will never know them as I know them; you will never experience them in my place. A consequence of this idea is that the psyche of another appears to me as radically inaccessible, at least in its own existence. I cannot reach other lives, other thought processes, since by hypothesis they are open only to inspection by a single individual: the one who owns them.

Since I cannot have direct access to the psyche of another, for the reasons just given, I must grant that I seize the other's psyche only indirectly, mediated by its bodily appearances. I see you in flesh and bone; you are there. I cannot know what you are thinking, but I can suppose it, guess at it from your facial expressions, your gestures, and your words—in short from a series of bodily appearances of which I am only the witness.

The question thus becomes this: How does it happen that, in the presence of this mannequin that resembles a man, in the presence of this body that gesticulates in a characteristic way, I come to believe that it is inhabited by a psyche? [9] How am I led to consider that this body before me encloses a psyche? How can I perceive across this body, so to speak, another's psyche? Classical psychology's conception of the body and the consciousness we have of it is here a second obstacle in the way of a solution of the problem. Here one wants to speak of the notion of *cenesthesia,* meaning a mass of sensations that would express to the subject the state of his different organs and different bodily functions. Thus my body for me, and your body for you, could be reached, and be knowable, by means of a cenesthesic sense.

A mass of sensations, by hypothesis, is as *individual* as the psyche itself. That is to say, if in fact my body is knowable by me only through the mass of sensations it gives me (a mass of sensations to which you obviously have no access and of which we have no concrete experience), then the consciousness I have of my body is impenetrable by you. You cannot represent yourself in the same way in which I feel my own body; it is likewise impossible for me to represent to myself the way in which you feel your body. How, then, can I suppose that, in back of this appearance before me, there is someone who experiences his body as I experience mine?

9. I use the vague term "psyche" on purpose, in order to avoid any theory of consciousness that might be implied by a more precise term.

Only one recourse is left for classical psychology—that of supposing that, as a spectator of the gestures and utterances of the other's body before me, I consider the totality of signs thus given, the totality of facial expressions this body presents to me, as the occasion for a kind of decoding. Behind the body whose gestures and characteristic utterances I witness, I project, so to speak, what I myself feel of my own body. No matter whether it is a question of an actual association of ideas or, instead, a judgment whereby I interpret the appearances, I transfer to the other the intimate experience I have of my own body.

The problem of the experience of others poses itself, as it were, in a system of four terms: (1) myself, my "psyche"; (2) the image I have of my body by means of the sense of touch or of cenesthesia, which, to be brief, we shall call the "introceptive image" of my own body; (3) the body of the other as seen by me, which we shall call the "visual body"; and (4) a fourth (hypothetical) term which I must re-constitute and guess at—the "psyche" of the other, the other's feeling of his own existence—to the extent that I can imagine or suppose it across the appearances of the other through his visual body.

Posed thus, the problem raises all kinds of difficulties. First, there is the difficulty of relating my knowledge or experience of the other to an association, to a judgment by which I would project into him the data of my intimate experience. The perception of others comes relatively early in life. Naturally we do not at an early age come to know the exact *meaning* of each of the emotional expressions presented to us by others. This exact knowledge is, if you like, late in coming; what is much earlier is the very fact that I perceive an expression, even if I may be wrong about what it means exactly. At a very early age children are sensitive to facial expressions, e.g., the smile. How could that be possible if, in order to arrive at an understanding of the global meaning of the smile and to learn that the smile is a fair indication of a benevolent feeling, the child had to perform the complicated task I have just mentioned? How could it be possible if, beginning with the visual perception of another's smile, he had to compare that visual perception of the smile with the movement that he himself makes when he is happy or when he feels benevolent—projecting to the other a benevolence of which he would have had intimate experience but which could not be grasped directly in the other? This complicated process would seem to be incompatible with the relative precociousness of the perception of others.

Again, in order for projection to be possible and to take place, it would be necessary for me to begin from the analogy between the facial expressions offered me by others and the different facial gestures I execute myself. In the case of the smile, for me to interpret the visible smile of the other requires that there be a way of comparing the visible smile of the other with what we may call the "motor smile"—the smile as felt, in the case of the child, by the child himself. But in fact do we have the means of making this comparison between the body of the other, as it appears in visual perception, and our own body, as we feel it by means of introception and of cenesthesia? Have we the means of systematically comparing the body of the other as seen by me with my body as sensed by me? In order for this to be possible there would have to be a fairly regular correspondence between the two experiences. The child's visual experience of his own body is altogether insignificant in relation to the kinesthetic, cenesthesic, or tactile feeling he can have of it. There are numerous regions of his body that he does not see and some that he will never see or know except by means of the mirror (of which we will speak shortly). There is no point-for-point correspondence between the two images of the body. To understand how the child arrives at assimilating the one to the other, we must, rather, suppose that he has other reasons for doing it than reasons of simple detail. If he comes to identify as bodies, and as animated ones, the bodies of himself and the other, this can only be because he globally identifies them and not because he constructs a point-for-point correspondence between the visual image of the other and the introceptive image of his own body.

These two difficulties are particularly apparent when it comes to accounting for the phenomenon of imitation. To imitate is to perform a gesture in the image of another's gesture—like the child, for example, who smiles because someone smiles at him. According to the principles we have been entertaining, it would be necessary for me to translate my visual image of the other's smile into a motor language. The child would have to set his facial muscles in motion in such a way as to reproduce the visible expression that is called "the smile" in another. But how could he do it? Naturally he does not have the other's internal motor feeling of his face; as far as he is concerned, he does not even have an image of himself smiling. The result is that if we want to solve the problem of the transfer of the other's conduct to me, we can in no way rest on the supposed analogy between the other's face and that of the child.

On the contrary, the problem comes close to being solved only on condition that certain classical prejudices are renounced. We must abandon the fundamental prejudice according to which the psyche is that which is accessible only to myself and cannot be seen from outside. My "psyche" is not a series of "states of consciousness" that are rigorously closed in on themselves and inaccessible to anyone but me. My consciousness is turned primarily toward the world, turned toward things; it is above all a relation to the world. The other's consciousness as well is chiefly a certain way of comporting himself toward the world. Thus it is in his conduct, in the manner in which the other deals with the world, that I will be able to discover his consciousness.

If I am a consciousness turned toward things, I can meet in things the actions of another and find in them a meaning, because they are themes of possible activity for my own body. Guillaume, in his book *l'Imitation chez l'enfant*,[10] says that we do not at first imitate others but rather the actions of others, and that we find others at the point of origin of these actions. At first the child imitates not persons but conducts. And the problem of knowing how conduct can be transferred from another to me is infinitely less difficult to solve than the problem of knowing how I can represent to myself a psyche that is radically foreign to me. If, for example, I see another draw a figure, I can understand the drawing as an action because it speaks directly to my own unique motility. Of course, the other *qua* author of a drawing is not yet a whole person, and there are more revealing actions than drawing—for example, using language. What is essential, however, is to see that a perspective on the other is opened to me from the moment I define him and myself as "conducts" at work in the world, as ways of "grasping" the natural and cultural world surrounding us.

But this presupposes a reform not only of the notion of the "psyche" (which we will replace henceforth by that of "conduct") but also of the idea we have of our own body. If my body is to appropriate the conducts given to me visually and make them its own, it must itself be given to me not as a mass of utterly private sensations but instead by what has been called a "postural," or "corporeal, schema." This notion, introduced long ago by Henry Head, has been taken over and enriched by Wallon, by certain German psychologists, and has finally been the subject of a study in its own right by Professor Lhermitte in *l'Image de notre corps*.[11]

For these authors, my body is no agglomeration of sensations (visual, tactile, "tenesthesic," or "cenesthesic"). It is first and foremost a *system* whose different introceptive and extroceptive aspects express each other reciprocally, including even the roughest of relations with surrounding space and its principal directions. The consciousness I have of my body is not the consciousness of an isolated mass; it is a *postural schema*. It is the perception of my body's position in relation to the vertical, the horizontal, and certain other axes of important coordinates of its environment.

In addition, the different sensory domains (sight, touch, and the

10. Paris, 1925.
11. Paris, 1939.

sense of movement in the joints) which are involved in the perception of my body do not present themselves to me as so many absolutely distinct regions. Even if, in the child's first and second years, the translation of one into the language of others is imprecise and incomplete, they all have in common a *certain style* of action, a certain *gestural* meaning that makes of the collection an already organized totality. Understood in this way, the experience I have of my own body could be transferred to another much more easily than the cenesthesia of classical psychology, giving rise to what Wallon calls a "postural impregnation" of my own body by the conducts I witness.

I can perceive, across the visual image of the other, that the other is an organism, that that organism is inhabited by a "psyche," because the visual image of the other is interpreted by the notion I myself have of my own body and thus appears as the visible envelopment of another "corporeal schema." My perception of my body would, so to speak, be swallowed up in a cenesthesia if that cenesthesia were strictly individual. On the contrary, however, if we are dealing with a schema, or a system, such a system would be relatively transferrable from one sensory domain to the other in the case of my own body, just as it could be transferred to the domain of the other.

Thus in today's psychology we have one system with two terms (my behavior and the other's behavior) which functions as a whole. To the extent that I can elaborate and extend my corporeal schema, to the extent that I acquire a better organized experience of my own body, to that very extent will my consciousness of my own body cease being a chaos in which I am submerged and lend itself to a transfer to others. And since at the same time the other who is to be perceived is himself not a "psyche" closed in on himself but rather a conduct, a system of behavior that aims at the world, he offers himself to my motor intentions and to that "intentional transgression" (Husserl) by which I animate and pervade him. Husserl said that the perception of others is like a "phenomenon of coupling" [*accouplement*]. The term is anything but a metaphor. In perceiving the other, my body and his are coupled, resulting in a sort of action which pairs them [*action à deux*]. This conduct which I am able only to see, I live somehow from a distance. I make it mine; I recover [*reprendre*] it or comprehend it. Reciprocally I know that the gestures I make myself can be the objects of another's intention. It is this transfer of my intentions to the other's body and of his intentions to my own, my alienation of the other and his alienation of me, that makes possible the perception of others.

All these analyses presuppose that the perception of others cannot be accounted for if one begins by supposing an ego and another that are *absolutely* conscious of themselves, each of which lays claim, as a result, to an absolute originality in relation to the other that confronts it. On the contrary, the perception of others is made comprehensible if one supposes that psychogenesis begins in a state where the child is unaware of himself and the other as different beings. We cannot say that in such a state the child has a genuine communication with others. In order that there be communication, there must be a sharp distinction between the one who communicates and the one with whom he communicates. But there is initially a state of pre-communication (Max Scheler), wherein the other's intentions somehow play *across* my body while my intentions play across his.

How is this distinction made? I gradually become aware of my body, of what radically distinguishes it from the other's body, at the same time that I begin to live my intentions in the facial expressions of the other and likewise begin to live the other's volitions in my own gestures. The progress of the child's experience results in his seeing that his body is, after all, closed in on itself. In particular, the visual image he acquires of his own body (especially from the mirror) reveals to him a hitherto unsuspected isolation of two subjects who are facing each other. The objectification of his own body discloses to the child his difference, his "insularity," and, correlatively, that of others.

Thus the development has somewhat the following character: There is a first phase, which we call pre-communication, in which there is not one individual over against another but rather an anonymous collectivity, an undifferentiated group life [*vie à plusieurs*]. Next, on the basis of this initial community, both by the objectification of one's own body and the constitution of the other in his difference, there occurs a segregation, a distinction of individuals—a process which, moreover, as we shall see, is never completely finished.

This kind of conception is common to many trends in contemporary psychology. One finds it in Guillaume and Wallon; it occurs in Gestalt theorists, phenomenologists, and psychoanalysts alike.

Guillaume shows that we must neither treat the origin of consciousness as though it were conscious, in an explicit way, of itself nor treat it as though it were completely closed in on itself. The first *me* is, as he says, virtual or latent, i.e., unaware of itself in its absolute difference. Consciousness of oneself as a unique individual, whose place can be taken by no one else, comes later and is not primitive. Since the primordial *me* is virtual or latent, egocentrism is not at all the attitude of a *me* that expressly grasps itself (as the term "egocentrism" might lead us to believe). Rather, it is the attitude of a *me* which is unaware of itself and lives as easily in others as it does in itself—but which, being unaware of others in their own separateness as well, in truth is no more conscious of them than of itself.

Wallon introduces an analogous notion with what he calls "syncretic sociability." Syncretism here is the indistinction between me and the other, a confusion at the core of a situation that is common to us both. After that the objectification of the body intervenes to establish a sort of wall between me and the other: a partition. Henceforth it will prevent me from confusing myself with what the other thinks, and especially with what he thinks of me; just as I will no longer confuse him with my thoughts, and especially my thoughts about him. There is thus a correlative constitution of me and the other as two human beings among all others.

Thus at first the *me* is both entirely unaware of itself and at the same time all the more demanding for being unaware of its own limits. The adult *me*, on the contrary, is a *me* that knows its own limits yet possesses the power to cross them by a genuine sympathy that is at least *relatively* distinct from the initial form of sympathy. The initial sympathy rests on the ignorance of oneself rather than on the perception of others, while adult sympathy occurs between "other" and "other"; it does not abolish the differences between myself and the other.

[2] THE PLACEMENT OF THE CORPOREAL SCHEMA
AND THE FIRST PHASES OF A PERCEPTION OF OTHERS
(FROM BIRTH TO SIX MONTHS)

WHAT HAS BEEN GAINED from these introductory remarks has been the correlation between consciousness of one's own body and perception of the other. To be aware that one has a body and that the other's body is animated by another psyche are two operations that are not simply logically symmetrical but form a real system. In both cases it is a question of becoming conscious of what might be called "incarnation." To notice, on the one hand, that I have a body which can be seen from outside and that for others I am nothing but a mannequin, gesticulating at a point in space and, on the other hand, to notice that the other has a psyche—i.e., that this body I see before me like a mannequin gesticulating at a point in space is animated by another psyche—are two moments of a single whole. This does not mean that the child's experience of this total phenomenon can assign a privilege to one of these aspects; rather, any progress realized in one aspect unbalances the totality and is the dialectical ferment that results in subsequent progress in the system. They are complementary operations, and the experience of my body and the body of the other form a totality and constitute a "form." In saying this, naturally I do not mean that the perception of others and the perception of one's own body always go hand in hand or that they develop at the same pace. On the contrary, we shall see that the perception of one's own body is ahead of the recognition of the other, and consequently if the two comprise a system, it is a system that becomes articulated in time. To say that a phenomenon is one of "form" (*Gestalt*) is in no way to say that it is innate in its different aspects or even in a single one of its aspects. Rather, it is to say that it develops according to a law of *internal* equilibrium, as if by *auto-organization*. Gestalt theorists have by no means limited the use of the notion of "form" to the instant or the present. They have, on the contrary, insisted on the phenomenon of form in time (melody). I said that perception of one's own body comes earlier than perception of the other. The child takes notice of his own body sooner than he does of the expressions of the other. That does not prevent the two phenomena from being internally linked. The perception of one's own body creates an imbalance as it develops: through its echo in the image of the other, it awakens an appeal to the forthcoming development of the perception of others. It echoes in another phase, in which the perception of others appears predominant, and so on throughout the development. The two phenomena can easily form a system, although they are emphasized only successively. Each of the phases of this development contains the germs which prepare the way for its being surpassed. And to say that the phenomenon is a formal one is by no means to say that it is, in each of its stages, completely at rest. Any form (e.g., those we perceive in space—colored forms) is actually subject to a play of forces from different directions. The imbalance can be infinitesimal at first and give rise to no appreciable change. Then when it passes a certain limit, a change occurs. In the same way there may well be something at the core of each phase of development which anticipates the next phase and which gives life to a series of re-structurations. The notion of form is essentially dynamic.

Let us now consider the state of the perception of one's own body and the state of the perception of others, each in its turn.

1. *One's own body from birth to six months*

THE BODY, as Henri Wallon suggests in his excellent analysis in *Les origines du caractère chez l'enfant*,[12] begins by being introceptive. At the beginning of life there emerges an entire phase in which extroceptivity (i.e., vision, hearing, and all other perceptions relating to the external world), even if it begins to operate, cannot in any case do so in collaboration with introceptivity. At this age the latter is the

12. 2d edition (Paris, 1949).

best organized means for bringing us into relation with things. In the earliest stage of the child's life, external perception is impossible for very simple reasons: visual accommodation and muscular control of the eyes are insufficient.

As has often been said, the body is at first "buccal" in nature. Stern has even spoken of a "buccal space" at the beginning of the child's life, meaning by this that the limit of the world for the child is the space that can be contained in, or explored by, his mouth. One could say more generally, as Wallon does, that the body is already a respiratory body. Not only the mouth but the whole respiratory apparatus gives the child a kind of experience of space. After that, other regions of the body intervene and come into prominence. All the regions linked to the functions of expression, for example, acquire an extreme importance in the months that follow. In waiting for the union that will arise between the data of external perception and those of introceptivity, the introceptive body functions as extroceptive. In another context, this is what psychoanalysts say about the origin of the child's experiences when they show, for example, that the child's relations to the mother's breast are his first relations with the world.

It is only between the third and the sixth month that a union occurs between the introceptive and the extroceptive domains. The different neural paths are not yet ready to function at birth. Myelinization, which makes their functioning possible, is late in taking place; this is particularly true of the connective fibers we speak of at present. It occurs between the third and the sixth month, connecting the mechanisms which furnish the various sensory data as well as those which correspond respectively to extroceptivity and introceptivity.

Up to that moment perception is impossible for yet another reason: it presupposes a minimal bodily equilibrium. The operation of a postural schema—that is, a global consciousness of my body's position in space, with the corrective reflexes that impose themselves at each moment, the global consciousness of the spatiality of my body—all this is necessary for perception (Wallon). In fact the effort at equilibrium continually accompanies all our perceptions except when we are lying on our back. But also, observes Wallon, it is above all in this position that the child's thinking and perception fade away; he falls asleep. This link between motility and perception shows at what point it is true to say that the two functions are only two aspects of a single totality and that the perception of one's entry into the world and of one's own body form a system.

When the necessary neural paths have been acquired, there remains a considerable gap between the precision of the consciousness of the body in certain domains and in others. You know, for example, that myelinization occurs much later in the nerve fibers corresponding to the activity of the feet than it does in those which correspond to the activity of the hands. The delay is about three weeks long. All the same, in the case of the hands there is a slight lag of about twenty-six days in the myelinization of the left hand as compared with the right. Consequently there is a phase in which the child calls up the physiological conditions for a precise perception of the right hand's movements but not yet those for a precise perception of the movements of the left hand.

It is not surprising, therefore, that the child does not really interest himself in his body or in its parts until relatively late. It is only on the 115th day of his life, or around the fourth month, that one notices the child actually paying attention to his right hand. Only in the twenty-third week of life, or around the sixth month, does one find the child systematically making the experiment of exploring one hand with the other. At that moment—having clasped his right hand with his left hand, for example—he interrupts his movement and looks attentively at his hands. At the twenty-fourth week, or at the end of the sixth month, the child is perplexed at the sight of a glove placed next to his hand. He is seen comparing the glove and his hand, looking attentively at the moving hand. All these experiments are aimed at familiarizing the child with the correspondence between the hand which touches and the hand which is touched, between the body as seen and the body as felt by introceptivity.

The consciousness of one's own body is thus fragmentary [*lacunaire*] at first and gradually becomes integrated; the corporeal schema becomes precise, restructured, and mature little by little.

2. *The other from birth to six months*

THIS ENTIRE PLACEMENT [*mise en place*] of the corporeal schema is at the same time a placing of the perception of others. Reactions to others, according to Guillaume in *l'Imitation chez l'enfant,* are extremely precocious. To tell the truth, it seems that the first forms of reaction to others described by Guillaume are not connected with a visual perception of others; they correspond, rather, to the data of introceptivity. Guillaume says that between the ninth and the eleventh day, he noticed an astonished and attentive expression in the child, directed toward faces and fleeting smiles. At sixteen days he found differences in the attitude of the child according to whether he was in the arms of his mother, his wet nurse, or his father.

In Wallon's view, it is not a question, in these different attitudes, of a veritable extroceptive perception of the mother, the father, and the nurse. Instead it is a question of differences felt by the child in the state of his body—differences in his well-being according to whether the nurse's breast is present or absent and also according to the way in which the child is held in the arms of each of the persons involved.

Up to the age of three months, according to Wallon, there is no external perception of others by the child, and what ought to be concluded when, for example, the child is seen to cry because someone goes away is that he has an "impression of incompleteness." Rather than truly perceiving those who are there, he feels incomplete when someone goes away. This negative experience does not mean that there is a precise perception of the other *qua* other in the preceding moment. The first external contact with others can be truly given only through extroceptivity. In so far as others are felt only as a kind of state of well-being in the baby's organism because he is held more firmly or more tenderly in their arms, we cannot say that they are actually perceived.

The first active extroceptive stimulus would be the voice. With it begin the reactions that can be called without any possible doubt *definite reactions to others*. At first the human voice as heard by the child provokes only cries when the child is afraid; then, at two months, it provokes smiles. At two or three months one observes that deliberately looking at the child makes him smile. At that moment there will be in the child at least one perception of a look as of something that makes him complete. At the same age the child responds to the cries of other children by calling out himself; there is a kind of contagion of cries that disappears later as the visual perception of others develops. Around that same age, too, the child cries when anyone at all leaves the room and not, as in the beginning, only at the departure of the wet nurse or the person who is feeding him.

At two months and five days one observes, says Wallon, an unmistakably visual experience of another—a recognition of the father at a distance of two yards. This assumes that the father presents himself in his habitual environment; in an unfamiliar setting, he would not be recognized. At three months the child cries out at all persons who come into his room, even when they are not persons from whom he can expect care.

Concerning relations with other children, here is roughly what happens: I said that at from two to three months there is a contagion of cries among babies and that afterward this contagion disappears, to the extent that visual perception of the other develops. Consequently for a child older than three months the contagion of cries is much rarer than before, and a baby of this age can look with cool detachment at another baby who is crying.

The first beginnings of an observation of others consist in fixations on *the parts of the body*. The child looks at the feet, the mouth, the hands; he does not look at the person. The difference is intuitively quite noticeable between a mere scrutiny of the parts of the body and a look oriented toward the other's look, which seeks to grasp the other as such. The scrutiny of the parts of the other's body considerably enriches the perception that the child can have of his own body. We see him systematically relating to himself, after six months, the different things he has learned about the other's body from looking at him. Still at five months there is no fraternization with children of the same age. At six months, at last, the child looks the other child in the face, and one has the impression that here, for the first time, he is perceiving another.

[3] AFTER SIX MONTHS: CONSCIOUSNESS OF ONE'S OWN BODY AND THE SPECULAR IMAGE

IT IS NOW up to us to describe the phase intervening after six months, which will be characterized by a sharp opposition to the first phase. It involves the development of perception of one's own body —a step which is considerably aided by the child's becoming acquainted with the image of his body in the mirror. This is a phenomenon of great importance, since the mirror furnishes the child with a perception of his own body that he could never have got by himself. On the other hand, there is an extraordinarily rapid development of contacts with others—so rapid, in fact, that Wallon was led to speak of and characterize the period between six months and one year as one of "incontinent sociability."

1. *The syncretic system "me-and-other" (after six months)*

AT THIS POINT we propose to examine simultaneously the development of the experience of one's own body (in its introceptive aspect and in the specular image [13]) and that of the consciousness of the other, beginning at six months.

The major fact that concerns the development of consciousness of one's own body is the acquisition of a representation or a visual image

13. *"L'image spéculaire."* Almost always this term designates the image of himself that is gradually acquired by the child from experiences of his own reflection in the mirror. When Merleau-Ponty refers merely to the physical, episodic event of a body's reflection in a mirror, he uses *"L'image du miroir."* The importance of distinguishing between the image as a physical event and as a development in the life history of the child has led me to translate this term throughout as "specular image," leaving "mirror-image" to refer to the former, narrower sense.—*Trans.*

of the body itself, in particular by means of the mirror. The study of this specular image, the recognition of this image and the different stages it passes through are the subjects we shall be concerned with at first.

On this point there is a contrast between the behavior of animals and of children. We cannot say that animals pay no attention to their images in the mirror or that they show no reaction to their specular images. But the conduct of animals is very different from that of children. The first information on the subject was given by Preyer in his now outdated book.[14] The story concerns a duck who, deprived of his mate's company by her death, developed the habit of sitting in front of a windowpane in which his body was reflected. This behavior, according to Wallon [Les origines du caractère chez l'enfant], would not be comparable to what one finds in the child. The animal, made incomplete by his mate's death, "completes" himself with his image in the windowpane. He does not take it to be an image of himself, since it is capable of taking the place of another living being; it is like a second animal facing him. Again, inversely, one could say that if in truth the reflected image represents for the animal what was formerly represented by the presence of his mate, the mate was, while he was perceiving her, only a kind of mirror image of himself. In both cases the conduct characteristic of the child (which we shall define shortly) does not yet appear.

Wallon describes the reactions of two dogs to their images in the mirror. One of the dogs displays reactions of fear and avoidance; when he sees his image in the mirror he turns and runs. The other dog, caressed by his master while looking at his image in the mirror, calmly stands still and at the same time turns his head toward his master, who caresses him. The image he sees in the mirror is not, for him, another dog, but neither is it *his own* visual image. The visual image is a kind of complement for him, and as soon as his master's caress recalls him to his body as given in introceptivity, he neglects the mirror image and turns toward the master. Here again, in other words, the animal does not display conduct that is characteristic of the symbol, of the external image as such. In the presence of the mirror he is disoriented, confused, and turns away hastily in order to return to the objects that for him are fundamental—that is, to return to introceptive experience.

The behavior of chimpanzees toward the mirror was studied by Köhler in his fine book, The Mentality of Apes.[15] There the author shows that when the chimpanzee is placed in front of a mirror and

14. Merleau-Ponty may be referring to Thierry Wilhelm Preyer, The Mind of the Child, trans. H. W. Brown (New York, 1893).—Trans.
15. New York, 1925.—Trans.

finds an image in it, he passes his hand behind it and shows signs of dissatisfaction at finding nothing behind the image. From then on he stubbornly refuses to interest himself in the mirror. Wallon interprets this as follows: At the moment when—through the manual exploration that could convince him that there was really only a simple image instead of another body—the chimpanzee was about to reach consciousness of the image or treat what is in the mirror as a simple reflection or symbol of his real body, he recoils from the object and treats it as foreign. Consciousness of the image *qua* image scarcely appears, and is only roughly outlined in him. Köhler, however, indicates that the chimpanzee seems to recognize himself in a portrait of himself when presented to him. A repeated experimental study of this phenomenon might well be made in order to see whether in fact chimpanzees are conscious of their portraits and, if so, why they do not achieve a full consciousness of the specular image.

These conducts, we have said, must be contrasted with those of the child. Let us begin by considering not the child's image of his own body in the mirror but instead the image he has of others' bodies. One notices, in effect, that he acquires the latter much more rapidly, that he distinguishes much more quickly between the other's specular image and the reality of the other's body than he does in the case of his own body. Thus it is possible that the experience he has of the other's specular image helps him arrive at an understanding of his own.

According to Guillaume [*l'Imitation chez l'enfant*], the consciousness of the other's image in the mirror comes at an early age. Guillaume observes grimaces before a mirror in the first weeks of life. Wallon thinks, however, that clear reactions to the specular image are not noticeable before the end of the third month.

At first there is a reaction of simple fixation on the specular image (around four or five months). This is followed by reactions of interest in the same image. At the same moment, one notices reactions in the child, e.g., to a portrait by Franz Hals. Finally, after six months, reactions other than the mimic or affective are seen to appear. These are genuine conducts. After five or six months, for example, there occurs the following:

A child smiles in a mirror at the image of his father. At this moment his father speaks to him. The child appears surprised and turns toward the father. As a result it seems that at this moment he *learns* something. What exactly does he learn? He is surprised, because at the moment before his father spoke, he did not have a precise awareness of the relation of image to model. He is surprised that the voice comes from another direction than that of the visible image in the mirror. The attention he gives to the phenomenon shows, in effect, that he is in the process of understanding something, that it is not a question of simple training. One might be tempted to say that we are here present at the formation of a conditioned reflex and that the mirror image becomes "comprehensible" by becoming the conditioned stimulus of responses that were formerly evoked by the father. In Wallon's eyes there can be no question either of a blind training or of an intellectual mastery of the image. Certainly one cannot say that the child comes into possession of a perfectly clear relation between the image and the model or that he learns to consider the mirror image as a spatial projection of the visible aspect of his father. The experience of which we are speaking occurs at about five or six months and does not give the child possession of a stable conduct. Just as the child studied by Wallon turned away from the specular image toward his father after a week, so several weeks later he still tried to grasp the image in the mirror with his hand; this means that he had not yet identified this image as a "simple image" that was nothing other than visible.

We should say that in this first phase of his apprenticeship, the child gives the image and the model an existence relatively independent of each other. There is the model, which is the father's body, the real father; there is in the mirror a sort of double or phantom of the father, having a "secondary existence" without the image being reduced to the simple state of a reflection of light and color in external space. When the child turns away from the mirror toward his father, we may indeed say that he recognizes his father in the image but in an altogether practical way. He turns toward his father because that is where the voice is coming from; but it cannot be said that at this point he has divested the specular image of its quasi-reality, the phantom existence it first had for him, nor can we try to render it with the aid of certain analogies borrowed from primitive thought. The image thus has an existence inferior to that of the father's real body—but it does have a sort of marginal existence.

Let us now consider the acquisition of the specular image of one's own body. It is around the age of eight months—hence later than in the case of the specular image of the other—that one clearly finds a reaction of surprise when the child sees his own image in the mirror. At thirty-five weeks the child still extends his hand toward his image in the mirror and appears surprised when his hand encounters the surface of the glass. At the same age he happens to look at his image in the glass when he is called. The illusion of reality, the quasi-reality he lends to the image, still remains, just as after several weeks the child still turns away from the specular image and toward his father. This confirms the fact that, if the child has an adaptive reaction, this does not entail that he has acquired a symbolic consciousness of the image.

Why does the specular image of one's own body develop later than that of the other's body? According to Wallon (whose analysis we are following here), it is because the problem to be solved is much more difficult in the case of one's own body. The child is dealing with two visual experiences of his father: the experience he has from looking at him and that which comes from the mirror. Of his own body, on the other hand, the mirror image is his only complete visual evidence. He can easily look at his feet and his hands but not at his body as a whole. Thus for him it is a problem first of understanding that the visual image of his body which he sees over there in the mirror is not himself, since he is not in the mirror but here, where he feels himself; and second, he must understand that, not being located there, in the mirror, but rather where he feels himself introceptively, he can nonetheless be seen by an external witness *at the very place at which he feels himself to be* and with the same visual appearance that he has from the mirror. In short, he must displace the mirror image, bringing it from the apparent or virtual place it occupies in the depth of the mirror back to himself, whom he identifies at a distance with his introceptive body.

Consequently, in the case of the image of his own body, we must admit, says Wallon, that the child begins by seeing the specular image as a sort of double of the real body—much more so indeed than in the case of the image of the other's body.

Many pathological facts bear witness to this kind of external perception of the self, this "autoscopy." First, it is found in many dreams, in which the subject figures as a quasi-visible character. There would also be phenomena of this kind in dying people, in certain hypnotic states, and in drowning people. What reappears in these pathological cases is comparable to the child's original consciousness of his own visible body in the mirror. "Primitive" people are capable of believing that the same person is in several places at the same time. This possibility of *ubiquity*, difficult for us to understand, can be illuminated by the initial forms of the specular image. The child knows well that he is there where his introceptive body is, and yet in the depth of the mirror he sees the same being present, in a bizarre way, in a visible appearance. There is a mode of spatiality in the specular image that is altogether distinct from adult spatiality. In the child, says Wallon, there is a kind of space clinging to the image. All images tend to present themselves in space, including the image of the mirror as well. According to Wallon, this spatiality of adherence will be reduced by intellectual development. We will learn gradually to return the specular image to the introceptive body and, reciprocally, to treat the quasi-locatedness and pre-spatiality of the image as an appearance that counts for nothing against the unique space of real things. Our intelligence would, so to speak, redistribute the spatial values, and we would learn to consider as relevant to the same place appearances which, on first sight, present themselves in different places. Thus an ideal space would be substituted for the space clinging to the images. It is necessary, in effect, that the new space be ideal, since for the child it is a question of understanding that what seems to be in different places is in fact in the same place. This can occur only in passing to a higher level of spatiality that is no longer the intuitive space in which the images occupy their own place.

This constitution of an ideal space would include all kinds of degrees. First, there would be, as we have just mentioned, the reduction of the image to a simple appearance lacking its own spatiality. This reduction occurs fairly early, at around one year. Guillaume describes an observation made on his own daughter, who steps before a mirror with a straw hat which she has been wearing since the morning. She puts her hand not to the image of the hat in the mirror but to the hat on her head; the image in the mirror suffices to call forth and regulate a movement adapted to the object itself. In this case one can say that the reduction has been accomplished, that the mirror image is no longer anything but a symbol, and that it returns the child's consciousness to the reflected objects in their proper places.

A counterproof: Each time there occur troubles with the symbolic consciousness—as, for example, in cases of aphasia or apraxia—one also finds troubles with spatiality. Apraxic subjects are known in particular for their difficulty in ordering movements adapted to objects by means of a mirror (or in imitating a subject who is facing them). For them the relation of the image to the model is disturbed and confused.

At one year, according to Wallon, one could say that this development is essentially complete. But this does not mean that the system of correspondence between the image of the body and the body itself is complete or that it is precise. This is shown by a whole series of events, certain of which come fairly late. For example, from twelve to fifteen months of age, the child is seen practicing a series of exercises that prepare for the habit of performing movements in front of the mirror. He is trying out the kind of movements that the apraxic is asked to perform. And this occurs after the first year, at between twelve and fifteen months; that is, the system at this moment is still quite fragmentary and the child needs to confirm it by repeated experiments. At sixty weeks (i.e., at more than a year), when the mother is sitting beside the child with a mirror in front of them and the child is asked to point to his mother, the child points to her in the mirror *while laughing* and turns back to her. The specular image has become the subject of a game, an amusement. But the very fact that the child thinks of using his specular image to play with shows that he is not so far removed from the experiments that first introduced him to the specular image.

The apprenticeship is not yet very stable. At fifty-seven weeks (thus at more than a year) Preyer's son looked at himself in the mirror, passed his hand behind the mirror, brought his hand back, and contemplated it. This, as we have seen, is exactly what chimpanzees do. The next day he turned away from the mirror, just like the chimpanzees. All the same, this fact would appear a bit difficult to admit if, as Guillaume thinks, the consciousness of the specular image has already been acquired at the age of one year. How could one revert after that age to the conduct of chimpanzees, which, as we have seen, is inferior to the level of consciousness of the image? Wallon proposes an explanation: In the case we are considering, he says, it is not so much a misunderstanding of the specular image; it is on the mirror, not on the image, that the inquiry bears. The child would have discovered once for all that what is portrayed over there on the mirror is only an appearance, a reflection, but it remains for him to understand *how* an object (the mirror) is capable of obtaining a duplicate of the surrounding objects. Wallon's interpretation is not entirely convincing. In order for there to be an exact consciousness of the image in its relation to the model, it seems necessary for there to be some understanding of the role of the mirror. In so far as the mirror is not at all understood, to the extent that the child expects to find in back of it something like the objects which outline themselves on its surface, he has not yet fully understood the existence of the reflection; he has not yet fully understood the image. If his consciousness of the image were entirely perfect, the child would no longer search behind the mirror for real objects similar to the ones reflected in it. The constitution of a specular image that would be in the fullest sense a *reflection* of the real object presupposes the gradual constitution of an entire naïve physics, into which would enter the causal relations that are designed to explain how the phenomenon of the reflection is possible.

The facts set forth by Preyer thus would seem to show that at fifty-seven weeks there still is no full understanding of the specular image. Hence we will not be astonished that even at sixty-one weeks Preyer's son still touched, licked, struck, and played with his image. Like the game of the child who laughed at his mother's image, this game seems to show that the child is not far from the time when the image was still a double, a phantom of the object. Wallon says that a child of twenty months kisses his image very ceremoniously before going to bed and even at thirty-one months the child is seen to play with his own image.

We have seen that Wallon considers that these games played by the

child with his own image represent a phase beyond the simple consciousness of the specular image. If the child plays with his own image
in the mirror, says Wallon, it is because he is amusing himself by
finding in the mirror a reflection which has all the appearances of an
animated being and yet is not one. Here it would be a question of
"animistic games," an activity which proclaims that animistic *beliefs*
have been suppressed. But why should it be so amusing somehow to
verify the animistic appearance if there remained in the subject no
traces of this amazing phenomenon which on first encounter so fascinated the child—namely, the presence of a quasi intention in a reflection? The child happily makes a sort of fairy dance before it and clings
to it, although it is not "for real."

This leads us to make a remark which perhaps will have to be
recalled in concluding. For adults like ourselves, the mirror image has
really become what Wallon would like it to be in an adult mind: a
simple reflection. Nonetheless there are two ways in which we can
consider the image—one, a reflective, analytic way according to which
the image is nothing but an appearance in a visible world and has
nothing to do with me; the other, a global and direct one, of the kind
which we use in immediate life when we do not reflect and which gives
us the image as something which *solicits* our belief. Let us compare the
mirror image to a painting. When I look at a painting of Charles XII of
Sweden, with his elongated face and that head which, according to his
contemporaries, only one idea could enter at a time, I know very well
that Charles XII has been dead for a long time and that what I am
looking at is no more than a painting. Nonetheless there is a *quasi-
person* who is smiling; that line joining nose and lips, that flashing in
the eyes are not simply things. This congealed movement is, all the
same, a *smile*. In the same way the image in the mirror, even for the
adult, when considered in direct unreflective experience, is not simply
a physical phenomenon: it is mysteriously inhabited by me; it is something of myself.

This experience allows us to understand the significance attached
to images in certain civilizations. There one is forbidden to make
images of men because this is similar to deliberately creating other
human beings—and this is not man's proper function. This group of
beliefs related to images can be understood only if images are more
than black-and-white sketches or simple signs of a person who remains
absolutely distinct from them. In a singular way the image incarnates
and makes appear the person represented in it, as spirits are made to
appear at a séance. Even an adult will hesitate to step on an image or
photograph; if he does, it will be with aggressive intent. Thus not only
is the consciousness of the image slow in developing and subject to

relapses, but even for the adult the image is never a simple reflection of the model; it is, rather, its "quasi-presence" (Sartre).

This also explains why the work of "reduction," even when done by the child in respect to the image in the mirror, never ends with a *general* result, such as a concept. The child must do the work all over again in respect to other analogous phenomena—shadows, for example. Wallon remarks that Preyer's son, at the age of four years, noticed for the first time that he cast a shadow and noticed it with fright. A little girl, four and a half years old, observed by Wallon, pretended that when she stepped on Wallon's shadow she was stepping on Wallon himself. The participationist beliefs with which, as we have said, the specular image is at first endowed have not been reduced by an intellectual critique that would apply indifferently to all phenomena of the same order. The progress consists in a restructuration of the specular image. The child puts this image at a distance, but this distance is not that of the concept.

Wallon would like to say that in the case of the shadow it is a matter of beginning the same development that has already been acquired in the case of the specular image. But this would be to say that the progressive reduction of the specular image is not, properly speaking, an intellectual phenomenon. A genuine intellectual event would obey the "all or nothing" law: either one knows or one does not know. One cannot "slightly know" the sum of two and three. The intellectual phenomenon is not susceptible to that series of gradations that one observes in the development of the specular image.

This leads us to ask whether, in the light of several other facts, there is room to reattempt to interpret the development of the specular image and relate it to phenomena other than those of knowledge. Wallon's book also contains indications along these lines. Wallon himself, in certain passages in *Les origines du caractère chez l'enfant*, suggests that the progress in experiencing one's own body is a "moment" in a global development that also involves the perception of others.

At the end of his analysis Wallon sharply criticizes the notion of cenesthesia, considered as a series of images given directly and immediately by my organs and bodily functions and representing these organs and functions to me. According to Wallon, this cenesthesia, when it exists, is the result of a very long development; it is a fact of adult psychology and altogether fails to express the relation between the child and his body. The child in no way distinguishes at first between what is furnished by introception and what comes from external perception. There is no distinction between the data of what the learned adult calls introceptivity and the data of sight. The specular image, given visually, participates globally in the existence of the body itself and leads a "phantom" life in the mirror, which "participates" in the life of the child himself. What is true of his own body, for the child, is also true of the other's body. The child himself feels that he is in the other's body, just as he feels himself to be in his visual image. It is this that Wallon suggests in showing by the examination of pathological cases: *that disorders in "cenesthesia" are closely linked with troubles in my relations with others.*

Sick people feel a voice speaking in the region of the epigastrium, in the throat, the chest, or the head. Classical psychiatrists thought that this must be a question of hallucinations involving different regions of the body. They translated and "put into images" the complaints of the sick, taking quite literally what the patients said.

Modern psychiatry shows, however, that what is essential and primary about the phenomena in question is not the location of voices in the subject's body, but rather a sort of "syncretism" that intervenes in his relations with others and causes alien voices to inhabit his own body. If the patient hears voices in his head, this is because he does not absolutely distinguish himself from others and because, for example, when he speaks, he can just as well believe that someone else is speaking. The patient, says Wallon, has the impression of being "without boundaries" in relation to the other, and this is what makes his acts, his speech, and his thoughts appear to him to belong to others or to be imposed by others.

This interpretation of the so-called cenesthesic disorders is closely connected with the analyses of Daniel Lagache in *Les hallucinations verbales et la parole.*[16] Lagache thinks that the question "How can we understand a subject who believes that he is hearing when it is he who is speaking?" can be answered only if one conceives language to be a kind of "we-operation" [*opération à deux*]. There is a sort of indistinction between the act of speaking and the act of hearing. The word is not understood or even heard unless the subject is ready to pronounce it himself, and, inversely, every subject who speaks carries himself toward the one who is listening. In a dialogue, the participants occupy both poles at once, and it is this that explains why the phenomenon of "speaking" can pass into that of "hearing." It is this primordial unity that reappears in pathological cases.

What this observation reveals when we rid ourselves of sensationalist prejudices, says Wallon, is the "inability to distinguish the active from the passive," myself from the other. Here we come very close to what the psychoanalysts call "projection" and "introjection," since

16. D. Lagache, *Les hallucinations verbales et la parole* (Paris, 1934).

these mechanisms consist, for the subject, in assuming as his own the conduct of another or in attributing to the other a conduct that is really his own.

There is thus a system (my visual body, my introceptive body, the other) which establishes itself in the child, never so completely as in the animal but imperfectly, with gaps. It is founded on the indistinction of the several elements that enter into it, rather than on an ordered relation and a two-way correspondence of its different elements. One may presume that, just as there is a global identification of the child with his visual image in the mirror, so also will there be a global identification of the child with others. If the child under six months of age does not yet have a visual notion of his own body (that is, a notion that locates his body at a certain point in visible space), that is all the more reason why, during this same period, he will not know enough to limit his own life to himself. To the extent that he lacks this visual consciousness of his body, he cannot separate what *he* lives from what *others* live as well as what he sees them living. Thence comes the phenomenon of "transitivism," i.e., the absence of a division between myself and others that is the foundation of syncretic sociability.

These remarks made by Wallon at the end of his book go much further than does his analysis of the specular image, and allow us to correct and complete the latter. Wallon's study of the specular image scarcely characterizes it in a positive way. It shows us how the child learns to consider the mirror image as unreal, to reduce it; hence the disillusionment with which the child deprives the specular image of the quasi-reality he gave it at first. But we must also ask why the specular image *interests* him and what it is for the child to know that *he has a visible image*. Wallon himself says that the child "amuses himself" with his image "to the point of excess." [17] But why is the image so *amusing?*

It is this that the psychoanalysts have tried to understand. Dr. Lacan begins by observing exactly what Wallon noticed: the child's extreme amusement in the presence of his image, his "jubilation" at seeing himself moving in the mirror. The child is not yet walking; he stands sometimes with difficulty. All traces of prenatal life have not yet been effaced in him; all neural connections have not yet matured. He is still far from being adapted to the physical world around him. Is it not surprising, under these conditions, that he takes such a lively, universal, and constant interest in the phenomenon of the mirror? Dr. Lacan's answer is that, when the child looks at himself in the mirror and recognizes his own image there, it is a matter of *identification* (in

17. *Les origines du caractère chez l'enfant*, p. 177.

the psychoanalytic sense of the word)—that is, of "the transformation occasioned in the subject when he assumes." [18] For the child, understanding the specular image consists in *recognizing as his own* this visual appearance in the mirror. Until the moment when the specular image arises, the child's body is a strongly felt but confused reality. To recognize his image in the mirror is for him to learn that *there can be a viewpoint taken on him*. Hitherto he has *never seen himself*, or he has only caught a glimpse of himself in looking out of the corner of his eye at the parts of his body he can see. By means of the image in the mirror he becomes capable of being a spectator of himself. Through the acquisition of the specular image the child notices that he is *visible*, for himself and for others. The passage from the introceptive *me* to the visual *me*, from the introceptive *me* to the "specular *I*" (as Lacan still says), is the passage from one form or state of personality to another. The personality before the advent of the specular image is what psychoanalysts call, in the adult, the ego (*soi*), i.e., the collection of confusedly felt impulses. The mirror image itself makes possible a contemplation of self. With the specular image appears the possibility of an ideal image of oneself—in psychoanalytic terms, the possibility of a super-ego. And this image would henceforth be either explicitly posited or simply implied by everything I see at each minute.

Thus one sees that the phenomenon of the specular image is given by psychoanalysts the importance it really has in the life of the child. It is the acquisition not only of a new content but of a new function as well: the narcissistic function. Narcissus was the mythical being who, after looking at his image in the water, was drawn as if by vertigo to rejoin his image in the mirror of water. At the same time that the image of oneself makes possible the knowledge of oneself, it makes possible a sort of alienation. I am no longer what I felt myself, immediately, to be; I am that image of myself that is offered by the mirror. To use Dr. Lacan's terms, I am "captured, caught up" by my spatial image. Thereupon I leave the reality of my lived *me* in order to refer myself constantly to the ideal, fictitious, or imaginary *me*, of which the specular image is the first outline. In this sense I am torn from myself, and the image in the mirror prepares me for another still more serious alienation, which will be the alienation by others. For others have only an exterior image of me, which is analogous to the one seen in the mirror. Consequently others will tear me away from my immediate inwardness much more surely than will the mirror. The specular image is the "symbolic matrix," says Lacan, "where the *I*

18. Cf. Jacques Lacan, "Le stade du miroir comme formateur du fonction du je," *Revue Française de Psychanalyse*, vol. 13 (October–December, 1949), pp. 449–55. Also the same author, "Les effets psychiques du mode imaginaire," *l'Evolution Psychiatrique* (January–March, 1947).

springs up in primordial form before objectifying itself in the dialectic of identification with the other."

The general function of the specular image would be to tear us away from our immediate reality; it would be a "de-realizing" function. The author insists that it is astonishing that such a phenomenon appears in a subject of whom we have said earlier that he is very far from maturity in the biological and motor spheres. The human child is that being who is capable of sensitivity to others and of considering himself one among other similar men long before the true state of physiological maturity. "Pre-maturation" and anticipation are essential phenomena for childhood; childhood makes possible both a development unknown to animality and an insecurity that is proper to the human child. For inevitably there is conflict between the *me* as I feel myself and the *me* as I see myself or as others see me. The specular image will be, among other things, the first occasion for aggressiveness toward others to manifest itself. That is why it will be assumed by the child both in jubilation and in suffering. The acquisition of a specular image, therefore, bears not only on our *relations of understanding* but also our *relations of being*, with the world and with others.

Thus in this phenomenon of the specular image, so simple at first glance, will be revealed to the child for the first time the possibility of an attitude of self-observation that will develop subsequently in the form of narcissism. For the first time the *me* ceases to confuse itself with what it experiences or desires at each moment. On this immediately lived *me* there is superimposed a constructed *me*, a *me* that is visible at a distance, an imaginary *me*, which the psychoanalysts call the super-ego. Henceforth the child's attention is captured by this "*me* above the *me*" or this "*me* before the *me*." From this moment on, the child also is drawn from his immediate reality; the specular image has a de-realizing function in the sense that it turns the child away from what he effectively is, in order to orient him toward what he sees and imagines himself to be. Finally, this alienation of the immediate *me*, its "confiscation" for the benefit of the *me* that is visible in the mirror, already outlines what will be the "confiscation" of the subject by the others who look at him.

An analysis of this kind extends what we have found in Wallon, while at the same time it is different. It is different mainly because it emphasizes the affective significance of the phenomenon. In reading Wallon one often has the feeling that in acquiring the specular image it is a question of a labor of understanding, of a synthesis of certain visual perceptions with certain introceptive perceptions. For psychoanalysts the visual is not simply one type of sensibility among others; it has an altogether different type of significance for the subject's life from those of other modes of sensibility. Is vision, the sense of spectacle, also the sense of the imaginary? Our images are predominantly visual, and this is no accident; it is by means of vision that one can sufficiently dominate and control objects. With the visual experience of the self, there is thus the advent of a new mode of relatedness to self. The visual makes possible a kind of schism between the immediate *me* and the *me* that can be seen in the mirror. The sensory functions themselves are thus redefined in proportion to the contribution they can make to the existence of the subject and the structures they can offer for the development of that existence.

In addition, the study of the phenomenon made by the psychoanalysts stresses both the anticipations and the regressions contained in its development.

"Pre-maturation," the anticipation by the child of adult forms of life, is for the psychoanalysts almost the definition of childhood. It is an advance made by the subject beyond his present means. The child always lives "beyond his means"; birth itself is "pre-mature," since the child comes into the world in a state in which independent life in his new environment is impossible for him. The first Oedipal impulse is a "psychological puberty," in contrast to the organic puberty of the individual, and is awakened by his relations with the adult world. The child lives in relations that belong to his future and are not actually realizable by him.

But while the child may anticipate, the adult may regress. Childhood is never radically liquidated; we never completely eliminate the corporeal condition that gives us, in the presence of a mirror, the impression of finding in it something of ourselves. This magic belief, which at first gives the specular image the value not of a simple reflection, of an "image" in the proper sense, but rather of a "double" of oneself—this belief never totally disappears. It re-forms itself in the emotional make-up of the adult. For this reduction to be possible, the "reduction" of the image must be not so much an irreversible progression of the understanding as a restructuration of our entire manner of being continually exposed to the accidents of emotional experience.

If the comprehension of the specular image were solely a matter of cognition, then once the phenomenon was understood its past would be completely reassimilated. Once the purely physical character of the reflection or of the phenomenon of the image was understood, there would remain nothing of the "presence" of the person reflected in his image. Since this is not the case, since the image-reflection is unstable, the operations that constitute it involve not only the intelligence proper but, rather, all the individual's relations with others.

Moreover, what distinguishes the psychoanalysts' remarks concerning the specular image is that they relate the specular image to identification with others. I understand all the more easily that what is in the mirror is my image for being able to represent to myself the other's viewpoint on me; and, inversely, I understand all the more the experience the other can have of me for seeing myself in the mirror in the aspect I offer him.

Wallon, we have said, accounts for the reduction of the specular image in terms of an intellectual operation. I first see in the mirror a double of myself; then an act of intellectual consciousness of my own experience makes me withdraw existence from this image and treat it as a simple symbol, reflection, or expression of the same body that is given in introceptivity. Intellectual activity operates at every moment of these reductions and integrations, and detaches the specular image from its spatial roots, transferring this visual appearance and introceptive experience to an ideal place in a space that is not the spatiality adhering to the sensed but the spatiality constructed out of the intelligence.

It is altogether undeniable that such a reduction occurs. But the question is one of knowing whether the intellectual operation in which it culminates can offer a *psychological explanation* for what takes place. The emergence of an ideal space, the redistribution, by the intelligence, of the spatial values that makes me withdraw from the image its own location in order to treat it as a simple modality of a unique placement of my body—is all this the *cause* or the *result* of the development?

Wallon remarks incidentally that we should not suppose that the child *begins by locating his own body in two places* or that there is a certain place where the tactile, introceptive body is situated and another place for the aspect, or visual appearance, of the body. If this were done, one would be realizing twice over in the child a rigorous form of spatiality that in fact belongs only to the adult. The child at first sees the image "over there" and feels his body "here." This does not mean that when he visually perceives the image and tactually perceives his body, he actually places each one at a distinct point in space in the same sense in which the adult, for example, perceives this microphone and that lamp *as being in two distinct places*. The two "spaces," says Wallon, are not immediately comparable, and any precise intuition of their mutual exteriority would require a sort of common denominator between them which is not immediately given by sense experience. In the case of the specular image, instead of a second body which the child would have and which would be located elsewhere than in his tactile body, there is a kind of *identity at a distance*, a *ubiquity* of the body; the body is at once present in the mirror and present at the point where I feel it tactually. But if this is the case, the two aspects that are to be co-ordinated are not really separated in the child and are in no way separated in the sense in which all objects in space are separated in adult perception. Since Wallon's analysis rests on the ideas (a) that what is involved is a redistribution of spatial values and the substitution of an ideal space for a perceived space and (b) that, as we know ourselves now, we do not have to overcome an absolute duality of visual image and sensed body, his work must be begun all over again. The reduction to unity is not a cataclysm, if it is true that there is no veritable duplicity or duality between the visual body and the introceptive body in spite of the phenomenon of distance that separates the image in the mirror from the felt body.

If the presence of others were allowed a role in the phenomenon of the specular image, one would have a better idea of the difficulty the child has to overcome. The child's problem is not so much one of understanding that the visual and the tactile images of the body—both located at two points in space—in reality comprise only one, as it is of understanding that the image in the mirror is *his* image, that it is what others see of him, the appearance he presents to other subjects; and the synthesis is less a synthesis of intellection than it is a synthesis of coexistence with others.

In looking at the matters more closely, moreover, we see that the two interpretations are not mutually exclusive. For we must consider the relation with others *not only as one of the contents of our experience but as an actual structure in its own right*. We can admit that what we call "intelligence" is only another name designating an original type of relation with others (the relation of "reciprocity") and that, from the start to the finish of the development, the living relation with others is the support, the vehicle, or the stimulus for what we abstractly call the "intelligence."

Thus understood, the phenomenon will necessarily be fragile and variable, as are our affective relations with others and with the world. The anticipations as well as the regressions are more easily conceived. Lacking this kind of concrete and effective interpretation, we should then have to suppose an intellectual control of our experience that never ceases—an activity which, as Wallon holds, operates at every moment to produce the reductions and the integrations. But we are absolutely unconscious of such an activity; in looking at the image in the mirror we are unaware of judging, of performing an intellectual act. We must thus suppose that there is an unperceived activity in us that constantly reduces perceived space, the space of the image, and succeeds in redistributing spatial values. On the contrary, if we suppose that the conquest of the image is only one aspect in the total continuum made up of all the lived relations with others and the world, it becomes easier to understand how this continuum, once at work, functions as though autonomously and how at the same time, participating in all the contingencies of our relations with others, it is susceptible to degradations and setbacks.

In our hypothesis it is a question of the acquisition of a certain *state of equilibrium* in our perception which, like any privileged state of equilibrium, tends to maintain itself unsheltered from the intervention of experience. Our interpretation would permit us to understand how the adult state can be distinct from the state of childhood without being immune to relapses into childhood.

2. *Syncretic sociability*

BETWEEN THE AGES of six and twelve months, says Wallon, there occurs an outburst of sociability. Wallon speaks of an "incontinent sociability." From the sixth to the seventh month the child, one notices, abandons the behavior of fixation on others without gestures. While this attitude formerly represented a good half of the child's conduct toward others, its frequency now falls to one quarter. Gestures toward his partners (other children) multiply, as do gestures oriented toward his own body. Movements aimed at the other are now four times as frequent as in the first six months of life. In the same period (between seven and twelve months), there are one third more movements directed toward others than there will be during the entire second year. Thus there is an abrupt forward thrust in relations with others, a sharp increase in the quantity and quality of these relations. The very nature of the child's conduct is modified. For example, it is at about seven months that the child begins to smile when he is looked at (and not merely when he is spoken to). Rarely at this time does the child smile at an animal or when alone. Social sensibility develops in an extraordinary manner, and it is remarkably more advanced than relations with the physical world, which at this time are still quite inadequate.

The general character of these relations with others has been competently described by Charlotte Bühler in her 1927 book, *Sociological and Psychological Studies on the First Year of Life*.[19] Mrs. Bühler observed children who found themselves together in the waiting room of a consultation clinic. She first remarks that before the age of three years, it is extremely rare that children are very interested in other children much younger than themselves, probably because until the

19. Charlotte Bühler, Hildegaard Hexter, Beatrix Tudor-Hart, *Soziologische und Psychologische Studien über das erste Lebensjahr* (Jena, 1927).

age of three the child does not emerge from his own situation or at least not enough to interest himself in subjects who are in an altogether different situation. This is why relations will be established only among children of relatively close ages, as elsewhere the most ordinary observation shows. Among other children of similar ages a frequent relation is that of the child who parades before another child who looks at him. Often one sees pairs of children, one of whom exhibits himself in his most remarkable activities (playing with this or that latest toy, talking, holding forth) while the other watches. This relation is often at the same time a relation of master and slave. In general this despotism requires a gap of at least three months between the children's ages, with the biggest child usually the master. This is not, however, an absolute rule. There are also cases of active despotism on the part of the smallest. This occurs often when the smallest has been brought up with special attention. When, for example, his approval is always sought, he becomes condescending and immediately adopts an attitude which is complementary to the one taken toward him. As Wallon remarks, there is an automatic logic of affective situations; any attitude taken toward the child immediately provokes in him the complementary attitude. Like all weak persons, he takes a show of excessive interest to be a mark of weakness. What characterizes the relation between the child who shows off and the child who watches him, says Wallon, is that the two children find themselves founded in and by the situation. The child who contemplates is truly identified with the one he is watching; he no longer exists except through his favorite comrade. As for the master, his despotism is naturally founded on the weakness of the slave, but also (and above all) it is founded on the slave's feeling of being a slave. As Wallon observes, what really counts, in order for a despotic relation to be established, is not that one party be stronger or more clever than the other; it is that the other recognize that he is weaker, less clever. What the master seeks, following Hegel's famous description of the relation between master and slave, is recognition [Anerkennung] by the slave, the consent of the slave to be a slave. The master is nothing without the humiliation of the slave; he would not feel alive without this abasement of the other. The relation in question, says Wallon, would include a confusion of self with another in the same situation of sentiments. The master exists through the recognition of his lordship by the slave, and the slave himself has no other function than to be there to admire and identify with the master. We have here a state of "combination with the other," as Wallon says, that is the mark of childish affective situations.

Under these conditions the importance of the relation of jealousy for the child is easily understood. In jealousy the couple made up of the child creating a spectacle and the child admiring him is of concern to the latter: the jealous child would like to be the one being watched. Wallon takes as an example the jealousy of dogs. If one is caressed, the other jumps forward to take his place. The desire to be caressed is not so much a positive desire as the feeling of being *deprived of the caresses* given the other. What is essential to jealousy is this feeling of privation, frustration, or exclusion. This jealousy appears at seven months, according to Guillaume; at nine months, according to Wallon. In any case it appears around the critical period we are speaking of. It is later that this jealousy is expressed in sulking. Sulking is the attitude of the child who renounces what it wanted to be and who consequently accepts the anguish of a repressed action.

One might say that the jealous person sees his existence invaded by the success of the other and feels himself dispossessed by him, and that in this sense jealousy is essentially a confusion between the self and the other. It is the attitude of the one who sees no life for himself other than that of achieving what the other has achieved, who does not define himself by himself but in relation to what others have. According to Wallon, all jealousy, even in the adult, represents a nondifferentiation of that kind between oneself and the other, a positive inexistence of the individual that gets confused with the contrast that exists between others and himself. Thus, says Wallon, we must consider adult jealousy as a regression to the mode of childish jealousy.

In relations of jealousy we often find phenomena of cruelty. The child tries to make the other suffer precisely because he is jealous of him, because everything the other has is stolen from him. In fact, however, cruelty is even more complex. I would not covet, in right and principle, what others have if I did not sympathize with them, if I did not consider others as "other myselves." Cruelty must, then, be understood as a "suffering sympathy" (Wallon). When I hurt the other, therefore, I am hurting myself. Consequently to like to hurt the other is to like to hurt oneself also. Here Wallon reaches the psychoanalytic idea of sado-masochism. "If sadism is a pursuit of the other's suffering, it is, however, a suffering felt to the point of pleasure as well as pain by the person who inflicts it."

It is thus with the jealous person. He likes to make himself suffer. He multiplies his investigations, he seeks information, he forms hypotheses that are always designed to stimulate his anguish or uneasiness. Wallon even indicates that in jealousy there is a sort of complacency that has as its end a heightening of the intensity of sexual passion. Wallon points out that the psychological explanation of certain groups of three people is to be found here. The trio would have no other meaning than to organize permanently an experience of jealousy that is sought by its initiators as an increase of anxiety and because it intensifies the reactions of aggressiveness and sexuality.

For the child, jealousy represents a stage wherein he participates in a total affective situation and senses the complementary life of his own without yet knowing how to isolate or affirm his own. He thus allows himself to be inwardly dominated by the one who plunders him [le dépouille]. Having, all told, nothing of his own, he defines himself entirely in relation to others and by the lack of what the others have. Here again we converge with psychoanalytic thought and its definition of jealousy.

Freud admits that a jealousy which seems to be directed toward one person is in reality directed toward another. A man's jealousy of his wife is the rivalry between that man and that woman in the presence of a third person who is the occasion of the jealousy. This leads us to say that in all jealous conduct there is an element of homosexuality. Wallon takes this kind of view when he admits that the jealous man is the one who lives, as his own, not only his own experiences but those of others as well, when he assumes the attitudes of the other (and, for example, the attitudes toward a third). Our relation with another is also always a relation with the other persons whom that other knows; our feelings toward another are interdependent with his feelings toward a third, and blend with them. Relations between two people are in reality more extensive relations, since they extend across the second person to those with whom the second person is vitally related. Likewise when Wallon writes of jealousy, "This feeling is the feeling of a rivalry in a person who does not know how to react except as a spectator possessed by the action of the rival," he is very close to the psychoanalytic considerations of the attitude of the "voyeur" (of which the voyeur, in the current sense of the term, is merely an extreme case). The jealous person allows himself to be trapped or captured by the other and, inversely, moreover, he would like to trap or capture the other in his turn. In his mind he plays all the roles of the situation he finds himself in and not only his own role, of which he has no separate notion.

These analyses also remind us of Proust. As a child, Proust begins to love Gilberte one day when he has been taken out to play in the Champs-Elysées and sees before him the group of children to which Gilberte, but not himself, belongs. His feeling of love is at first the feeling of being excluded. It is not so much that he finds Gilberte lovable as it is that he feels himself outside the group of children.

One is also reminded of the famous analysis of the narrator's jealousy toward Albertine. He cannot tolerate the fact that something of Albertine escapes him completely—for example, her past before he met her. The sole fact that she has a past suffices to make him suffer, and this suffering almost confuses itself with his love. When she is not there he no longer feels anything for Albertine and even believes that he no longer loves her; he can only love her without suffering when she is inanimate in sleep (or, later, when she has disappeared in death). But even at this moment his love consists in *contemplating* her in sleep; that is to say, it remains under the law of jealousy, which is identification of oneself with a seen spectacle.

The negative attitudes of jealousy and cruelty are not the child's only attitudes, although they are quite frequent. There are also attitudes of sympathy. Sympathy must, in Wallon's eyes, be understood to be a primordial and irreducible phenomenon. It appears in the child on a foundation of mimesis, at the moment when, all the same, consciousness of self and consciousness of others begin to be distinguished from one another. Mimesis is the ensnaring of me by the other, the invasion of me by the other; it is that attitude whereby I assume the gestures, the conducts, the favorite words, the ways of doing things of those whom I confront. Wallon shows great insight in relating mimesis to the postural function that allows me to govern my body. It is a manifestation of a unique system which unites my body, the other's body, and the other himself. Mimesis, or mimicry, is the power of assuming conducts or facial expressions as my own; this power is given to me with the power I have over my own body. It is the "postural function appropriate to the needs of expression" (Wallon). The constant regulation of bodily equilibrium, without which no function (and in particular no perceptual function) would be possible in the child, is not merely the capacity to reunite the minimal conditions for balancing the body but is more generally the power I have to realize with my body gestures that are analogous to those I see. Wallon speaks of a kind of "postural impregnation" that is resolved into gestures of imitation. He cites the example of a child who is observed watching a chirping bird for a long time and who, after this "postural impregnation," sets himself to reproducing the bird's sounds as well as something of the bird's bearing. Not only the perception of another child but even that of an animal quite different from the child himself shows up, thanks to the postural function, in attitudes which resemble those of the other and have their same expressive value. In sum, our perceptions arouse in us a reorganization of motor conduct, without our already having learned the gestures in question. We know the famous example of the spectators at a football game who make the proper gesture at the moment when the player would make it. Authors like Guillaume have tried to explain this phenomenon in terms of the awakening of the memory of gestures already made. On such accounts we would substitute ourselves for the other in thought; we would perform, on our own, acts we already knew how to perform. In fact, however, phenomena of this kind are documented facts, certified even in the case of acts that have never been executed—as, for example, in the case of the child just mentioned who imitates a bird. In Wallon's eyes there is, as a result, a necessity for acknowledging that the body has a capacity for "meditation," for the "inward formulation" of gestures. I see unfolding the different phases of the process, and this perception is of such a nature as to arouse in me the preparation of a motor activity related to it. It is this fundamental correspondence between perception and motility—the power of perception to organize a motor conduct that Gestalt theorists have insisted on—that allows the perception of fear to translate itself into an original motor organization. This is what would be the function of mimesis, or mimicry, in its most fundamental and irreducible form.

Sympathy would emerge from this. Sympathy does not presuppose a genuine distinction between self-consciousness and consciousness of the other but rather the absence of a distinction between the self and the other. It is the simple fact that I live in the facial expressions of the other, as I feel him living in mine. It is a manifestation of what we have called, in other terms, the system "me-and-other."

Before passing to the crisis at three years, let us try to shed light from another viewpoint on what we were able to say about the period from six months to three years, by insisting on two points: first, on the conception of the personality that seems to be immanent in this phase of childhood development and, finally on the expression which the phenomenon of pre-communication finds in the language of the child.

In the period of pre-communication, of which we spoke earlier, the personality is somehow immersed in the situation and is a function of the child himself or the other beings with whom he lives. A frequent example is that of children who fully recognize their father only on condition that he is found in his customary setting. A child said, for example, that his real father was in Vienna and that the father on vacation with him in the country was not his real father.

But the child confuses himself with his situation. One recalls the example of a child who had a glass in his hand (against his father's wishes), put it down and, on hearing the sound of breaking glass five minutes later, started and became just as agitated as if he still had the glass in his hand. He created a sort of magic link between the forbidden thing he had done several minutes earlier and the breaking of the glass, far away from him. In a case like this one, there is in the child no distinct conception of moments of time, nor is there any distinct conception of causal relations. The child confuses himself with his situation. He is someone who has been holding a glass in his hand, someone who has had a relation with the glass, so that the subsequent breaking of the glass concerns him.

Elsa Köhler, in her book on the personality of the three-year-old,[20] tells the story of a child who had eaten her brother's candy while her brother and parents were away. The moment the father returned, the little girl ran up to him, telling him enthusiastically how much fun she had had eating her brother's candy and trying to make him share her pleasure. The father reprimanded her; the little girl cried and appeared convinced that she had done something wrong. A short time later the mother appeared, and *the same scene was repeated.* How are we to explain this? At bottom it is the problem of children who, as their parents say, "go right back and do it again." In order to understand why—immediately following a scene of repentance, tears, and good resolutions—the child repeats exactly the same offense, it is necessary to think that she establishes no connection between the arrival of her mother and that of her father; the two events must be absolutely distinct in her eyes. The child *is*, in fact, the situation and has no distance from it. The situation is taken in its most immediate meaning, and all that happened before is nothing, canceled from the time when a new situation—the mother's return—arises. This incapacity to distinguish between different situations, to adopt a conduct that is autonomous in its relation to the situations and constant in relation to the variable conditions, is what makes the child's attitude understandable. The child was really not the same when she underwent her father's reproaches, deferred to them, and made good resolutions as when her mother returned several minutes later.

William Stern tells of how his son, at the birth of a younger sister, suddenly identified himself with his elder sister, pretended to have her name, and gave her another name. This seems to show that the child identifies himself absolutely with his family situation; and from the birth of the new child, which makes the youngest into a relatively older child, he takes over absolutely the role of the eldest, even to the point of usurping the place of the rightful eldest.

Hence, perhaps, the possibility of understanding how the child can feel himself to be several persons and can simultaneously play several roles—resembling the ill in this respect. Wallon mentions the case of a patient of Janet who declared that she was at the same time both the daughter of the Virgin and the Virgin herself and who showed this, in effect, by all her mimicry, playing the roles of both the expectant mother and the child.

Hence also the real meaning of the child's dialogues with himself. When the child chats with himself (a familiar occurrence to anyone

20. Elsa Köhler, *Die Persönlichkeit des dreijährigen Kindes* (Leipzig, 1926).

who has raised children), there is an actual plurality of roles; one role converses with another.

Finally, we are in a position to understand the frequent phenomena of what is called "transitivism" in the sick and also in the child. Transitivism consists in attributing to others what belongs to the subject himself. For example, a patient will pity another patient for having had a crisis which, in fact, he himself underwent during the night—as though it were the other who had suffered the crisis. Transitivism is also the attitude of hypochondriacs who look for signs of ill health in the faces of others. All that we are, all that happens to us can furnish us with explanatory categories and in every case plays the role of exploratory tools for knowing the other. Everything that happens to us makes us sensitive to a certain aspect of the other and makes us seek in the other the equivalent of, or something that corresponds to, what has happened to us. This is why Goethe was right in saying that for each of us our circle of friends is what we ourselves are. Our *Umwelt* is what we are, because what happens to us does not happen only to us but to our entire vision of the world. Transitivism is, in other words, the same notion that psychoanalysts are using when they speak of *projection,* just as mimesis is the equivalent of *introjection.*

There are striking examples of transitivism in children, too. Wallon mentions one of them, borrowed from the work of Charlotte Bühler. It is the case of a little girl who, when seated beside her maid and another little girl, seemed uneasy and unexpectedly slapped her companion. When asked why, she answered that it was her companion who was naughty and who hit her. The child's air of sincerity ruled out any deliberate ruse. We have here a manifestly aggressive child who gives an unprovoked slap and explains herself right afterward by saying that it is the other child who slapped her. Psychoanalysts have stressed the childlike attitude that consists in imputing the wrong to the other (*"You're* the one who's lying!"). The child who seemed uneasy was passing through a phase of anxiety, and this anxiety impregnated her entire view of things and people around her—in particular her view of the little girl sitting beside her. This little girl appeared to her to be surrounded by the same anguishing aura. The child was living her anxiety, and the gestures appropriate to lessening it, not as interior events but as qualities of things in the world and of others. In the absence of a reduction of the anxiety to its subjective source and a concentration of the anxiety within the child in whom it was actually located, the anxiety was lived as something that has an external as well as an internal origin. Slapping her companion was the little girl's response to the aggression of the anxiety that came from outside.

The child's own personality is at the same time the personality of the other, that indistinction of the two personalities that makes transitivism possible; this presupposes an entire structure in the child's consciousness. The guilty act of taking the glass, that has just occurred, and the breaking of the glass are now joined in a quasi-magic way. Similarly there is a sort of spatial syncretism—i.e., a presence of the same psychic being in several spatial points, a presence of me in the other and the other in me. In a general way there is an inability to conceive space and time as environments that contain a series of perspectives which are absolutely distinct from one another. The child switches from perspective to perspective, erasing them in the identity of the thing, unaware even of the different profiles or different perspectives in which space can present itself. It is an aspect of the same structure of consciousnesss that expresses itself in certain childish persons we studied last year [*rabattement*]. The reduction of external perception to what can be seen from a single point of view—in short, the perspective given—is possible only much later. There is also an indistinction between the symbol and what it symbolizes. Words and things are not absolutely distinguished; of this we have already had more than one reminder.

The absence of what we call in the adult the symbolic consciousness, the fusion of sign and referent [*signifié*], the different moments of time and of space in the thing are so many evidences of the same fact.

The syncretic relations with others that show up in the child's conception of personality also show up clearly in the child's use of language. The child's first words, considered by the psychologists and the linguists as standing for sentences (word-sentences), can be the equivalent of entire sentences only through the effects of syncretism. The first word-sentences, as we have already seen, aim just as much at the actions of others as at one's own actions or conducts. When the child (even the very young child) says "hand" (hand-hand), this means his father's hand as well as the hand represented by a photograph or his own hand. This seems to presuppose a kind of abstraction, a recognition of the same object in a plurality of cases. And in fact the object identified is greatly different (for example, there is not a great resemblance between a child's hand and the photograph of an adult's hand). In reality, however, there is no abstraction here. There is simply no radical distinction in the child between his own hand and that of another. The child's extraordinary facility in recognizing the parts of the body in a drawing or an even rougher sketch, the promptness and skill with which he identifies parts of his own body in the bodies of animals that scarcely resemble the human body or familiar domestic animals, the plasticity of vision that allows him to recognize homologous structures of the body in quite different organisms—all this can be explained by the state of neutral indistinction between self and other in which he lives. The child's own body is for him a way of understanding other bodies through "postural impregnation" (Wallon). The child's person, says Wallon, is in a way scattered through all the images his action gives rise to, and it is because of this that he is apt to recognize himself in everything.

This explains the relative ease with which children understand the modern way of painting and drawing. It is altogether startling to see certain children much more apt to understand this drawing or that painting by Picasso than the adults around them. The adult hesitates before this kind of drawing because his cultural formation has trained him to take as canonical the perspective inherited from the Italian Renaissance, a perspective that works by projection of different external data on a single plane. To the extent that the child is a stranger to this cultural tradition and has not yet received the training that will integrate him within it, he recognizes with great freedom in a number of traits what the painter meant to show. If you like, the child's thought processes are general from the start and at the same time are very individual. They are expressive thought processes that get to the essentials by means of a concrete corporeal recovery [reprise] of objects and conducts as given.

This allows us to understand why the use of the word I comes relatively late to the child. He will use it when he has become conscious of his own proper perspective, distinct from those of others, and when he has distinguished all of the perspectives from the external object. In the initial state of perception there is consciousness not of being enclosed in a perspective and of guessing—picking out across it an object which is outside—but of being in direct touch with things across a personal-universal vision. The I arises when the child understands that every you that is addressed to him is for him an I; that is, that there must be a consciousness of the reciprocity of points of view in order that the word I may be used.

Guillaume points out that in the early months of the second year the child is first seen to acquire a large number of names of persons. Finally, around the sixteenth month, he acquires his own name, which at first he uses only in very limited cases, i.e., in answering questions like "What is your name?" or to designate the situations in which he is placed along with other children—for example, in the distribution of gifts. In this case the child can employ his own name because of the collective operation in which he is involved just like one of the others. The use of his own name in these circumstances does not indicate that he is conscious of his privileged perspective, which seems to escape him completely at sixteen months or thereabouts. For example, when he wants to say "I want to write," he uses the infinitive, without a subject. Guillaume's son said "write" for "I want to write," but he said "Papa write"; that is, he used the subject only when the subject was another person. When it was he himself who was involved, he never expressed the subject at all. And the "Paul writes" that he finally came to say grew somehow within the formula "Papa writes." The use of his own name was learned from the use of other people's names.

Use of the pronoun *I* comes still later than use of the proper name, at least as it is understood in its full meaning, i.e., in its relative meaning. The pronoun *I* has its full meaning only when the child uses it not as an individual sign to designate his own person—a sign that would be assigned once for all to himself and to nobody else—but when he understands that each person he sees can in turn say *I* and that each person is an *I* for himself and a *you* for others. It is when he understands that even though others call him *you* he can nonetheless say *I*, that the pronoun *I* is acquired in all its significance. Thus it is not because a child of around nineteen months finds he has used the sound "I" that we say that he has acquired the use of the pronoun. In order for it to have been a real acquisition, he must have grasped the relations between the different pronouns and the passage from one of their designata to the others. In other cases the sound "I" is used mechanically, like the body [*physique*], but it is not used in its fullest linguistic and grammatical meaning. Only at nineteen months did Guillaume's son use *me* or *I* in their fullest senses. At nineteen months he used *mine* and *yours* in a systematic way; at twenty months he used *mine, yours, his, everybody's*.[21] At this moment the operation of distribution is conceived in the same way whether it is addressed to the child or to others. The use of *I* takes the place of the child's first name and occurs regularly only at the end of the second year. While the name is an attribute of the person alone, the pronoun designates either the speaker or the person he is speaking to. The same pronoun can serve to designate different persons, while each person has only one proper name.

3. The "crisis at three years"

THIS CRISIS HAS BEEN well described by Elsa Köhler in her book on the personality of the three-year-old as well as by Wallon in *Les origines du caractère chez l'enfant*.

At around three years the child stops lending his body and even his thoughts to others, as we have seen happen in the phase of syncretic

21. *"A moi," "à toi," "à lui," "à chacun."*

sociability. He stops confusing himself with the situation or the role in which he may find himself engaged. He adopts a proper perspective or viewpoint of his own—or rather he understands that, whatever the diversity of situations or roles, he is *someone* above and beyond these different situations and roles.

The acquisition of perspective in drawing (which will occur later) can serve us here as a symbol; it will only be possible for a subject to whom the notion of an individual *perspective* is a familiar one. The child cannot understand what it is to portray the things before him as one sees them from a single viewpoint, unless he has come to the idea that he sees them from a single point instead of living in them. There must thus be a kind of duplication of the immediately given sensory spectacle in which the child was at first engulfed and of a subject who is henceforth capable of re-ordering and re-distributing his experience in accordance with the directions chosen by this thought processes. Wallon indicates a certain number of typical attitudes by which one can disclose the advent of this distance between the child on the one hand and the spectacle of others and the world on the other. It is at around the age of three years that one sees in the child the deliberate decision to do everything all alone. Wallon also shows the change in the child's reactions to the look of the other. Up to the age of three years, in general, except in pathological cases, the other's look encourages the child or helps him. Beginning at three years a whole quite different set of reactions is seen to arise; they bring to mind certain pathological reactions. The other's look becomes an annoyance for the child, and everything happens as though, when he is looked at, his attention is displaced from the task he is carrying out to a representation of himself in the process of carrying it out.

This is related to certain pathological phenomena.[22] Wallon mentions the case of a hemiplegic described by Davidson, in whom a convulsive laugh broke out, shaking him all over, whenever he was looked at. Wallon also mentions the case of a subject whose job was testing automobiles. When alone the subject drove skillfully at ninety miles an hour, but when he had a passenger he was tormented by irrepressible tics. This extreme sensitivity to the other's look had shown up very early in this subject—after convulsions at the age of two and a half years. Wallon again recalls the case of general paralytics who, when looked at, show questioning, approving, or satisfied expressions, as though it were absolutely necessary that their faces show something, as though the other's look demanded these expressions of them.

Some subjects who are perfectly normal are afraid of seeming in-

22. Cf. Henri Wallon, "La maladresse," *Journal de Psychologie Normale*, vol. 25 (1928), pp. 61–78.

significant when being photographed. We can also mention idiots who howl when anyone looks at them. If the three-year-old child is inhibited by the other's look, it is because from this point on he is not simply what he is in his own eyes; he feels himself also to be that which others see him to be. The phenomenon of the specular image, mentioned earlier, becomes generalized. The specular image teaches the child that he is not only what he believed he was by inner experience but that he is in addition that figure he sees in the mirror. The other's look tells me, as does the image in the mirror, that I am *also* that being who is limited to a point in space, that I am that visible "stand-in" [*doublure*] in whom I would recognize only with difficulty the lived *me*. To be sure, as we have seen, this *me* scarcely distinguishes itself from the other before the age of three years. But for this very reason there was never any question of being controlled or inhibited by others; and when this phenomenon appears, it is because the indistinction of myself and the other is at an end.

The ego, the *I*, cannot truly emerge at the age of three years without doubling itself with an *ego in the eyes of the other*. In the case of this phenomenon it is not a question of shame, in the sense in which it exists later on as the shame of being naked (which appears only around the age of five or six), any more than it is the fear of being reprimanded. It is simply a question of the fear experienced by the child when he is looked at.

At the same age the child wants attention and will go to the point of misbehaving in order to get it. Conducts of duplicity that until now were absent are seen to emerge at this time. The child interferes with the play of others for the sake of his own pleasure. He also changes his attitude toward giving. When he gives an object away, he often does it while saying that he does not like the object any more. A thoughtless gift, given earlier, disappears. The child takes things away from others solely for the fun of it; as soon as he has taken them he abandons them. The gift is transformed in the transaction.

In sum, the child constantly calls into play the relation of "me-and-other," which as a result ceases to be a unity, an undifferentiated system, as it is in the preceding phase.

These remarks lead us to ask ourselves to what extent the crisis at three years brings about a transformation and a total re-structuration in the child and whether the state of undifferentiation, of pre-communication, of which we have been speaking until now, is visibly abolished. Wallon himself writes that the already surpassed forms of activity are not abolished. Syncretic sociability is perhaps not liquidated in the third-year crisis. This state of indistinction from others, this mutual impingement of the other and myself at the heart of a situation in which we are confused, this presence of the same subject in several roles—all are met with again in adult life. The crisis at three years pushes syncretism farther away rather than suppressing it altogether. Certainly after three years a neutral or objective ground is set up between me and the other; a "lived distance" divides us, as Minkowski says. There is no longer that dizzying proximity of others which made possible certain disorders, certain hallucinations, as well as transitivism.

The child understands, for example, that there is a way of accusing the other that amounts to a confession. Unlike the child, an adult will no longer say, "*You're* the one who's lying." The adult understands that certain resentments disclose in the person expressing them precisely the faults for which he reproaches another. He must be capable of certain meannesses in order to suspect others of them. The adult is conscious of transitivism and the projections whereby we lend others our own ways of being. But if transitivism is thus pushed out of a whole sector of his life, does this mean that it has completely disappeared? The indistinction between me and the other does not inevitably reappear except in certain situations that for the adult are limiting situations but are quite important in his life.

Could one conceive of a love that would not be an encroachment on the freedom of the other? If a person wanted in no way to exert an influence on the person he loved and consequently refrained from choosing on her behalf or advising her or influencing her in any way, he would act on her precisely by that abstention, and would incline her all the more strongly toward choosing in such a way as to please him. This apparent detachment, this will to remain without responsibility arouses in the other an even more lively desire to come closer. There is a paradox in accepting love from a person without wanting to have any influence on her freedom. If one loves, one finds one's freedom precisely in the act of loving, and not in a vain autonomy. To consent to love or be loved is to consent also to influence someone else, to decide to a certain extent on behalf of the other. To love is inevitably to enter into an undivided situation with another.

From the moment when one is joined with someone else, one suffers from her suffering. If physical pain is involved, in which one can participate only metaphorically, one strongly feels his inadequacy. One is not what he would be without that love; the perspectives remain separate—and yet they overlap. One can no longer say "This is mine, this is yours"; the roles cannot be absolutely separated. And to be joined with someone else is, in the end, to live her life, at least in intention. To the very extent that it is convincing and genuine, the experience of the other is necessarily an alienating one, in the sense that it tears me away from my lone self and creates instead a mixture of myself and the other.

As Alain has said, to love someone is to swear and affirm more than one knows about what the other will be. In a certain measure, it is to relinquish one's freedom of judgment. The experience of the other does not leave us at rest within ourselves, and this is why it can always be the occasion for doubt. If I like, I can always be strict and put in doubt the reality of the other's feelings toward me; this is because such feelings are never *absolutely* proved. This person who professes to love does not give every instant of her life to her beloved, and her love may even die out if it is constrained. Certain subjects react to this evidence as though it were a refutation of love and refuse to be trusting and believe in an unlimited affirmation of the basis of an always-finite number of professions.[23] The ensnaring love of the child is the love that never has enough proofs, and ends by imprisoning and trapping the other in its immediacy.

The normal, non-pathological attitude consists in having confidence above and beyond what can be proved, in resolutely skirting these doubts that can be raised about the reality of the other's sentiments, by means of the generosity of the *praxis,* by means of an action that proves itself in being carried out.

But if these matters are as we have depicted them, all relations with others, if deep enough, bring about a state of insecurity, since the doubt we mentioned always remains possible and since love itself creates its own proper truth and reality. The state of union with another, the dispossession of me by the other, are thus not suppressed by the child's arrival at the age of three years. They remain in other zones of adult life. This is a particular case of what Piaget has called *displacement* [*décalage*]. The same conduct, overcome at a certain level, is not yet (and perhaps will never be) overcome at a higher level. Transitivism, which has been surpassed in the realm of immediate daily life, is never surpassed in the realm of feelings. That is why, as the psychoanalysts have shown, syncretic sociability can be found in the sick to the extent to which they regress in the direction of the conduct of children and show themselves incapable of making the transition to *praxis,* to the selfless, outgoing attitude of the adult.

We might ask what kind of relationship must be established between the crisis at three years mentioned by Wallon and the Oedipal phase of development which certain psychoanalysts locate at the same moment and which accompanies the emergence of the super-ego, the true "objective" relation, and the surpassing of narcissism.

23. The word *abandonniques* appears in the text at this point without explanation.—*Trans.*

PART II

Philosophy of Art

5 / Eye and Mind [1]

Translated by Carleton Dallery

"What I am trying to translate to you is more mysterious;
it is entwined in the very roots of being, in the impalpable
source of sensations." J. Gasquet, *Cézanne*

[I]

SCIENCE MANIPULATES THINGS and gives up living in them.
It makes its own limited models of things; operating upon these indices
or variables to effect whatever transformations are permitted by their
definition, it comes face to face with the real world only at rare intervals. Science is and always has been that admirably active, ingenious,
and bold way of thinking whose fundamental bias is to treat everything
as though it were an object-in-general—as though it meant nothing to
us and yet was predestined for our own use.

But classical science clung to a feeling for the opaqueness of the
world, and it expected through its constructions to get back into the
world. For this reason classical science felt obliged to seek a transcendent or transcendental foundation for its operations. Today we find—not
in science but in a widely prevalent philosophy of the sciences—an
entirely new approach. Constructive scientific activities see themselves

1. "L'Oeil et l'esprit" was the last work Merleau-Ponty saw published. It appeared in the inaugural issue of *Art de France*, vol. I, no. 1 (January, 1961). After
his death it was reprinted in *Les Temps Modernes*, no. 184–85, along with seven
articles devoted to him. It has now been published, in book form, by Editions
Gallimard (1964). Both the *Art de France* article and the book contain illustrations
chosen by Merleau-Ponty. According to Professor Claude Lefort, "L'Oeil et l'esprit"
is a preliminary statement of ideas that were to be developed in the second part of
the book Merleau-Ponty was writing at the time of his death—*Le visible et l'invisible* (part of which was published posthumously by Gallimard in February,
1964). The translator wishes to acknowledge his immense debt to George Downing,
who spent many long hours working over the final revisions of the translation. Also,
thanks are due to Michel Beaujour, Arleen B. Dallery, and Robert Reitter for their
advice and encouragement.—*Trans.*

[159]

and represent themselves to be autonomous, and their thinking deliberately reduces itself to a set of data-collecting techniques which it has invented. To think is thus to test out, to operate, to transform—on the condition that this activity is regulated by an experimental control that admits only the most "worked-out" phenomena, more likely produced by the apparatus than recorded by it. From this state of affairs arise all sorts of vagabond endeavors.

Today more than ever, science is sensitive to intellectual fads and fashions. When a model has succeeded in one order of problems, it is tried out everywhere else. At the present time, for example, our embryology and biology are full of "gradients." Just how these differ from what tradition called "order" or "totality" is not at all clear. This question, however, is not raised; it is not even permitted. The gradient is a net we throw out to sea, without knowing what we will haul back in it. Or again, it is the slender twig upon which unforeseeable crystallizations will form. Certainly this freedom of operation will serve well to overcome many a pointless dilemma—provided only that we ask from time to time why the apparatus works in one place and fails in others. For all its fluency, science must nevertheless understand itself; it must see itself as a construction based on a brute, existent world and not claim for its blind operations that constituting value which "concepts of nature" were able to have in an idealist philosophy. To say that the world is, by nominal definition, the object x of our operations is to treat the scientist's knowledge as if it were absolute, as if everything that is and has been was meant only to enter the laboratory. Thinking "operationally" has become a sort of absolute artificialism, such as we see in the ideology of cybernetics, where human creations are derived from a natural information process, itself conceived on the model of human machines. If this kind of thinking were to extend its reign to man and history; if, pretending to ignore what we know of them through our own situations, it were to set out to construct man and history on the basis of a few abstract indices (as a decadent psychoanalysis and a decadent culturalism have done in the United States)—then, since man really becomes the *manipulandum* he takes himself to be, we enter into a cultural regimen where there is neither truth nor falsity concerning man and history, into a sleep, or a nightmare, from which there is no awakening.

Scientific thinking, a thinking which looks on from above, and thinks of the object-in-general, must return to the "there is" which underlies it; to the site, the soil of the sensible and opened world such as it is in our life and for our body—not that possible body which we may legitimately think of as an information machine but that actual body I call mine, this sentinel standing quietly at the command of my words and my acts. Further, *associated bodies* must be brought forward along with my body—the "others," not merely as my congeners, as the zoologist says, but the others who haunt me and whom I haunt; the "others" along *with* whom I haunt a single, present, and actual Being as no animal ever haunted those beings of his own species, locale, or habitat. In this primordial historicity, science's agile and improvisatory thought will learn to ground itself upon things themselves and upon itself, and will once more become philosophy. . . .

But art, especially painting, draws upon this fabric of brute meaning which activism [or operationalism—*Trans.*] would prefer to ignore. Art and only art does so in full innocence. From the writer and the philosopher, in contrast, we want opinions and advice. We will not allow them to hold the world suspended. We want them to take a stand; they cannot waive the responsibilities of men who speak. Music, at the other extreme, is too far beyond the world and the designatable to depict anything but certain outlines of Being—its ebb and flow, its growth, its upheavals, its turbulence.

Only the painter is entitled to look at everything without being obliged to appraise what he sees. For the painter, we might say, the watchwords of knowledge and action lose their meaning and force. Political regimes which denounce "degenerate" painting rarely destroy paintings. They hide them, and one senses here an element of "one never knows" amounting almost to a recognition. The reproach of escapism is seldom aimed at the painter; we do not hold it against Cézanne that he lived hidden away at Estaque during the war of 1870. And we recall with respect his "C'est effrayant, la vie," even when the lowliest student, ever since Nietzsche, would flatly reject philosophy if it did not teach how to live fully [*à être de grands vivants*]. It is as if in the painter's calling there were some urgency above all other claims on him. Strong or frail in life, he is incontestably sovereign in his own rumination of the world. With no other technique than what his eyes and hands discover in seeing and painting, he persists in drawing from this world, with its din of history's glories and scandals, *canvases* which will hardly add to the angers or the hopes of man—and no one complains.[2]

What, then, is this secret science which he has or which he seeks? That dimension which lets Van Gogh say he must go "further on"? What is this fundamental of painting, perhaps of all culture?

2. Il est là, fort ou faible dans la vie, mais souverain sans conteste dans sa rumination du monde, sans autre "technique" que celle que ses yeux et ses mains se donnent à force de voir, à force de peindre, acharné à tirer de ce monde où sonnent les scandales et les gloires de l'histoire des *toiles* qui n'ajouteront guère aux colères ni aux espoirs des hommes, et personne ne murmure.

[2]

THE PAINTER "takes his body with him," says Valéry. Indeed we cannot imagine how a *mind* could paint. It is by lending his body to the world that the artist changes the world into paintings. To understand these transubstantiations we must go back to the working, actual body—not the body as a chunk of space or a bundle of functions but that body which is an intertwining of vision and movement.

I have only to see something to know how to reach it and deal with it, even if I do not know how this happens in the nervous machine. My mobile body makes a difference in the visible world, being a part of it; that is why I can steer it through the visible. Conversely, it is just as true that vision is attached to movement. We see only what we look at. What would vision be without eye movement? And how could the movement of the eyes bring things together if the movement were blind? If it were only a reflex? If it did not have its antennae, its clairvoyance? If vision were not prefigured in it?

In principle all my changes of place figure in a corner of my landscape; they are recorded on the map of the visible. Everything I see is in principle within my reach, at least within reach of my sight, and is marked upon the map of the "I can." Each of the two maps is complete. The visible world and the world of my motor projects are each total parts of the same Being.

This extraordinary overlapping, which we never think about sufficiently, forbids us to conceive of vision as an operation of thought that would set up before the mind a picture or a representation of the world, a world of immanence and of ideality. Immersed in the visible by his body, itself visible, the see-er does not appropriate what he sees; he merely approaches it by looking, he opens himself to the world. And on its side, this world of which he is a part is not *in itself*, or matter. My movement is not a decision made by the mind, an absolute doing which would decree, from the depths of a subjective retreat, some change of place miraculously executed in extended space. It is the natural consequence and the maturation of my vision. I say of a thing that it is moved; but my body moves itself, my movement deploys itself. It is not ignorant of itself; it is not blind for itself; it radiates from a self. . . .

The enigma is that my body simultaneously sees and is seen. That which looks at all things can also look at itself and recognize, in what it sees, the "other side" of its power of looking. It sees itself seeing; it touches itself touching; it is visible and sensitive for itself. It is not a self through transparence, like thought, which only thinks its object by assimilating it, by constituting it, by transforming it into thought. It is a self through confusion, narcissism, through inherence of the one who sees in that which he sees, and through inherence of sensing in the sensed—a self, therefore, that is caught up in things, that has a front and a back, a past and a future. . . .

This initial paradox cannot but produce others. Visible and mobile, my body is a thing among things; it is caught in the fabric of the world, and its cohesion is that of a thing. But because it moves itself and sees, it holds things in a circle around itself.[3] Things are an annex or prolongation of itself; they are incrusted into its flesh, they are part of its full definition; the world is made of the same stuff as the body. This way of turning things around [*ces renversements*], these antinomies,[4] are different ways of saying that vision happens among, or is caught in, things—in that place where something visible undertakes to see, becomes visible for itself by virtue of the sight of things; in that place where there persists, like the mother water in crystal, the undividedness [*l'indivision*] of the sensing and the sensed.

This interiority no more precedes the material arrangement of the human body than it results from it. What if our eyes were made in such a way as to prevent our seeing any part of our body, or if some baneful arrangement of the body were to let us move our hands over things, while preventing us from touching our own body? Or what if, like certain animals, we had lateral eyes with no cross blending of visual fields? Such a body would not reflect itself; it would be an almost adamantine body, not really flesh, not really the body of a human being. There would be no humanity.

But humanity is not produced as the effect of our articulations or by the way our eyes are implanted in us (still less by the existence of mirrors which could make our entire body visible to us). These contingencies and others like them, without which mankind would not exist, do not by simple summation bring it about that there *is* a single man.

The body's animation is not the assemblage or juxtaposition of its parts. Nor is it a question of a mind or spirit coming down from somewhere else into an automaton; this would still suppose that the body itself is without an inside and without a "self." There is a human body when, between the seeing and the seen, between touching and the touched, between one eye and the other, between hand and hand, a blending of some sort takes place—when the spark is lit between sensing and sensible, lighting the fire that will not stop burning until

3. Cf. *Le visible et l'invisible* (Paris, 1964), pp. 273, 308–11.—*Trans.*

4. See *Signes* (Paris, 1960), pp. 210, 222–23, especially the footnotes, for a clarification of the "circularity" at issue here.—*Trans.*

some accident of the body will undo what no accident would have sufficed to do. . . .

Once this strange system of exchanges is given, we find before us all the problems of painting. These exchanges illustrate the enigma of the body, and this enigma justifies them. Since things and my body are made of the same stuff, vision must somehow take place in them; their manifest visibility must be repeated in the body by a secret visibility. "Nature is on the inside," says Cézanne. Quality, light, color, depth, which are there before us, are there only because they awaken an echo in our body and because the body welcomes them.

Things have an internal equivalent in me; they arouse in me a carnal formula of their presence. Why shouldn't these [correspondences] in their turn give rise to some [external] visible shape in which anyone else would recognize those motifs which support his own inspection of the world?[5] Thus there appears a "visible" of the second power, a carnal essence or icon of the first. It is not a faded copy, a trompe-l'oeil, or another *thing*. The animals painted on the walls of Lascaux are not there in the same way as the fissures and limestone formations. But they are not *elsewhere*. Pushed forward here, held back there, held up by the wall's mass they use so adroitly, they spread around the wall without ever breaking from their elusive moorings in it. I would be at great pains to say *where* is the painting I am looking at. For I do not look at it as I do at a thing; I do not fix it in its place. My gaze wanders in it as in the halos of Being. It is more accurate to say that I see according to it, or with it, than that I *see it*.

The word "image" is in bad repute because we have thoughtlessly believed that a design was a tracing, a copy, a second thing, and that the mental image was such a design, belonging among our private bric-a-brac. But if in fact it is nothing of the kind, then neither the design nor the painting belongs to the in-itself any more than the image does. They are the inside of the outside and the outside of the inside, which the duplicity of feeling [*le sentir*] makes possible and without which we would never understand the quasi presence and imminent visibility which make up the whole problem of the imaginary. The picture and the actor's mimicry are not devices to be borrowed from the real world in order to signify prosaic things which are absent. For the imaginary is much nearer to, and much farther away from, the actual—nearer because it is in my body as a diagram of the life of the actual, with all its pulp and carnal obverse [*son envers*

5. Cet équivalent interne, cette formule charnelle de leur présence que les choses suscitent en moi, pourquoi à leur tour ne susciteraient-ils pas un tracé, visible encore, où tout autre regard retrouvera les motifs qui soutiennent son inspection du monde?

charnel] exposed to view for the first time. In this sense, Giacometti [6] says energetically, "What interests me in all paintings is resemblance —that is, what is resemblance for me: something which makes me discover more of the world." And the imaginary is much farther away from the actual because the painting is an analogue or likeness only according to the body; because it does *not* present the *mind* with an occasion to rethink the constitutive relations of things; because, rather, it offers to our *sight* [*regard*], so that it might join with them, the inward traces of vision, and because it offers to vision its inward tapestries, the imaginary texture of the real. [7]

Shall we say, then, that we look out from the inside, that there is a third eye which sees the paintings and even the mental images, as we used to speak of a third ear which grasped messages from the outside through the noises they caused inside us? But how would this help us when the real problem is to understand how it happens that our fleshly eyes are already much more than receptors for light rays, colors, and lines? They are computers of the world, which have the gift of the visible as it was once said that the inspired man had the gift of tongues. Of course this gift is earned by exercise; it is not in a few months, or in solitude, that a painter comes into full possession of his vision. But that is not the question; precocious or belated, spontaneous or cultivated in museums, his vision in any event learns only by seeing and learns only from itself. The eye sees the world, sees what inadequacies [*manques*] keep the world from being a painting, sees what keeps a painting from being itself, sees—on the palette—the colors awaited by the painting, and sees, once it is done, the painting that answers to all these inadequacies just as it sees the paintings of others as other answers to other inadequacies.

It is no more possible to make a restrictive inventory of the visible than it is to catalogue the possible usages of a language or even its vocabulary and devices. The eye is an instrument that moves itself, a means which invents its own ends; it is *that which* has been moved by some impact of the world, which it then restores to the visible through the offices of an agile hand.

In whatever civilization it is born, from whatever beliefs, motives, or thoughts, no matter what ceremonies surround it—and even when it appears devoted to something else—from Lascaux to our time, pure or

6. G. Charbonnier, *Le monologue du peintre* (Paris, 1959), p. 172.

7. Beaucoup plus loin, puisque le tableau n'est un analogue que selon le corps, qu'il n'offre pas à l'esprit une occasion de repenser les rapports constitutifs des choses, mais au regard, pour qu'il les épouse, les traces de la vision du dedans, à la vision ce qui la tapisse intérieurement, la texture imaginaire du réel.

impure, figurative or not, painting celebrates no other enigma but that of visibility.

What we have just said amounts to a truism. The painter's world is a visible world, nothing but visible: a world almost demented because it is complete when it is yet only partial. Painting awakens and carries to its highest pitch a delirium which is vision itself, for to see is *to have at a distance;* painting spreads this strange possession to all aspects of Being, which must in some fashion become visible in order to enter into the work of art. When, apropos of Italian painting, the young Berenson spoke of an evocation of tactile values, he could hardly have been more mistaken; painting evokes nothing, least of all the tactile. What it does is much different, almost the inverse. It gives visible existence to what profane vision believes to be invisible; thanks to it we do not need a "muscular sense" in order to possess the voluminosity of the world. This voracious vision, reaching beyond the "visual givens," opens upon a texture of Being of which the discrete sensorial messages are only the punctuations or the caesurae. The eye lives in this texture as a man lives in his house.

Let us remain within the visible in the narrow and prosaic sense. The painter, whatever he is, *while he is painting* practices a magical theory of vision. He is obliged to admit that objects before him pass into him or else that, according to Malebranche's sarcastic dilemma, the mind goes out through the eyes to wander among objects; for the painter never ceases adjusting his clairvoyance to them. (It makes no difference if he does not paint from "nature"; he paints, in any case, because he has seen, because the world has at least once emblazoned in him the ciphers of the visible.) He must affirm, as one philosopher has said, that vision is a mirror or concentration of the universe or that, in another's words, the *idios kosmos* opens by virtue of vision upon a *koinos kosmos;* in short, that the same thing is both out there in the world and here in the heart of vision—the same or, if one prefers, a *similar* thing, but according to an efficacious similarity which is the parent, the genesis, the metamorphosis of Being in his vision. It is the mountain itself which from out there makes itself seen by the painter; it is the mountain that he interrogates with his gaze.

What exactly does he ask of it? To unveil the means, visible and not otherwise, by which it makes itself a mountain before our eyes. Light, lighting, shadows, reflections, color, all the objects of his quest are not altogether real objects; like ghosts, they have only visual existence. In fact they exist only at the threshold of profane vision; they are not seen by everyone. The painter's gaze asks them what they do to suddenly cause something to be and to be *this* thing, what they do to compose this worldly talisman and to make us see the visible.

We see that the hand pointing to us in *The Nightwatch* is truly there only when we see that its shadow on the captain's body presents it simultaneously in profile. The spatiality of the captain lies at the meeting place of two lines of sight which are incompossible and yet together. Everyone with eyes has at some time or other witnessed this play of shadows, or something like it, and has been made by it to see a space and the things included therein. But it works in us without us; it hides itself in making the object visible. To see the object, it is necessary *not* to see the play of shadows and light around it. The visible in the profane sense forgets its premises; it rests upon a total visibility which is to be re-created and which liberates the phantoms captive in it. The moderns, as we know, have liberated many others; they have added many a blank note [*note sourde*] to the official gamut of our means of seeing. But the interrogation of painting in any case looks toward this secret and feverish genesis of things in our body.

And so it is not a question asked of someone who doesn't know by someone who does—the schoolmaster's question. The question comes from one who does not know, and it is addressed to a vision, a seeing, which knows everything and which we do not make, for it makes itself in us. Max Ernst (with the surrealists) says rightly, "Just as the role of the poet since [Rimbaud's] famous *Lettre du voyant* consists in writing under the dictation of what is being thought, of what articulates itself in him, the role of the painter is to grasp and project what is seen in him." [8] The painter lives in fascination. The actions most proper to him—those gestures, those paths which he alone can trace and which will be revelations to others (because the others do not lack what he lacks or in the same way)—to him they seem to emanate from the things themselves, like the patterns of the constellations.

Inevitably the roles between him and the visible are reversed. That is why so many painters have said that things look at them. As André Marchand says, after Klee: "In a forest, I have felt many times over that it was not I who looked at the forest. Some days I felt that the trees were looking at me, were speaking to me. . . . I was there, listening. . . . I think that the painter must be penetrated by the universe and not want to penetrate it. . . . I expect to be inwardly submerged, buried. Perhaps I paint to break out." [9]

We speak of "inspiration," and the word should be taken literally. There really is inspiration and expiration of Being, action and passion so slightly discernible that it becomes impossible to distinguish between what sees and what is seen, what paints and what is painted.

It can be said that a human is born at the instant when something

8. Charbonnier, *op. cit.*, p. 34.
9. *Ibid.*, pp. 143–45.

that was only virtually visible, inside the mother's body, becomes at one and the same time visible for itself and for us. The painter's vision is a continued birth.

In paintings themselves we could seek a figured philosophy [10] of vision—its iconography, perhaps. It is no accident, for example, that frequently in Dutch paintings (as in many others) an empty interior is "digested" by the "round eye of the mirror." [11] This prehuman way of seeing things is the painter's way. More completely than lights, shadows, and reflections, the mirror image anticipates, within things, the labor of vision. Like all other technical objects, such as signs and tools, the mirror arises upon the open circuit [that goes] from seeing body to visible body. Every technique is a "technique of the body." A technique outlines and amplifies the metaphysical structure of our flesh. The mirror appears because I am seeing-visible [voyant-visible], because there is a reflexivity of the sensible; the mirror translates and reproduces that reflexivity. My outside completes itself in and through the sensible. Everything I have that is most secret goes into this visage, this face, this flat and closed entity about which my reflection in the water has already made me puzzle. Schilder [12] observes that, smoking a pipe before a mirror, I feel the sleek, burning surface of the wood not only where my fingers are but also in those ghostlike fingers, those merely visible fingers inside the mirror. The mirror's ghost lies outside my body, and by the same token my own body's "invisibility" can invest the other bodies I see.[13] Hence my body can assume segments derived from the body of another, just as my substance passes into them; man is mirror for man. The mirror itself is the instrument of a universal magic that changes things into a spectacle, spectacles into things, myself into another, and another into myself. Artists have often mused upon mirrors because beneath this "mechanical trick," they recognized, just as they did in the case of the trick of perspective,[14] the

10. ". . . une philosophie figurée . . ." Cf. Bergson (Ravaisson), note 46 below.—Trans.

11. P. Claudel, Introduction à la peinture hollandaise (Paris, 1935).

12. P. Schilder, The Image and Appearance of the Human Body (London, 1935; New York, 1950), pp. 223–24. [". . . the body-image is not confined to the borderlines of one's own body. It transgresses them in the mirror. There is a body-image outside ourselves, and it is remarkable that primitive peoples even ascribe a substantial existence to the picture in the mirror" (p. 278). Schilder's earlier, shorter study, Das Körperschema (Berlin, 1923), is cited several times in The Structure of Behavior and in Phenomenology of Perception. Schilder's later work is of especial interest with regard to Merleau-Ponty's own elaborations of the meaning of the human body; it is worth examining for that reason, as well as for the chance it provides to discern some fundamental coincidences between Merleau-Ponty and certain American pragmatists.]

13. Cf. Schilder, Image, pp. 281–82.—Trans.

14. Robert Delaunay, Du cubisme à l'art abstrait (Paris, 1957).

metamorphosis of seeing and seen which defines both our flesh and the painter's vocation. This explains why they have so often liked to draw themselves in the act of painting (they still do—witness Matisse's drawings), adding to what *they* saw then, what *things* saw of them. It is as if they were claiming that there is a total or absolute vision, outside of which there is nothing and which closes itself over them. Where in the realm of the understanding can we place these occult operations, together with the potions and idols they concoct? What can we call them? Consider, as Sartre did in *Nausea,* the smile of a long-dead king which continues to exist and to reproduce itself [*de se produire et de se reproduire*] on the surface of a canvas. It is too little to say that it is there as an image or essence; it is there as itself, as that which was always most alive about it, even now as I look at the painting. The "world's instant" that Cézanne wanted to paint, an instant long since passed away, is still thrown at us by his paintings.[15] His Mount Saint Victor is made and remade from one end of the world to the other in a way that is different from, but no less energetic than, that of the hard rock above Aix. Essence and existence, imaginary and real, visible and invisible—a painting mixes up all our categories in laying out its oneiric universe of carnal essences, of effective likenesses, of mute meanings.

[3]

How CRYSTAL CLEAR everything would be in our philosophy if only we could exorcise these specters, make illusions or object-less perceptions out of them, keep them on the edge of a world that doesn't equivocate!

Descartes' *Dioptric* is an attempt to do just that. It is the breviary of a thought that wants no longer to abide in the visible and so decides to construct the visible according to a model-in-thought. It is worthwhile to remember this attempt and its failure.

Here there is no concern to cling to vision. The problem is to know "how it happens," but only so far as it is necessary to invent, whenever the need arises, certain "artificial organs"[16] which correct it. We are to reason not so much upon the light we see as upon the light which, from

15. "A minute in the world's life passes! to paint it in its reality! and forget everything for that. To become that minute, be the sensitive plate, . . . give the image of what we see, forgetting everything that has appeared before our time. . . ." Cézanne, quoted in B. Dorival, *Paul Cézanne,* trans. H. H. A. Thackthwaite (London, 1948), p. 101.—*Trans.*

16. Descartes, *La Dioptrique,* Discours VII [conclusion]. Edition Adam et Tannery, VI, p. 165.

outside, enters our eyes and commands our vision. And for that we are to rely upon "two or three comparisons which help us to conceive it [light]" in such a way as to explain its known properties and to deduce others.[17] The question being so formulated, it is best to think of light as an action by contact—not unlike the action of things upon the blind man's cane. The blind, says Descartes, "see with their hands." [18] The Cartesian concept of vision is modeled after the sense of touch.

At one swoop, then, he removes action at a distance and relieves us of that ubiquity which is the whole problem of vision (as well as its peculiar virtue). Why should we henceforth puzzle over reflections and mirrors? These unreal duplications are a class of things; they are real effects like a ball's bouncing. If the reflection resembles the thing itself, it is because this reflection acts upon the eyes more or less as a thing. would. It deceives the eye by engendering a perception which has no object but which does not affect our idea of the world. In the world there is the thing itself, and outside this thing itself there is that other thing which is only reflected light rays and which happens to have an ordered correspondence with the real thing; there are two individuals, then, bound together externally by causality. As far as the thing and its mirror image are concerned, their resemblance is only an external denomination; the resemblance belongs to thought. [What for us is] the "cross-eyed" [louche] relationship of resemblance is—in the things—a clear relationship of projection.

A Cartesian does not see himself in the mirror; he sees a dummy, an "outside," which, he has every reason to believe, other people see in the very same way but which, no more for himself than for others, is not a body in the flesh. His "image" in the mirror is an effect of the mechanics of things. If he recognizes himself in it, if he thinks it "looks like him," it is his thought that weaves this connection. The mirror image is nothing that belongs to him.

Icons lose their powers.[19] As vividly as an etching "represents" forests, towns, men, battles, storms, it does not resemble them. It is only a bit of ink put down here and there on the paper. A figure flattened down onto a plane surface scarcely retains the forms of things; it is a deformed figure that ought to be deformed—the square becomes a lozenge, the circle an oval—in order to represent the object. It is an image only as long as it does not resemble its object. If not through resemblance, how, then, does it act? It "excites our thought" to

17. Ibid., Discours I. Adam et Tannery, p. 83. [Oeuvres et lettres de Descartes, ed. André Bridoux, Edition Pléiade, p. 181. Page references from the Bridoux selections have been added in the belief that this volume is more widely accessible today than the Adam and Tannery complete edition.]

18. Ibid., Adam et Tannery, p. 84. [Bridoux, p. 182.]

19. This paragraph continues the exposition of the Dioptric.—Trans.

"conceive," as do signs and words "which in no way resemble the things they signify." [20] The etching gives us sufficient indices, unequivocal means for forming an idea of the thing represented that does not come from the icon itself; rather, it arises in us as it is "occasioned." The magic of intentional species—the old idea of effective resemblance as suggested by mirrors and paintings—loses its final argument if the entire potency of a painting is that of a text to be read, a text totally free of promiscuity between the seeing and the seen. We need no longer understand how a painting of things in the body could make them felt in the soul—an impossible task, since the very resemblance between this painting and those things would have to be seen in turn, since we would "have to have other eyes in our head with which to apperceive it," [21] and since the problem of vision remains whole even when we have given ourselves these likenesses which wander between us and the real things. What the light designs upon our eyes, and thence upon our brain, does not resemble the visible world any more than etchings do. There is nothing more going on between the things and the eyes, and the eyes and vision, than between the things and the blind man's hands, and between his hands and thoughts.

Vision is not the metamorphosis of things themselves into the sight of them; it is not a matter of things' belonging simultaneously to the huge, real world and the small, private world. It is a thinking that deciphers strictly the signs given within the body. Resemblance is the result of perception, not its mainspring. More surely still, the mental image, the clairvoyance which renders present to us what is absent, is nothing like an insight penetrating into the heart of Being. It is still a thought relying upon bodily indices, this time insufficient, which are made to say more than they mean. Nothing is left of the oneiric world of analogy. . . .

What interests us in these famous analyses is that they make us aware of the fact that any theory of painting is a metaphysics. Descartes does not say much about painting, and one might think it unfair on our part to make an issue out of a few pages on copper engravings. And yet even if he speaks of them only in passing, that in itself is significant. Painting for him is not a central operation contributing to the definition of our access to Being; it is a mode or a variant of thinking, where thinking is canonically defined according to intellectual possession and evidence. It is this option that is expressed within the little he does say, and a closer study of painting would lead to another philosophy. It is significant too that when he speaks of "pic-

20. *Ibid.*, Discours IV. Adam et Tannery, pp. 112–14. [Bridoux, pp. 203–4; in English, *Descartes: Philosophical Writings*, ed. and trans. N. Kemp Smith, Modern Library Edition, pp. 145–47.]

21. *Ibid.*, p. 130. [Bridoux, p. 217; Smith, p. 148.]

tures" he takes line drawings as typical. We shall see that all painting is present in each of its modes of expression; one drawing, even a single line, can embrace all its bold potential.

But what Descartes likes most in copper engravings is that they preserve the forms of objects, or at least give us sufficient signs of their forms. They present the object by its outside, or its envelope. If he had examined that other, deeper opening upon things given us by secondary qualities, especially color, then—since there is no ordered or projective relationship between them and the true properties of things and since we understand their message all the same—he would have found himself faced with the problem of a conceptless universality and a conceptless opening upon things. He would have been obliged to find out how the indecisive murmur of colors can present us with things, forests, storms—in short the world; obliged, perhaps, to integrate perspective, as a particular case, with a more ample ontological power. But for him it goes without saying that color is an ornament, mere coloring [*coloriage*], and that the real power of painting lies in design, whose power in turn rests upon the ordered relationship existing between it and space-in-itself as taught to us by perspective-projection. Pascal is remembered for speaking of the frivolity of paintings which attach us to images whose originals would not touch us; this is a Cartesian opinion. For Descartes it is unarguably evident that one can paint only existing things, that their existence consists in being extended, and that design, or line drawing, alone makes painting possible by making the representation of extension possible. Thus painting is only an artifice which presents to our eyes a projection similar to that which the things themselves in ordinary perception would and do inscribe in our eyes. A painting makes us see in the same way in which we actually see the thing itself, even though the thing is absent. Especially it makes us see a *space* where there is none.[22]

The picture is a flat thing contriving to give us what we would see in the [actual] presence of "diversely contoured" things, by offering sufficient diacritical signs of the missing dimension, according to height and width.[23] Depth is a *third dimension* derived from the other two.

It will pay us to dwell for a moment upon this third dimension. It has, first of all, something paradoxical about it. I see objects which hide each other and which consequently I do not see; each one stands behind the other. I see it [the third dimension] and it is not visible,

22. The system of means by which painting makes us see is a scientific matter. Why, then, do we not methodically produce perfect images of the world, arriving at a universal art purged of personal art, just as the universal language would free us of all the confused relationships that lurk in existent languages?

23. *Dioptrique*, Discours IV, *loc. cit.* [Note 20 above.]

since it goes toward things from, as starting point, this body to which I myself am fastened. But the mystery here is a false one. I don't really see it [the third dimension], or if I do, it is only another *size* [measured by height and width]. On the line which lies between my eyes and the horizon, the first [vertical] plane forever hides all the others, and if from side to side I think I see things spread out in order before me, it is because they do not completely hide each other. Thus I see each thing to be outside the others, according to some measure otherwise reckoned [*autrement compté*].[24] We are always on this side of space or beyond it entirely. It is never the case that things really *are* one behind the other. The fact that things overlap or are hidden does not enter into their definition, and expresses only my incomprehensible solidarity with one of them—my body. And whatever might be positive in these facts, they are only thoughts that I formulate and not attributes of the things. I know that at this very moment another man, situated else-where—or better, God, who is everywhere—could penetrate their "hid-ing place" and see them openly deployed. Either what I call depth is nothing, or else it is my participation in a Being without restriction, a participation primarily in the being of space beyond every [particular] point of view. Things encroach upon one another *because each is outside of the others*. The proof of this is that I can see depth in a painting which everyone agrees has none and which organizes for me an illusion of an illusion. . . . This two-dimensional being,[25] which makes me see another [dimension], is a being that is opened up [*troué*] —as the men of the Renaissance said, a window. . . .

But in the last analysis the window opens only upon those *partes extra partes,* upon height and width seen merely from another angle— upon the absolute positivity of Being.

It is this identity of Being, or this space without hiding places which in each of its points is only what it is, neither more nor less, that underlies the analysis of copper engravings. Space is in-itself; rather, it is the in-itself *par excellence*. Its definition is *to be* in itself. Every point of space is and is thought to be right where it is—one here, another there; space is the evidence of the "where." Orientation, polarity, envel-opment are, in space, derived phenomena inextricably bound to my presence. *Space* remains absolutely in itself, everywhere equal to itself, homogeneous; its dimensions, for example, are interchangeable.

Like all classical ontologies, this one builds certain properties of beings into a structure of Being. Reversing Leibniz's remark, we might say that in doing this, it is true and false: true in what it denies and

24. Discours V of the *Dioptrique*, especially Descartes' diagrams, helps con-siderably to clarify this compressed passage.—*Trans.*
25. That is, the painting.—*Trans.*

false in what it affirms. Descartes' space is true over against a too empirical thought which dares not construct. It was necessary first to idealize space, to conceive of that being—perfect in its genus, clear, manageable, and homogeneous—which our thinking glides over without a vantage point of its own: a being which thought reports entirely in terms of three rectangular dimensions. This done, we were enabled eventually to find the limits of construction, to understand that space does not have three dimensions or more or fewer, as an animal has either four or two feet, and to understand that the three dimensions are taken by different systems of measurement from a single dimensionality, a polymorphous Being, which justifies all without being fully expressed by any. Descartes was right in setting space free. His mistake was to erect it into a positive being, outside all points of view, beyond all latency and all depth, having no true thickness [épaisseur].

He was right also in taking his inspiration from the perspectival techniques of the Renaissance; they encouraged painting to freely produce experiences of depth and, in general, presentations of Being. These techniques were false only in so far as they pretended to bring an end to painting's quest and history, to found once and for all an exact and infallible art of painting. As Panofsky has shown concerning the men of the Renaissance,[26] this enthusiasm was not without bad faith. The theoreticians tried to forget the spherical visual field of the ancients, their angular perspective which relates the apparent size not to distance but to the angle from which we see the object. They wanted to forget what they disdainfully called the *perspectiva naturalis*, or *communis*, in favor of a *perspectiva artificialis* capable in principle of founding an exact construction. To accredit this myth, they went so far as to expurgate Euclid, omitting from their translations that eighth theorem which bothered them so much. But the painters, on the other hand, knew from experience that no technique of perspective is an exact solution and that there is no projection of the existing world which respects it in all aspects and deserves to become the fundamental law of painting. They knew too that linear perspective was so far from being an ultimate breakthrough that, on the contrary, it opens several pathways for painting. For example, the Italians took the way of representing the object, but the northern painters discovered and worked out the formal technique of *Hochraum*, *Nahraum*, and *Schrägraum*. Thus plane projection does not always provoke our thought to reach the true form of things, as Descartes believed. Beyond a certain degree of deformation, it refers back, on the contrary, to our own vantage point. And the painted objects are left to retreat into a remoteness out

26. E. Panofsky, *Die Perspektive als symbolische Form*, in *Vorträge der Bibliotek Warburg*, IV (1924–25).

of reach of all thought. Something in space escapes our attempts to look at it from "above."

The truth is that no means of expression, once mastered, resolves the problems of painting or transforms it into a technique. For no symbolic form ever functions as a stimulus. Wherever it has been put to work and has acted, has *gone* to work, it has been put to work and has acted with the entire context of the *oeuvre*, and not in the slightest by means of a *trompe-l'oeil*. The *Stilmoment* never gets rid of the *Wermoment*.[27] The language of painting is never "instituted by nature"; it is to be made and remade over and over again. The perspective of the Renaissance is no infallible "gimmick." It is only a particular case, a date, a moment in a poetic information of the world which continues after it.

Yet Descartes would not have been Descartes if he had thought to *eliminate* the enigma of vision. There is no vision without thought. But *it is not enough* to think in order to see. Vision is a conditioned thought; it is born "as occasioned" by what happens in the body; it is "incited" to think by the body. It does not *choose* either to be or not to be or to think this thing or that. It has to carry in its heart that heaviness, that dependence which cannot come to it by some intrusion from outside. Such bodily events are "instituted by nature" in order to bring us to see this thing or that. The thinking that belongs to vision functions according to a program and a law which it has not given itself. It does not possess its own premises; it is not a thought altogether present and actual; there is in its center a mystery of passivity.

As things stand, then, everything we say and think of vision has to make a *thought* of it. When, for example, we wish to understand how we see the way objects are situated, we have no other recourse than to suppose the soul to be capable, knowing where the parts of its body are, of "transferring its attention from there" to all the points of space that lie in the prolongation of [i.e., beyond] the bodily members.[28] But so far this is only a "model" of the event. For the question is, how does the soul know this space, its own body's, which it extends toward things, this primary *here* from which all the *there's* will come? This space is

27. *Ibid.*

28. Descartes, *op. cit.*, Adam et Tannery, VI, p. 135 [Bridoux, p. 220; Smith, p. 154. Here is Smith's translation of the passage under discussion: "Our knowledge of it (the situation of an object) does not depend on any image or action which comes to us from the object, but solely on the situation of the small parts of the brain whence the nerves take their origin. For this situation—a situation which changes with every change however small in the points at which these nerve-fibers are located—is instituted by nature in order to secure, not only that the mind be aware of the location of each part of the body which it animates, relatively to all the others, but also that it be able to transfer its attention to all the positions contained in the straight line that can be imaged as drawn from the extremity of each of these parts, and as prolonged to infinity."]

not, like them, just another mode or specimen of the extended; it is the place of the body the soul calls "mine," a place the soul inhabits. The body it animates is not, for it, an object among objects, and it does not derive from the body all the rest of space as an implied premise. The soul thinks with reference to the body, not with reference to itself, and space, or exterior distance, is stipulated as well within the natural pact that unites them. If for a certain degree of accommodation and eye convergence the soul takes note of a certain distance, the thought which draws the second relationship from the first is as if immemorially enrolled in our internal "works" [fabrique]. "Usually this comes about without our reflecting upon it—just as, when we clasp a body with our hand, we conform the hand to the size and shape of the body and thereby sense the body, without having need to think of those movements of the hand." [29] For the soul, the body is both natal space and matrix of every other existing space. Thus vision divides itself. There is the vision upon which I reflect; I cannot think it except as thought, the mind's inspection, judgment, a reading of signs. And then there is the vision that really takes place, an honorary or instituted thought, squeezed into a body—its own body, of which we can have no idea except in the exercise of it and which introduces, between space and thought, the autonomous order of the compound of soul and body. The enigma of vision is not done away with; it is relegated from the "thought of seeing" to vision in act.

Still this de facto vision and the "there is" which it contains do not upset Descartes' philosophy. Being thought united with a body, it cannot, by definition, really be thought [conceived]. One can practice it, exercise it, and, so to speak, exist it; yet one can draw nothing from it which deserves to be called true. If, like Queen Elizabeth,[30] we want at all costs to think something about it, all we can do is go back to Aristotle and scholasticism, to conceive thought as a corporeal something which cannot be conceived but which is the only way to formulate, for our understanding, the union of soul and body. The truth is that it is absurd to submit to pure understanding the mixture of understanding and body. These would-be thoughts are the hallmarks of "ordinary usage," mere verbalizations of this union, and can be allowed only if they are not taken to be thoughts. They are indices of an order of existence—of man and world as existing—about which we do not have to think. For this order there is no terra incognita on our map of

29. Ibid., Adam et Tannery, p. 137. [Bridoux, p. 222; Smith, p. 155. Smith's translation is given here.]

30. No doubt Merleau-Ponty is speaking of Princess Elizabeth, Descartes' correspondent. Cf. Phénoménologie de la perception, pp. 230–32 (C. Smith translation, pp. 198–99), and Descartes' letter to Elizabeth of June 28, 1643 (Bridoux, pp. 1157–61).
—Trans.

Being. It does not confine the reach of our thoughts, because it, just as much as they, is sustained by a truth which grounds its obscurity as well as our own lights.[31]

We have to push Descartes this far to find in him something like a metaphysics of depth [*de la profondeur*]. For we do not attend the birth of this truth; God's being for us is an abyss. An anxious trembling quickly mastered; for Descartes it is just as vain to plumb that abyss as it is to think the space of the soul and the depth of the visible. Our very position, he would say, disqualifies us from looking into such things. Here is the Cartesian secret of equilibrium: a metaphysics which gives us decisive reasons to be no longer involved with metaphysics, which validates our evidences while limiting them, which opens up our thinking without rending it.

The secret has been lost for good, it seems. If we ever again find a balance between science and philosophy, between our models and the obscurity of the "there is," it must be of a new kind. Our science has rejected the justifications as well as the restrictions which Descartes assigned to its domain. It no longer pretends to deduce its invented models from the attributes of God. The depth of the existing world and that of the unfathomable God come no longer to stand over against the platitudes [and flatness] of "technicized" thinking. Science gets along without the excursion into metaphysics which Descartes had to make at least once in his life; it takes off from the point he ultimately reached. Operational thought claims for itself, in the name of psychology, that domain of contact with oneself and with the world which Descartes reserved for a blind but irreducible experience. It is fundamentally hostile to philosophy as thought-in-contact, and if operational thought rediscovers the sense of philosophy it will be through the very excess of its ingenuousness [*sa désinvolture*]. It will happen when, having introduced all sorts of notions which for Descartes would have arisen from confused thought—quality, scalar structures, solidarity of observer and observed—it will suddenly become aware that one cannot summarily speak of all these beings as *constructs*. As we await this moment, philosophy maintains itself against such thinking, entrenching itself in that dimension of the compound of soul and body, that dimension of the existent world, of the abyssal Being that Descartes opened up and so quickly closed again. Our science and our philosophy are two faithful and unfaithful consequences of Cartesianism, two monsters born from its dismemberment.

Nothing is left for our philosophy but to set out toward the prospection of the actual world. We *are* the compound of soul and body, and so

31. That is, the obscurity of the "existential" order is just as necessary, just as grounded in God, as is the clarity of true thoughts ("nos lumières").—*Trans.*

there must be a thought of it. To this knowledge of position or situation Descartes owes what he himself says of it [this compound] or what he says sometimes of the presence of the body "against the soul," or the exterior world "at the end" of our hands. Here the body is not the means of vision and touch but their depository.

Our organs are no longer instruments; on the contrary, our instruments are detachable organs. Space is no longer what it was in the *Dioptric,* a network of relations between objects such as would be seen by a witness to my vision or by a geometer looking over it and reconstructing it from outside. It is, rather, a space reckoned starting from me as the zero point or degree zero of spatiality. I do not see it according to its exterior envelope; I live in it from the inside; I am immersed in it. After all, the world is all around me, not in front of me. Light is viewed once more as action at a distance. It is no longer reduced to the action of contact or, in other words, conceived as it might be by those who do not see in it.[32] Vision reassumes its fundamental power of showing forth more than itself. And since we are told that a bit of ink suffices to make us see forests and storms, light must have its *imaginaire.* Light's transcendence is not delegated to a reading mind which deciphers the impacts of the light-thing upon the brain and which could do this quite as well if it had never lived in a body. No more is it a question of speaking of space and light; the question is to make space and light, which are *there,* speak to us. There is no end to this question, since the vision to which it addresses itself is itself a question. The inquiries we believed closed have been reopened.

What is depth, what is light, τί τὸ ὄν? What are they—not for the mind that cuts itself off from the body but for the mind Descartes says is suffused throughout the body? And what are they, finally, not only for the mind but for themselves, since they pass through us and surround us?

Yet this philosophy still to be done is that which animates the painter—not when he expresses his opinions about the world but in that instant when his vision becomes gesture, when, in Cézanne's words, he "thinks in painting." [33]

[4]

THE ENTIRE MODERN HISTORY of painting, with its efforts to detach itself from illusionism and to acquire its own dimensions, has a metaphysical significance. This is not something to

32. "those who do not see in it," i.e., the blind (note 18, above).—*Trans.*

33. B. Dorival, *Paul Cézanne* (Paris, 1948), p. 103 *et seq.* [*trans.* Thackthwaite, *op. cit.,* pp. 101–3].

be demonstrated. Not for reasons drawn from the limits of objectivity in history and from the inevitable plurality of interpretations, which would prevent the linking of a philosophy and an event; the metaphysics we have in mind is not a body of detached ideas [*idées séparées*] for which inductive justifications could be sought in the experiential realm. There are, in the flesh of contingency, a structure of the event and a virtue peculiar to the scenario. These do not prevent the plurality of interpretations but in fact are the deepest reasons for this plurality. They make the event into a durable theme of historical life and have a right to philosophical status. In a sense everything that could have been said and that will be said about the French Revolution has always been and is henceforth within it, in that wave which arched itself out of a roil of discrete facts, with its froth of the past and its crest of the future. And it is always by looking more deeply into *how it came about* that we give and will go on giving new representations of it. As for the history of art works, if they are great, the sense we give to them later on has issued from them. It is the work itself that has opened the field from which it appears in another light. It changes *itself* and *becomes* what follows; the interminable reinterpretations to which it is *legitimately* susceptible change it only in itself. And if the historian unearths beneath its manifest content the surplus and thickness of meaning, the texture which held the promise of a long history, this active manner of being, then, this possibility he unveils in the work, this monogram he finds there—all are grounds for a philosophical meditation. But such a labor demands a long familiarity with history. We lack everything for its execution, both the competence and the place. Just the same, since the power or the fecundity of art works exceeds every positive causal or filial relation, there is nothing wrong with letting a layman, speaking from his memory of a few paintings and books, tell us how painting enters into his reflections; how painting deposits in him a feeling of profound discordance, a feeling of mutation within the relations of man and Being. Such feelings arise in him when he holds a universe of classical thought, en bloc, up against the explorations [*recherches*] of modern painting. This is a sort of history by contact, perhaps, never extending beyond the limits of one person, owing everything nevertheless to his frequentation of others. . . .

"I believe Cézanne was seeking depth all his life," says Giacometti.[34] Says Robert Delaunay, "Depth is the new inspiration." [35] Four centuries after the "solutions" of the Renaissance and three centuries after Descartes, depth is still new, and it insists on being sought, not

34. Charbonnier, *op. cit.*, p. 176.
35. Delaunay, *op. cit.*, p. 109.

"once in a lifetime" but all through life. It cannot be merely a question of an unmysterious interval, as seen from an airplane, between these trees nearby and those farther away. Nor is it a matter of the way things are conjured away, one by another, as we see happen so vividly in a perspective drawing. These two views are very explicit and raise no problems. The enigma, though, lies in their bond, in what is between them. The enigma consists in the fact that I see things, each one in its place, precisely because they eclipse one another, and that they are rivals before my sight precisely because each one is in its own place. Their exteriority is known in their envelopment and their mutual dependence in their autonomy. Once depth is understood in this way, we can no longer call it a third dimension. In the first place, if it were a dimension, it would be the *first* one; there are forms and definite planes only if it is stipulated how far from me their different parts are. But a *first* dimension that contains all the others is no longer a dimension, at least in the ordinary sense of a *certain relationship* according to which we make measurements. Depth thus understood is, rather, the experience of the reversibility of dimensions, of a global "locality"—everything in the same place at the same time, a locality from which height, width, and depth are abstracted, of a voluminosity we express in a word when we say that a thing is *there*. In search of depth Cézanne seeks this deflagration of Being, and it is all in the modes of space, in form as much as anything. Cézanne knows already what cubism will repeat: that the external form, the envelope, is secondary and derived, that it is not that which causes a thing to take form, that this shell of space must be shattered, this fruit bowl broken—and what is there to paint, then? Cubes, spheres, and cones (as he said once)? Pure forms which have the solidity of what could be defined by an internal law of construction, forms which all together, as traces or slices of the thing, let it appear between them like a face in the reeds? This would be to put Being's solidity on one side and its variety on the other. Cézanne made an experiment of this kind in his middle period. He opted for the solid, for space—and came to find that inside this space, a box or container too large for them, the things began to move, color against color; they began to modulate in instability.[36] Thus we must seek space and its content *as* together. The problem is generalized; it is no longer that of distance, of line, of form; it is also, and equally, the problem of color.

Color is the "place where our brain and the universe meet," he says in that admirable idiom of the artisan of Being which Klee liked to

36. F. Novotny, *Cézanne und das Ende der wissenschaftlichen Perspective* (Vienna, 1938).

cite.[37] It is for the benefit of color that we must break up the form-spectacle. Thus the question is not of colors, "simulacra of the colors of nature." [38] The question, rather, concerns the dimension of color, that dimension which creates identities, differences, a texture, a materiality, a something—creates them from itself, for itself. . . .

Yet (and this must be emphasized) there is no one master key of the visible, and color alone is no closer to being such a key than space is. The return to color has the merit of getting somewhat nearer to "the heart of things," [39] but this heart is beyond the color envelope just as it is beyond the space envelope. The *Portrait of Vallier* sets white spaces between the colors which take on the function of giving shape to, and setting off, a being more general than the yellow-being or green-being or blue-being. Also in the water colors of Cézanne's last years, for example, space (which had been taken to be evidence itself and of which it was believed that the question of *where* was not to be asked) radiates around planes that cannot be assigned to any place at all: "a superimposing of transparent surfaces," "a flowing movement of planes of color which overlap, which advance and retreat." [40]

Obviously it is not a matter of adding one more dimension to those of the flat canvas, of organizing an illusion or an objectless perception whose perfection consists in simulating an empirical vision to the maximum degree. Pictorial depth (as well as painted height and width) comes "I know not whence" to alight upon, and take root in, the sustaining support. The painter's vision is not a view upon the *outside*, a merely "physical-optical" [41] relation with the world. The world no longer stands before him through representation; rather, it is the painter to whom the things of the world give birth by a sort of concentration or coming-to-itself of the visible. Ultimately the painting relates to nothing at all among experienced things unless it is first of all "autofigurative." [42] It is a spectacle of something only by being a "spectacle of nothing," [43] by breaking the "skin of things" [44] to show how the things become things, how the world becomes world. Apollinaire said that in a poem there are phrases which do not appear to have been *created*, which seem to have *formed themselves*. And Henri

37. W. Grohmann, *Paul Klee* (Paris, 1954), p. 141 [New York, 1956].

38. Delaunay, *op. cit.*, p. 118.

39. Klee, *Journal* . . . , French trans. P. Klossowski (Paris, 1959).

40. George Schmidt, *Les aquarelles de Cézanne*, p. 21. [*The Watercolors of Cézanne* (New York, 1953).]

41. Klee, *op. cit.*

42. "The spectacle is first of all a spectacle of itself before it is a spectacle of something outside of it."—*Translator's note from Merleau-Ponty's 1961 lectures.*

43. C. P. Bru, *Esthétique de l'abstraction* (Paris, 1959), pp. 99, 86.

44. Henri Michaux, *Aventures de lignes*.

Michaux said that sometimes Klee's colors seem to have been born slowly upon the canvas, to have emanated from some primordial ground, "exhaled at the right place" [45] like a patina or a mold. Art is not construction, artifice, meticulous relationship to a space and a world existing outside. It is truly the "inarticulate cry," as Hermes Trismegistus said, "which seemed to be the voice of the light." And once it is present it awakens powers dormant in ordinary vision, a secret of preexistence. When through the water's thickness I see the tiling at the bottom of a pool, I do not see it *despite* the water and the reflections there; I see it through them and because of them. If there were no distortions, no ripples of sunlight, if it were without this flesh that I saw the geometry of the tiles, then I would cease to see it *as* it is and where it is—which is to say, beyond any identical, specific place. I cannot say that the water itself—the aqueous power, the sirupy and shimmering element—is *in* space; all this is not somewhere else either, but it is not in the pool. It inhabits it, it materializes itself there, yet it is not contained there; and if I raise my eyes toward the screen of cypresses where the web of reflections is playing, I cannot gainsay the fact that the water visits it, too, or at least sends into it, upon it, its active and living essence. This internal animation, this radiation of the visible is what the painter seeks under the name of depth, of space, of color.

Anyone who thinks about the matter finds it astonishing that very often a good painter can also make good drawings or good sculpture. Since neither the means of expression nor the creative gestures are comparable, this fact [of competence in several media] is proof that there is a system of equivalences, a Logos of lines, of lighting, of colors, of reliefs, of masses—a conceptless presentation of universal Being. The effort of modern painting has been directed not so much toward choosing between line and color, or even between the figuration of things and the creation of signs, as it has been toward multiplying the systems of equivalences, toward severing their adherence to the envelope of things. This effort might force us to create new materials or new means of expression, but it could well be realized at times by the reexamination and reinvestment of those which existed already.

There has been, for example, a prosaic conception of the line as a positive attribute and a property of the object in itself. Thus, it is the outer contour of the apple or the border between the plowed field and the meadow, considered as present in the world, such that, guided by points taken from the real world, the pencil or brush would only have to pass over them. But this line has been contested by all modern painting, and probably by all painting, as we are led to think by da

45. *Ibid.*

Vinci's comment in his *Treatise on Painting:* "The secret of the art of drawing is to discover in each object the particular way in which a certain flexuous line, which is, so to speak, its generating axis, is directed through its whole extent. . . ." [46] Both Ravaisson and Bergson sensed something important in this, without daring to decipher the oracle all the way. Bergson scarcely looked for the "sinuous outline" [*serpentement*] outside living beings, and he rather timidly advanced the idea that the undulating line "could be no one of the visible lines of the figure," that it is "no more here than there," and yet "gives the key to the whole." [47] He was on the threshold of that gripping discovery, already familiar to the painters, that there are no lines visible in themselves, that neither the contour of the apple nor the border between field and meadow is in *this* place or that, that they are always on the near or the far side of the point we look at. They are always between or behind whatever we fix our eyes upon; they are indicated, implicated, and even very imperiously demanded by the things, but they themselves are not things. They were supposed to circumscribe the apple or the meadow, but the apple and the meadow "form themselves" from themselves, and come into the visible as if they had come from a pre-spatial world behind the scenes.

Yet this contestation of the prosaic line is far from ruling out all lines in painting, as the impressionists may have thought. It is simply a matter of freeing the line, of revivifying its constituting power; and we are not faced with a contradiction when we see it reappear and triumph in painters like Klee or Matisse, who more than anyone believed in color. For henceforth, as Klee said, the line no longer imitates the visible; it "renders visible"; it is the blueprint of a genesis of things. Perhaps no one before Klee had "let a line muse." [48] The beginning of the line's path establishes or installs a certain level or mode of the linear, a certain manner for the line to be and to make itself a line, "to go line." [49] Relative to it, every subsequent inflection will have a dia-critical value, will be another aspect of the line's relationship to itself, will form an adventure, a history, a meaning of the line—all this according as it slants more or less, more or less rapidly, more or less subtly. Making its way in space, it nevertheless corrodes prosaic space and the *partes extra partes;* it develops a way of extending itself actively into that space which sub-tends the spatiality of a thing quite

46. Ravaisson, cited by Bergson, "La vie et l'oeuvre de Ravaisson," in *La pensée et le mouvant* (Paris, 1934), pp. 264–65. [The passage quoted here is from M. L. Andison's translation of that work, *The Creative Mind* (New York, 1946), p. 229. It remains moot whether these are Ravaisson's or da Vinci's words.]

47. Bergson, *ibid.*

48. Michaux, *op. cit.* ["laissé rêver une ligne"]

49. *Ibid.* ["d'aller ligne"]

as much as that of a man or an apple tree. This is so simply because, as Klee said, to give the generating axis of a man the painter "would have to have a network of lines so entangled that it could no longer be a question of a truly elementary representation." [50]

In view of this situation two alternatives are open, and it makes little difference which one is chosen. First, the painter may, like Klee, decide to hold rigorously to the principle of the genesis of the visible, the principle of fundamental, indirect, or—as Klee used to say—absolute painting, and then leave it up to the *title* to designate by its prosaic name the entity thus constituted, in order to leave the painting free to function more purely as a painting. Or alternatively he may choose with Matisse (in his drawings) to put into a single line both the prosaic definition [*signalement*] of the entity and the hidden [*sourde*] operation which composes in it such softness or inertia and such force as are required to constitute it as *nude*, as *face*, as *flower*.

There is a painting by Klee of two holly leaves, done in the most figurative manner. At first glance the leaves are thoroughly indecipherable, and they remain to the end monstrous, unbelievable, ghostly, *on account of their exactness* [*à force d' exactitude*]. And Matisse's women (let us keep in mind his contemporaries' sarcasm) were not immediately women; they became women. It is Matisse who taught us to see their contours not in a "physical-optical" way but rather as structural filaments [*des nervures*], as the axes of a corporeal system of activity and passivity. Figurative or not, the line is no longer a thing or an imitation of a thing. It is a certain disequilibrium kept up within the indifference of the white paper; it is a certain process of gouging within the in-itself, a certain constitutive emptiness—an emptiness which, as Moore's statues show decisively, upholds the pretended positivity of the things. The line is no longer the apparition of an entity upon a vacant background, as it was in classical geometry. It is, as in modern geometries, the restriction, segregation, or modulation of a pre-given spatiality.

Just as it has created the latent line, painting has made itself a movement without displacement, a movement by vibration or radiation. And well it should, since, as we say, painting is an art of space and since it comes about upon a canvas or sheet of paper and so lacks the wherewithal to devise things that actually move. But the immobile canvas could suggest a change of place in the same way that a shooting star's track on my retina suggests a transition, a motion not contained in it. The painting itself would offer to my eyes almost the same thing offered them by real movements: a series of appropriately mixed, instantaneous glimpses along with, if a living thing is involved, atti-

50. Grohmann, *op. cit.*, p. 192.

tudes unstably suspended between a before and an after—in short, the outsides of a change of place which the spectator would read from the imprint it leaves. Here Rodin's well-known remark reveals its full weight: the instantaneous glimpses, the unstable attitudes, petrify the movement, as is shown by so many photographs in which an athlete-in-motion is forever frozen. We could not thaw him out by multiplying the glimpses. Marey's photographs, the cubists' analyses, Duchamp's *La Mariée* do not move; they give a Zenonian reverie on movement. We see a rigid body as if it were a piece of armor going through its motions; it is here and it is there, magically, but it does not *go* from here to there. Cinema portrays movement, but *how*? Is it, as we are inclined to believe, by copying more closely the changes of place? We may presume not, since slow-motion shows a body floating among objects like an alga but not moving *itself*.

Movement is given, says Rodin,[51] by an image in which the arms, the legs, the trunk, and the head are each taken at a different instant, an image which therefore portrays the body in an attitude which it never at any instant really held and which imposes fictive linkages between the parts, as if this mutual confrontation of incompossibles could, and could alone, cause transition and duration to arise in bronze and on canvas. The only successful instantaneous glimpses of movement are those which approach this paradoxical arrangement—when, for example, a walking man is taken at the moment when both his feet are touching the ground; for then we almost have the temporal ubiquity of the body which brings it about that the man *bestrides* space. The picture makes movement visible by its internal discordance. Each member's position, precisely by virtue of its incompatibility with the others' (according to the body's logic), is otherwise dated or is not "in time" with the others; and since all of them remain visibly within the unity of a body, it is the body which comes to bestride time [*la durée*]. Its movement is something premeditated between legs, trunk, arms, and head in some virtual "control center," and it breaks forth only with a subsequent change of place. When a horse is photographed at that instant when he is completely off the ground, with his legs almost folded under him—an instant, therefore, when he must be moving— why does he look as if he were leaping in place? Then why do Géricault's horses really *run* on canvas, in a posture impossible for a real horse at the gallop? It is just that the horses in *Epsom Derby* bring me to see the body's grip upon the soil and that, according to a logic of body and world I know well, these "grips" upon space are also ways of taking hold of time [*la durée*]. Rodin said very wisely, "It is the artist who is truthful, while the photograph is mendacious; for, in reality,

51. Rodin, *L'art.* Interviews collected by Paul Gsell (Paris, 1911).

time never stops cold." [52] The photograph keeps open the instants which the onrush of time closes up forthwith; it destroys the overtaking, the overlapping, the "metamorphosis" [Rodin] of time. But this is what painting, in contrast, makes visible, because the horses have in them that "leaving here, going there," [53] because they have a foot in each instant. Painting searches not for the outside of movement but for its secret ciphers, of which there are some still more subtle than those of which Rodin spoke. All flesh, and even that of the world, radiates beyond itself. But whether or not one is, depending on the times and the "school," attached more to manifest movement or to the monumental, the art of painting is never altogether outside time, because it is always within the carnal [dans le charnel].

Now perhaps we have a better sense of what is meant by that little verb "to see." Vision is not a certain mode of thought or presence to self; it is the means given me for being absent from myself, for being present at the fission of Being from the inside—the fission at whose termination, and not before, I come back to myself.

Painters always knew this. Da Vinci [54] invoked a "pictorial science" which does not speak with words (and still less with numbers) but with oeuvres which exist in the visible just as natural things do and which nevertheless communicate through those things "to all the generations of the universe." This silent science, says Rilke (apropos of Rodin), brings into the oeuvre the forms of things "whose seal has not been broken"; [55] it comes from the eye and addresses itself to the eye. We must understand the eye as the "window of the soul." "The eye . . . through which the beauty of the universe is revealed to our contemplation is of such excellence that whoever should resign himself to losing it would deprive himself of the knowledge of all the works of nature, the sight of which makes the soul live happily in its body's prison, thanks to the eyes which show him the infinite variety of creation: whoever loses them abandons his soul in a dark prison where all hope of once more seeing the sun, the light of the universe, must vanish." The eye accomplishes the prodigious work of opening the soul to what is not soul—the joyous realm of things and their god, the sun.

A Cartesian can believe that the existing world is not visible, that the only light is that of the mind, and that all vision takes place in God. A painter cannot grant that our openness to the world is illusory or

52 Ibid., p. 86.
53. Michaux, op. cit.
54. Cited by Delaunay, op. cit., p. 175.
55. Rilke, Auguste Rodin, French translation by Maurice Betz (Paris, 1928), p. 150. [English translation by Jessie Lamont and Hans Trausil (New York, 1919; republished 1945).]

indirect, that what we see is not the world itself, or that the mind has to do only with its thoughts or with another mind. He accepts with all its difficulties the myth of the windows of the soul; it must be that what has no place is subjected to a body—even more, that what has no place be initiated *by* the body to all the others and to nature. We must take literally what vision teaches us: namely, that through it we come in contact with the sun and the stars, that we are everywhere all at once, and that even our power to imagine ourselves elsewhere—"I am in Petersburg in my bed, in Paris, my eyes see the sun"—or to intend [*viser*] real beings wherever they are, borrows from vision and employs means we owe to it. Vision alone makes us learn that beings that are different, "exterior," foreign to one another, are yet absolutely *together*, are "simultaneity"; this is a mystery psychologists handle the way a child handles explosives. Robert Delaunay says succinctly, "The railroad track is the image of succession which comes closest to the parallel: the parity of the rails." The rails converge and do not converge; they converge *in order to* remain equidistant down below. The world is in accordance with my perspective *in order to* be independent of me, is for me in *order to be* without me, and to be the world. The "visual quale" [56] gives me, and alone gives me, the presence of what is not me, of what *is* simply and fully. It does so because, like texture, it is the concretion of a universal visibility, of a unique space which separates and reunites, which sustains every cohesion (and even that of past and future, since there would be no such cohesion if they were not essentially relevant to the same space). Every visual something, as individual as it is, functions also as a dimension, because it gives itself as the result of a dehiscence of Being. What this ultimately means is that the proper essence [*le propre*] of the visible is to have a layer [*doublure*] of invisibility in the strict sense, which it makes present as a certain absence. "In their time, our bygone antipodes, the impressionists, were perfectly right in making their abode with the castaways and the undergrowth of daily life. As for us, our heart throbs to bring us closer to the depths. . . . These oddities will become . . . realities . . . because instead of being held to the diversely intense restoration of the visible, they will annex to it the proper share [*la part*] of the invisible, occultly apperceived." [57] There is that which reaches the eye directly [*de face*], the frontal properties of the visible; but there is also that which reaches it from below—the profound postural latency where the body raises itself to see—and that which reaches vision from above like the phenomena of flight, of swimming, of movement, where it participates no longer in the heaviness of origins but in free

56. Delaunay, *op. cit.*, pp. 115, 110.
57. Klee, *Conférence d'Iena* (1924), according to Grohmann, *op. cit.*, p. 365.

accomplishmఁnts.[58] Through it, then, the painter touches the two extremities. In the immemorial depth of the visible, something moved, caught fire, and engulfed his body; everything he paints is in answer to this incitement, and his hand is "nothing but the instrument of a distant will." Vision encounters, as at a crossroads, all the aspects of Being. "[A] certain fire pretends to be alive; it awakens. Working its way along the hand as conductor, it reaches the support and engulfs it; then a leaping spark closes the circle it was to trace, coming back to the eye, and beyond." [59]

There is no break at all in this circuit; it is impossible to say that nature ends here and that man or expression starts here. It is, therefore, mute Being which itself comes to show forth its own meaning. Herein lies the reason why the dilemma between figurative and nonfigurative art is badly posed; it is true and uncontradictory that no grape was ever what it is in the most figurative painting and that no painting, no matter how abstract, can get away from Being, that even Caravaggio's grape is the grape itself.[60] This precession of what is upon what one sees and makes seen, of what one sees and makes seen upon what is—this is vision itself. And to give the ontological formula of painting we hardly need to force the painter's own words, Klee's words written at the age of thirty-seven and ultimately inscribed on his tomb: "I cannot be caught in immanence." [61]

[5]

BECAUSE DEPTH, color, form, line, movement, contour, physiognomy are all branches of Being and because each one can sway all the rest, there are no separated, distinct "problems" in painting, no really opposed paths, no partial "solutions," no cumulative progress, no irretrievable options. There is nothing to prevent a painter from going back to one of the devices he has shied away from—making it, of course, speak differently. Rouault's contours are not those of Ingres. Light is the "old sultana," says Georges Limbour, "whose charms withered away at the beginning of this century." [62] Expelled first by the painters of materials [les peintres de le matière],

58. Klee, Wege des Naturstudiums (1923), as found in G. di San Lazzaro, Klee.
59. Klee, cited by Grohmann, op. cit., p. 99.
60. A. Berne-Joffroy, Le dossier Caravage (Paris, 1959), and Michel Butor, "La Corbeille de l'Ambrosienne," Nouvelle Revue Française, 1959, pp. 969–89.
61. Klee, Journal, op. cit. ["Je suis insaissable dans l'immanence."]
62. G. Limbour, Tableau bon levain à vous de cuire la pâte: l'art brut de Jean Dubuffet (Paris, 1953), pp. 54–55.

it reappears finally in Dubuffet as a certain texture of matter. One is never immune to this kind of turning back or to the least expected convergences; some of Rodin's fragments are almost statues by Germain Richier *because they were both sculptors*—that is to say, enmeshed in a single, identical network of Being. For the same reason nothing is ever finally acquired and possessed for good.

In "working over" a favorite problem, even if it is just the problem of velvet or wool, the true painter unknowingly upsets the givens of all the other problems. His quest is total even where it looks partial. Just when he has reached proficiency in some area, he finds that he has reopened another one where everything he said before must be said again in a different way. The upshot is that what he has found he does not yet have. It remains to be sought out; the discovery itself calls forth still further quests. The idea of a universal painting, of a totalization of painting, of a fully and definitively achieved painting is an idea bereft of sense. For painters the world will always be yet to be painted, even if it lasts millions of years . . . it will end without having been conquered in painting.

Panofsky shows that the "problems" of painting which magnetize its history are often solved obliquely, not in the course of inquiries instigated to solve them but, on the contrary, at some point when the painters, having reached an impasse, apparently forget those problems and permit themselves to be attracted by other things. Then suddenly, altogether off guard, they turn up the old problems and surmount the obstacle. This unhearing [*sourde*] historicity, advancing through the labyrinth by detours, transgression, slow encroachments and sudden drives, does not imply that the painter does not know what he wants. It does imply that what he wants is beyond the means and goals at hand and commands from afar all our *useful* activity.

We are so fascinated by the classical idea of intellectual adequation that painting's mute "thinking" sometimes leaves us with the impression of a vain swirl of significations, a paralyzed or miscarried utterance. Suppose, then, that one answers that no thought ever detaches itself completely from a sustaining support; that the only privilege of speaking-thought is to have rendered its own support manageable; that the figurations of literature and philosophy are no more settled than those of painting and are no more capable of being accumulated into a stable treasure; that even science learns to recognize a zone of the "fundamental," peopled with dense, open, rent [*déchirés*] beings of which an exhaustive treatment is out of the question—like the cyberneticians' "aesthetic information" or mathematical-physical "groups of operations"; that, in the end, we are never in a position to take stock of everything objectively or to think of progress in itself; and that the whole of human history is, in a certain sense, stationary. *What,* says the understanding, like [Stendhal's] Lamiel, *is it only that?*

Is this the highest point of reason, to realize that the soil beneath our feet is shifting, to pompously name "interrogation" what is only a persistent state of stupor, to call "research" or "quest" what is only trudging in a circle, to call "Being" that which never fully *is*?

But this disappointment issues from that spurious fantasy [63] which claims for itself a positivity capable of making up for its own emptiness. It is the regret of not being everything, and a rather groundless regret at that. For if we cannot establish a hierarchy of civilizations or speak of progress—neither in painting nor in anything else that matters—it is not because some fate holds us back; it is, rather, because the very first painting in some sense went to the farthest reach of the future. If no painting comes to be *the* painting, if no work is ever absolutely completed and done with, still each creation changes, alters, enlightens, deepens, confirms, exalts, re-creates, or creates in advance all the others. If creations are not a possession, it is not only that, like all things, they pass away; it is also that they have almost all their life still before them.

Le Tholonet, July–August 1960

63. "Mais cette deception est celle du faux imaginaire, qui . . ."

PART III

Philosophy of History and Politics

6 / The Crisis of the Understanding[1]

Translated by Nancy Metzel and John Flodstrom

MAX WEBER's notions of freedom and of truth are both very exacting and very vague. But he was aware that they occur only in certain cultures, by means of certain historical choices which are never completely realized. They do not fully assimilate the confused world out of which they have arisen. They are thus not of divine right and have no other justification than that which they effectively bring to man, no other titles than those which are acquired in a struggle in which they are in principle at a disadvantage, since they cannot subsist without struggle; before they can arise it is equally essential that they legitimatize their adversaries and confront them. Because he remains faithful to the spirit of search and of knowledge, Weber is a liberal. His liberalism is completely new because he admits that truth always leaves a margin of doubt, that it does not exhaust the reality of the past and still less that of the present, and that history is the natural seat of violence. It does not ingenuously consider itself to be the law of things, as did previous liberalisms; it perseveres in becoming such a law through a history in which it is not predestined.

In the first place, Weber believes that he is able to juxtapose the order of truth and that of violence. We know history in the same way that Kant says we know nature; the historian's understanding, like the physicist's, forms an "objective" truth to the degree that it is constructed. The objective element is only one aspect of a coherent representation which can be idefinitely corrected and made more precise but never merges with the thing in itself. The historian cannot look at the past without finding a meaning, without contrasting the important and the subordinate, the essential and the accidental, plans and accomplishments, preparations and declines. These vectors which are traced

1. "La crise de l'entendement," *Les aventures de la dialectique* (Paris, 1955), pp. 15–42.

through the dense whole of facts have already distorted the original reality in which everything is equally real. We have imposed our own interests upon it. The historian's invasion of history cannot be avoided, but care must be taken to guarantee that the historical understanding, like the Kantian subject, works according to certain rules which assure intersubjective value to its representation of the past. The meanings— or, as Weber calls them, the ideal types—that the historian introduces into the facts must not be taken as keys to history. They are only precise guideposts for appreciating the divergence between what we think and what has been, and for bringing into the open what has been left out of our interpretation. Each perspective is there only in order to prepare for others. It is well founded only if we understand that it is partial and that the real is still beyond it. Knowledge is never categorical; it is always conditional. We can never be the past; it is only a spectacle before us, which is there for us to question. The questions come from us, and thus the responses in principle do not exhaust historical reality, since historical reality does not depend upon them for its existence.

On the contrary, the present is us; it awaits our consent or our refusal. Suspension of judgment, which is obligatory with respect to the past, is here impossible. To wait for things to take shape before deciding is to decide to let them happen in their own manner. The proximity of the present, which is what makes us responsible for it, nevertheless does not give us access to the thing itself. In fact, because of lack of distance we can see only one side of it. Knowledge and practice confront the same infinitely complex historical reality, but they respond to it in two opposed fashions: knowledge by multiplying views through provisional, open, motivated (that is to say, conditional) conclusions; practice through absolute, partial, unjustifiable decisions.

But how can we abide by this dualism of the past and of the present? It is evidently not absolute. I will tomorrow have to construct an image of that which I now see. I cannot pretend not to know it when I see it. The past which I contemplate has been lived. From the moment when I first desire to study its origins, I cannot deny that it has been a present. Because of the fact that the order of knowledge is not the only order, because it is not enclosed in itself, and because it contains at least the gaping chasm of the present, the whole of history is still action and action already history. History is the same whether we contemplate it as a spectacle or assume it as a responsibility. The condition of the historian is not very different from that of the acting man. He puts himself in the place of those whose actions have been decisive, reconstitutes the horizon of their decision, and redoes what they have done (with this difference: he knows the context better than they, and he is already aware of the consequences). Not that history consists in penetrating the states of mind of great men. Even the search for motives, says Weber, involves ideal types. It is not a question of coinciding with what has been lived but rather of deciphering the total meaning of what has been done. In order to understand an action, its horizon must be restored—not merely the perspective of the actor but also the "objective" context.

History could thus be said to be imaginative action or even the spectacle that one has of an action. Conversely, action consults history, which teaches us, says Weber, not indeed what must be willed but the true meaning of our volitions. Knowledge and action are two poles of a single existence. Our relationship to history is not merely a relation of understanding, that of spectacle and spectator. We would not be spectators if we were not involved in the past. Action would not be serious if it did not bring some sort of finality to the whole enterprise of the past, if it did not give the drama its last act. History is a strange object, an object which is ourselves. Our irreplaceable life, our fierce liberty find themselves already prefigured, already implicated, already played out in other freedoms which today are past. Weber is obliged to go beyond the regime of the double truth, the dualism of the objective understanding and moral feeling, and look beyond the formula of this singular situation.

He has nowhere given this formula. His methodological writings postdate his scientific practice. It is for us to discover in his work as historian how he accommodates himself to this object, which centers around individual subjects, and how he forges a method out of this difficulty. By going beyond the past considered as spectacle, he attempts to comprehend the past itself by making it enter our own lives. We cannot be content with the past as we ourselves have seen it. The very attempt to discover the past as it actually was always implies a spectator, and there is a danger that we will discover the past only as it is for us.

Perhaps it is of the nature of history to be undefined in the present, and to become completely real only when it has once been given as a spectacle to a posterity which passes judgment upon it. Is it perhaps the case that only successive generations (*"generations appelantes,"* as Péguy called them) are in the position to see whether that which has been brought about really deserved to be, to correct the deceptions of recorded history, and to reinstate other possibilities? Is our image of the past preceded only by sequences of events which form neither a system nor even perspectives and whose truth is in abeyance? Is it perhaps the definition of history to exist completely only through that which comes after, to be in this sense suspended into the future? If this is true, the intervention of the historian is not a defect in historical knowledge. That facts interest the historian, that they speak to a man of culture, that they can be recaptured in the intentions of the historical subject threaten historical knowledge with subjectivity. But they also promise it a superior objectivity, if only one can successfully distinguish that which belongs to reason from that which is arbritrary, and determine the close relationships which our "metamorphoses" violate but without which they would be impossible.

Let us now attempt to understand the relationship between Protestantism and the capitalistic spirit. The historian begins by abstracting these two historical types. Weber does not consider speculation, or venture capitalism, which depends upon power politics. He takes as his object an economic system within which one can expect continuous returns from a durable and profitable enterprise—a system which involves a minimum of accountancy and organization, encourages free labor, and tends toward a regular market. In the same way he limits his discussion of the Protestant ethic to the Calvinism of the sixteenth and seventeenth centuries, considered more as it was generally interpreted than as it was originated by Calvin. These facts are chosen as interesting and historically important because they reveal a certain logical structure which is the key to another series of facts. How does the historian know this when he begins? Strictly speaking, he doesn't know. He foresees certain results that are indicated by his analysis. This analysis is justified to the extent that it renders readable those facts which are not contributed by the initial definitions. However, it is not certain that they designate essences. They were not developed by the next genus and specific difference and do not follow, as geometric definitions do, the genesis of an ideal being. They give only, as Weber says, a "provisional illustration" of the point of view chosen, and the historian chooses this point of view in the same way that you remember the word of an author or someone's gesture: when you first approach the work you become aware of a certain style.

It was one of Franklin's works that led Weber to his first view of the relationship between Calvinism and capitalism. Dating from the age of the maturity of Puritanism and preceding the adult age of capitalism, Franklin represented the transition from one to the other. His famous words are striking and illuminating because they express an ethic of labor: It is a duty to augment your capital and to increase it without enjoying that which you have gained. Production and accumulation are in themselves holy. You miss the essential point if you believe that Franklin attempts here to disguise interest as virtue. On the contrary, he goes so far as to say that God uses interest to lead him to the faith. If he writes that time is money, it is because he has learned from the Puritan tradition that spiritually time is precious and that we are in the world to give evidence at each moment of the glory of God. The useful could only become a value after it had been sanctified. What inspired the pioneers of capitalism was not the philosophy of the enlightenment and immanence, the joy of life that will come later. The "righteous, strict, and formalistic" character that brought them success can only be understood in terms of their feeling for the temporal calling and the economic ethic of Puritanism. Many of these elements of capitalism have existed here and there throughout history, but if it is only in Western Europe that you find the rational capitalistic enterprise in the sense that Weber defines it, this is perhaps because no other civilization has a theology which sanctifies temporal labor, demands a disciplined conduct of life, and joins the glory of God to the transformation of nature. Franklin's work presents us with a vital choice in its pure state, a mode of *Lebensführung* which relates Puritanism to the capitalistic spirit, defines Calvinism as disciplined conduct of life and capitalism as rationalization; finally, if the initial intuition is confirmed it discovers an intelligible transition from one to the other. If, in extending the ethic of labor back to its Calvinistic origins and toward its capitalistic consequences, Weber succeeds in understanding the basic structure of the facts, it is because he has discovered an objective meaning in them. It is because he has pierced the appearances in which reason is enclosed and gone beyond provisional and partial perspectives to reestablish the anonymous intention, the dialectic of a whole.

Going back from the disciplined conduct of life to its premises, Weber finds in Calvinism the feeling of an infinite distance between God and his creatures. In themselves they merit only eternal death; they can do nothing and are worth nothing and have no control over their destiny. God decides their election or their dereliction. They do not even know what they truly are. Alone on the other side of things, only God knows if they are to be saved or damned. The Calvinistic consciousness oscillates between culpability and vindication, both of which are equally unmerited, between an anguish without limits and a security without conditions. Both other people and the world have this same relation to God. Because of this infinite distance no third party can intervene in the relationship. The ties which man has with others and with the world are of a different order than those which he has with God. He cannot expect, on the whole, any succor from a church where the sinners are as numerous as the righteous or any aid from sermons and sacraments which will do nothing to alter the *decretum horrible*. The church is not a place where man will find another natural life. It is an institution created by will and attached to predetermined ends. For the Catholic it is as if a running account is open to him, and it is not until the end of his life that the balance is made of what he has and what he owes. The solitude of the Calvinist signifies that he confronts the absolute continually and that he does so futilely because he knows nothing of his destiny. At each moment the whole question of his salvation or damnation is posed and remains unanswered. There is no gain in Christian life; it can never be self-sufficient. "The glory of God and personal salvation remain always above the threshold of consciousness." [2]

Summoned to break the vital alliance that we have with time, with others, and with the world, the Calvinist pushes to its limits a demystification that is also a depoetization or a disenchantment [*Entzauberung*]. The sacraments, the church as the place of salvation, human feelings which always would sanctify creatures are rejected as magic. This absolute anguish finds no relaxation in brotherly relations with created things. The created is the material upon which one works. It is to be transformed and organized to manifest the glory of God. The conscious control which is useless for salvation draws man into a temporal enterprise that takes on the value of a duty. Plans, methods, balance sheets are useless from God's point of view, since from that side everything is done and we can know nothing. All that is left to us is to put the world in order, to change the natural aspect and to rationalize life. This is the only means that we have to bring God's reign to earth. Salvation will not result from any of our acts. But the same anguish which we feel before that which we do not control, the same energy that we would expend to implement our salvation, even though we cannot do so, is expended in a temporal enterprise which is under our control. This temporal enterprise becomes even in Puritanism a presumption of salvation. The terror of man in the face of a supernatural destiny over which he has no control weighs heavily upon every one of the Puritan's activities in the world. By an apparent paradox, because he wishes to respect the infinite distance between God and man, he endows the useful and even the comfortable with a dignity and a religious meaning. He discredits leisure and even poverty in order to bring the rigors of asceticism into worldly use. In the Calvinist's estimation the goods of the world are precipitated by, and survive in relationship to, being and the absolute.

Let us now return from the consideration of the Calvinist ethic to the spirit of capitalism. Weber cites one of Wesley's phrases that marks this transition: "Religion necessarily produces the spirit of industry and frugality, and these cannot but produce riches. But as wealth

2. Max Weber, *Die Protestantische Ethik und der Geist des Kapitalismus* (Tübingen, 1934), p. 37.

increases so will pride, passion, and the love of worldly things. So although the form of religion remains, the spirit gradually declines." Franklin's generation left to its successors the possibility of becoming rich in good conscience. But they will forget the motive and concentrate on gaining the best of this world and the next. Once crystallized in the world by the Protestant ethic, capitalism will develop according to its own logic. Weber does not believe that it is sustained by the motive that brought it into existence or that it is the truth of Calvinism.

> The capitalistic economy is currently an immense cosmos into which individuals are born. It is for them, in so far as they are individuals, given as an actual, unalterable order within which they have to live. It imposes upon them, in so far as they are involved in market relationships, the norms of their economic behavior. Today's capitalism, newly come to the domination of economic life, trains and produces through economic selection the economic subjects that it needs, whether they be entrepreneurs or laborers. However, it is at this point that we begin to understand the limits of the concept of selection in the explanation of historical facts. In order that the type of behavior [*Lebensführung*] could be chosen with respect to the calling suitable for capitalism, it had not only to exist in several individuals but it must have appeared as a manner of life common to human groups. It is this appearance that needs to be explained.[3]

There are thus a religious efficacy and an economic efficacy. Weber describes them as interwoven, exchanging positions so that first one and then the other plays the role of tutor. The effect turns back on its cause, carrying and transforming it in its turn. Furthermore, Weber does not simply integrate spiritual motives and material causes. He renews the concept of historical matter. An economic system is, as he says, a cosmos, a human choice become a situation. It is because of this that he can examine the disciplined conduct of life in terms of its religious motives and the descent of its capitalistic downfall as they are all connected in a single fabric. History has a meaning, but there is no pure development of the idea. Its meaning comes into contact with contingency at the moment when human initiative founds a system of life in taking up again the various givens. And the historical understanding which reveals an interior to history still leaves us in the presence of empirical history, with its depth and its chances which it does not subordinate to any hidden reason. Such is the philosophy without dogmatism which one observes all through Weber's studies. To go beyond this we must interpret freely. Let us do this without imputing to Weber more than he would have wished to say.

These intelligible nuclei of history are typical ways of treating natural being, of responding to others and to death. They appear at the

3. *Ibid.,* p. 37.

point where men and the givens of nature or of the past meet, arising as symbolic matrices which have no preexistence and which can, for a longer or shorter time, influence history itself and then disappear, not by external forces but through an internal disintegration or because one of their secondary elements becomes predominant and changes their nature. The "rationalization" by which Weber defines capitalism is a fecund scheme of the kind that can also be used to explain art, science, the organization of the state, mysticism, or Western economy. It emerges here and there in history and, like historical types, is borne out only through the encounter of these givens, when, each confirming the other, they organize themselves into a system. For Weber capitalism presupposes a certain technology of production and therefore presupposes science in the Western sense. But it also presupposes a certain type of law, a government based upon formal rules, without which adventurous and speculative capitalism is possible but not the bourgeois enterprise. To these conditions Weber adds a "rational conduct of life," which has been the historical contribution of Protestantism. Law, science, technology, and Western religion are prime examples of this "rationalizing" tendency. But only after the fact. Each of these elements acquires its historical meaning only through its encounter with the others. History has often produced one of them in isolation (Roman law, the fundamental principles of calculus in India), without its being developed to the degree that it would have to be in capitalism. The encounter of these givens establishes the rationality which each possesses in outline form. To the degree that interactions accumulate, the development of the system in its own sense becomes more and more probable. Capitalistic production pushes more and more in the direction of the development of technology and the applied sciences. At the start it is not an all-powerful idea; it is a sort of historical imagination which sows here and there elements capable of one day being integrated. The meaning of a system in its beginnings is like the pictorial meaning of a painting which directs the painter's movements less than it is a result of them and progresses with them. Or again, it can be compared to the meaning of a spoken language, which is not transmitted in conceptual terms in the minds of those who speak, or in some ideal model of language, but which is, rather, the focal point of a series of verbal operations which converge almost by chance. Historians come to talk of "rationalism" or "capitalism" when the affinity of these products of the historical imagination becomes clear. But history does not work according to a model; it is in fact the very advent of meaning. To say that there has been an affinity between the elements of rationality before they crystallize into a system is only a manner of saying that, taken up and developed by human intentions, they ought to confirm one another and form a whole. Just as before the coming of the bourgeois enterprise, the elements which it joins did not belong to the same world, each must be said to be drawn by the others to develop a meaning which is common to them all, but which no one of them embodies.

The disciplined conduct of life whose principles have been established by Calvinism is finished by capitalism, but finished in both senses of the word. It is realized because it is, even more so than capitalism, activity in the world; it is destroyed as rigorous code because capitalism strives to eliminate its own transcendent motives. There is, Weber says, an elective affinity between the elements of an historical totality:

> Given the prodigious interweaving of the reciprocal influences among the material foundations, the forms of social and political organization, and the spiritual content of the cultural age of the Reformation, we must first of all try to discover whether and to what point certain elective affinities [*Wahlverwandtschaften*] can be recognized between such a form of religious belief and the ethic of a calling. We will also clarify, in so far as this can be done, the modalities and the general direction of the influence which the religious movement, by reason of these elective affinities, exercised upon the material culture. Only when this is sufficiently clarified can we attempt to determine to what extent the contents of modern culture can be imputed, in their historical development, to religious motives and to what extent to others.[4]

This relation is supple and reversible. If Protestant morality and capitalism are two institutional ways of stating the relationship of man to man, there is no reason why Protestant morality should not in such a case support the incipient capitalism. Nor is there anything to prevent capitalism from perpetuating certain typically Protestant modes of behavior in history, or even from displacing it as the driving force of history and substituting itself for it, allowing certain motives to perish and asserting others as its exclusive theme. The ambiguity of historical facts, their *Vielseitigkeit*, the plurality of their aspects, far from condemning historical knowledge to the realm of the provisional (as Weber said at first), is the very thing that agglomerates the dust of facts, which allows us to read in a religious fact the first draft of an economic system, or in an economic system a position taken with regard to the Absolute. Religion, law, and economy make up one single history because any fact in any one of the three orders arises, in a sense, from the two others. This is so because they are all bound up in the unique fiber of human choices.

This is a difficult position to hold and one which is threatened on

4. *Ibid.*, p. 83.

both sides. Since Weber tries to preserve the individuality of the past while still situating it in a developmental process, perhaps even in a hierarchy, he will be reproached at times for concluding too little and at times for presuming too much. Does he not leave us without the means to criticize the past? Does he not give the same degree of reality and the same value to all civilizations, because the system of real and imaginary means by which man has managed his relations with the world and with other men has always managed to function, somehow or other? If we wish to go so far as to try to understand the past even in its phantasms, are we not inevitably led to justify it and thereby rendered unable to judge it? On the other hand, when Weber presents us with a logic of history, the objection can always be made that, as Malraux has shown, the decision to investigate and understand all civilizations is a deed which belongs to a civilization which is different from them, which transforms them. It transforms the crucifix into a work of art. That which had been a means of capturing the holy becomes an object of knowledge.

One final objection can be made. Historical consciousness is caught in this indefensible paradox: fragments of human life, each of which had been lived as absolute and which are in principle concealed to the disinterested onlooker, are brought together in the imagination in a single act of attention, compared, and considered as moments in a single developmental process. We must choose, then, between a history which judges, situates, and organizes—at the risk of finding in the past only a reflection of the troubles and problems of the present—and an indifferent, agnostic history which strings civilizations together as individuals which cannot be compared.

Weber is not oblivious of these difficulties; indeed it is they which have set his thought in action. The path which he seeks lies between history considered as a succession of unique facts and the arrogance of a philosophy which lays claim to have grasped the past in its categories and reduces it to our thoughts about it. He is opposed to both of them because of our interest in the past; it is ours and we are its. The dramas which have been lived inevitably remind us of our own and of us; we must view them from a single perspective, either because our own acts present us with the same problems in a clearer manner or, on the contrary, because our own difficulties have been more accurately defined in the past. We have just as much right to judge the past as the present. Moreover, it precedes the judgments we pass upon it. It has judged itself; having been lived by men, it has introduced values into history, and we cannot describe it without confirming or weakening their historical status. In most past mystifications those involved were to a certain extent aware of the deception. To be "objective" we are asked only to approach the past with its appropriate criteria. Weber reconciles evaluative history with objective history by calling upon the past to testify concerning itself. It is through Wesley that he can disclose the moment at which religion becomes mystification. An ideology which is a mystification is never completely ignorant of the fact. It requires a great deal of complaisance to justify the capitalistic world by means of Calvinistic principles; if these principles are fully articulated they will expose the ruse of attempting to turn them to one's own purposes. The men of the past could not completely hide the truth of their era from themselves; they did not need us in order to catch a glimpse of it. It is there, ready to appear; we have only to make a sign to reveal it.

Thus the very attempt to understand the past completely presupposes that we have already ordered the facts, placed them in a hierarchy, in a progression or a regression. In so doing we recapture the very movement of the past. It is true that the *Kulturmensch* is a modern type. History appears as a spectacle only to those who have a personal interest in all the various solutions which have been put at their disposal. History thus stands in contrast to both the narrow and the profound passions which it considers. Truth, says Weber, "is that which *seeks* to be recognized by all those who *seek* the truth." [5]

The decision to question each time a fundamental choice that is diffused in his thoughts, his desires, and his actions and of which he has never made an accounting is the result of living in a time that has tasted of the tree of knowledge. Scientific history is in principle opposed to naïve history—which it would, however, like to recapture. It is presupposed in that which it reconstructs. But this is not a vicious circle; it is the postulate of all historical thought. And Weber steps in conscientiously at this point. As Karl Löwith has shown, Weber is aware that scientific history is itself a product of history, a moment of the "rationalization," a moment of the history of capitalism. [6]

This same history turns back upon itself, presuming that clarification is possible. This presumption cannot be demonstrated. It is justified only in so far as it can give us a coherent image of the universal history of culture. Nothing guarantees in advance that the attempt will be successful, but it is sufficient to know that to choose any other hypothesis is to choose chaos and that the truth which is sought is not, in principle, beyond our grasp. Of that we are certain. We discover that we possess the power of a radical choice by which we give meaning to our lives, and through this power we become sensitive to all the uses

5. *Gesammelte Aufsätze zur Wissenschaftslehre* (Tübingen, 1922), p. 184.
6. "Max Weber und Karl Marx," *Archiv für Sozialwissenschaft und Sozialpolitik,* LVII (1932).

that humanity has made of it. Through it other cultures are opened up to us and made understandable. What we assume in order to understand history is that freedom understands the uses of freedom. What we contribute ourselves is only the prejudice of not having any prejudices, the fact that we belong to a cultural order where our choices, even those which are opposed to each other, tend to be complementary. "Culture is a closed segment abstracted from the infinity of events which is endowed with meaning and signification only for man. The transcendental condition of all cultural science is not that we find this or that culture valuable but the fact that we are 'cultural men,' endowed with the capacity consciously to take a position with regard to the world and to give meaning to it. Whatever this meaning might be, its consequence is that in living we abstract certain phenomena of human coexistence and in order to judge them we take a position (positive or negative) with regard to their significance." [7]

Historical understanding thus does not introduce a system of categories arbitrarily chosen; it only presupposes the possibility that we have a past which is ours and that we can recapture in our freedom the work of so many other freedoms. It assumes that we can clarify the choices of others through our own and ours through theirs, that we adjust one by the other and finally arrive at the truth.

There is no greater respect, no more profound objectivity than this claim of going to the very source of history. History is not an external god, a hidden reason of which we need only record our conclusions. It is the metaphysical fact that the same life, our own, is played out both within us and outside us, in our present and in our past, and that the world is a system to which we have various accesses or, if you prefer, various likenesses.

Because this type of economy, this type of knowledge, law, and religion depend upon the same fundamental choice and are historical accomplices, we can assume, the circumstances permitting, that the facts will arrange themselves, that the development can interpret the logic of an initial choice, and that history can become an experience of mankind. Even if the Calvinistic choice has transcendent motives which capitalism ignores, we can still say that in tolerating certain ambiguities it takes responsibility for what follows, and thus we can treat this sequence as a logical development. The Calvinist confronts and juxtaposes the finite and the infinite, carries to the extreme the consciousness that we have of not being the source of our own being, and organizes the obsession with the other world, at the same time closing the routes of access to it. In so doing he paves the way for the fanaticism of the bourgeois enterprise, authorizes the ethic of labor, and

7. *Gesammelte Aufsätze zur Wissenschaftslehre,* pp. 180–81.

eliminates the consideration of the transcendent. Thus the course of history clarifies the errors and the contradictions of the fundamental choice, and the historical failure proves counter to Calvinism. In the factual sciences there is no proof by absurdity or crucial experiment. We know that certain solutions are impossible. We do not gain an enveloping understanding from the working operations of history which would reveal a true situation. At best we rectify errors which occur along the way, but the new aim is not immune to errors which will have to be rectified anew. History eliminates the irrational; but the rational continues to be imagined and to be created, and it has not the power of replacing the false with the true.

One historical solution of the human problem, one end of history could be conceived only if humanity were a thing to be known—if in it knowledge were able to exhaust being and could come to a state that really contained all that it had been and all that it could ever be. Whereas, on the contrary, in the depth of social reality each decision brings unexpected consequences, and man responds to these surprises by inventions which transform the problem. There is no situation without hope, but there is no choice which terminates the deviations or which can extenuate its inventive power and exhaust its history. There are only advances. The capitalistic rationalization is one of them, since it is the resolution of taking our given condition in hand through knowledge and action. It can be demonstrated that the appropriation of the world by man, that demystification, is better because it faces difficulties that other historical regimes have avoided. But this progress is bought by regressions, and there is no guarantee that the progressive elements of history will be disengaged from experience and be added up later. Demystification is also de-poetization and disenchantment. We must keep the capitalistic refusal of the sacred as external but renew in it the demands of the absolute that it has abolished. We have no grounds for affirming that this recovery will be made.

Capitalism is a shell that the religious animal has secreted for his domicile, and it survives him. "No one knows yet who will inhabit this shell in the future: whether at the end of its prodigious development there will be new prophets or a vigorous renaissance of all thoughts and ideals or whether finally, if none of this occurs, mechanism will produce only petrification [*Versteinerung*] hidden under a kind of anxious importance. According to this hypothesis, the prediction will become a reality for the last men of this particular development of culture. Specialists without spirit, libertines without heart, this nothingness imagines itself to be elevated to a level of humanity never before attained." [8] If the system comes to life again, it will be through

8. *Ibid.,* p. 204.

the intervention of new prophets or by a resurrection of past culture, by an invention or reinvention which does not come from anything in that system. Perhaps history will eliminate, together with false solutions to the human problem, certain valid acquisitions as well. It will not locate its errors precisely in a total system. It does not accumulate truths; it works on a question that is confusedly posed and is not sheltered from regressions and setbacks. Projects change so much in the course of things that the generations of men who make the accounting are not those who have had the experience. What the facts have taught them has not been passed on.

Weber's phenomenology is thus not systematic like Hegel's. It does not lead to an absolute knowledge. Man's freedom and the contingency of history exclude definitively "the idea that the end of the cultural sciences, even though remote, is to construct a closed system of concepts in which reality will be confined according to a definitive order and from which it can be deduced. The course of unforeseeable events is transformed endlessly, stretching to eternity. The problems that move men are constantly posed anew and from other aspects. That which becomes meaningful and significant in the infinite flow of the individual constantly changes the field and it becomes a historical concept, just as the relations of thought are variable under which it is considered and posited as an object of science. The principles of the cultural sciences will keep changing in a future without limits as long as a sclerosis of life and of spirit does not disaccustom humanity, as in China, to posing new questions to an inexhaustible life. A system of the cultural sciences, even if confined to an area which is systematic and objectively valid for questions and for the domains which these questions are called upon to treat, will be nonsense in itself. An attempt of this type could only reassemble pell-mell the multiple, specific, heterogeneous, disparate points of view under which reality is presented to us each time as 'culture,' i.e., each time it is made significant in its specificity." [9]

The intelligible wholes of history never cease to confront contingency, and the movement by which history turns back on itself to attempt to grasp itself, to dominate itself, to justify itself, is also without guarantee. History admits of dialectical facts of adumbrative significations. It is not a coherent system. Like a distracted interlocutor it allows the debate to become sidetracked; it forgets the data of the problem along the way. Historical epochs become ordered around a question of human possibilities rather than around an immanent solution of which history will be the result.

Because its aim is to recover the fundamental choices of the past,

9. *Ibid.,* p. 185.

science is, for Weber, a methodical extension of the experience of the present. But have this experience and its practical options benefited from historical understanding? For only if they have would Weber have reconciled theory and practice.

Weber is not a revolutionary. It is true that he writes that Marxism is "the most important instance of the construction of ideal types" and that all those who have employed its concepts know how fruitful they are—on the condition that they take as *meanings* what Marx describes as *forces*. But for him this transposition is incompatible with both Marxist theory and practice. As historical materialism, Marxism is a causal explanation through economics; and in its revolutionary practices Weber never sees the fundamental choice of the proletariat appear. It thus happens that, as has been said, this great mind judges the revolutionary movements which he witnessed in Germany after 1918 as if he were a provincial, bourgeois German. The Munich riot had placed at the head of the revolutionary government the most moralistic of his students. ("God, in his wrath, has made him a politician," Weber will say while defending him before the tribunal at the time of the repression.) [10] Weber confines himself to these minor facts and does not see a new historical significance in the revolutions after 1917. He is against the revolution because he does not consider it to be a revolution—that is to say, the creation of a historical whole. He describes it as essentially a military dictatorship and for the rest, a carnival of intellectuals dressed up as politicians.

Weber is a liberal. But as we said at the beginning, his is a different kind of liberalism from those which preceded him. Raymond Aron writes that his politics is, like that of Alain, a "politics of the understanding." Only, from Alain to Weber the understanding has learned to doubt itself. Alain recommends a policy which is not quite adequate: do each day that which is just and don't worry about the consequences. However, this maxim is inoperative every time we approach a critical situation, and understanding is then against his principles, sometimes revolutionary, sometimes submissive. Weber himself well knows that it functions easily only within certain critical limits, and he consciously gives himself the task of keeping history within the region where it is free from antinomies. He does not make an isolated instance of it. Since we cannot even be sure that the history within which we find ourselves is in the end rational, those who choose truth and freedom cannot find those who make other choices guilty of absurdity, nor can they even flatter themselves of having "gone beyond" them. "It is the destiny of a cultural epoch which has tasted of the tree of knowledge to know that we cannot decipher the meaning of world

10. Marianne Weber, *Max Weber, ein Lebensbild* (Tübingen, 1926).

events, regardless of how completely we might study them. We ought, rather, to be in the condition to create it ourselves and to know that world-views can never be the product of factual knowledge. Thus the highest ideals, those which move us most powerfully, can only become valid by being opposed to the ideals of other men, which are as sacred to them as ours are to us." [11]

Weber's liberalism does not demand a political utopia. It does not consider the formal universe of democracy to be an absolute. He admits that all politics is violence—even, in its own fashion, democratic politics. His liberalism is militant, suffering, heroic. He recognizes the rights of his adversaries, refuses to hate them, does not try to avoid confronting them, and in order to refute them relies only upon their own contradictions and upon the discussions which expose them. Though he rejects nationalism, Communism, and pacifism, he does not want to outlaw them; he does not cease trying to understand them. He who under the Empire decided against submarine warfare and in favor of a white peace declared himself jointly responsible with the patriot who would kill the first Pole who entered Danzig. He opposed the pacifist left, which made Germany alone responsible for the war and exonerated in advance the foreign occupation, because he thought that these abuses of self-accusation paved the way for a violent nationalism in the future. Still, he testified in favor of the students who were involved in pacifist propaganda. Though he did not believe in the revolution, he made public his esteem for Liebknecht and Rosa Luxemburg.

Weber is against political discrimination within the university. Perhaps, he says, anarchist opinions might allow a scholar to see an aspect of history of which he would not have become aware had it not been for them. Though he scrupulously left out of his teaching anything which might have favored some cause or have exhibited his personal beliefs, he is in favor of professors who become engaged in politics. However, they should do this outside the classroom—in essays which are open to discussion and in public gatherings where the adversary can respond. The academic soliloquy should not be fraudulently used for the purposes of propaganda. . . . Thus he holds both ends of the chain. He thereby makes truth work together with decision, knowledge with struggle. In this way he makes sure that freedom should never be made the point of honor of a repression.[12]

Is this better than a compromise? Has he succeeded in uniting, except in his own person, the meanings of force and of freedom? When he wished to found a political party upon these bases, Weber was so

11. *Gesammelte Aufsätze zur Wissenschaftslehre*, p. 154.
12. On all these points see Marianne Weber, *op. cit.*

easily eliminated and he returned so quickly to his studies that it was thought he did not adhere to it too strongly. It was thought that he felt there was an insurmountable obstacle in it and that a party which did not play according to the rules of the game would be a utopia. Nevertheless this failure is perhaps only Weber's. Perhaps it leaves intact the political wisdom which he sketched out at least once, even if he did not know how to put it into practice. For he does not content himself with setting values and efficacity, feeling and responsibility in opposition to one another. He makes an attempt to show what must be done to get beyond these alternatives. The taste for violence, he says, is a hidden weakness; the ostentation of virtuous feelings is a secret violence. These are two sorts of histrionics or neurosis, and there is a *force*, that of true politics, which is beyond these.

His secret is to not try to form an image of himself and of his life. Because he has set himself and success at a distance, he does not become complacent in his intentions; he does not accept the judgment of others without recourse. Because his action is a "work," a devotedness to a "thing" [*Sache*] which grows outside him, it has a rallying power of the sort which is always lacking in undertakings which are done out of vanity. "Lack of distance" from oneself, from things, and from others is the professional disease of academic and intellectual circles. For them action is only a flight from oneself, a decadent mode of self-love. On the contrary, having once and for all decided to "bear the irrationality of the world," the politician is patient or intractable when he must be—that is to say, when he has compromised as much as he will allow himself and when the very sense of what he is doing is involved. Precisely because he is not a man of the ethics of the heart, when he says no to others and to things, even this is an action, and it is this which shows the inadequacy of the sterile promises of the politics of the heart. "When today, in the agitation of a time which we believe to be productive although agitation is not always a true passion, suddenly we see politics of the heart appearing everywhere, its advocates proclaiming, 'It is the world that is stupid and common, not I; I refuse the responsibility for the consequences'—then I often point out that there must be a degree of interior equilibrium that lies behind this ethics of the heart. I have the impression that in nine cases out of ten they are braggarts who do not really feel the seriousness of their action and who are intoxicated by romantic sentiments. This does not particularly arouse my humane interest or disturb me at all; on the contrary, what is disturbing is that a mature man, regardless of whether he is young or old, who feels actually responsible with his whole soul for consequences and who practices the ethics of responsibility, can come to the point of saying: *here I stand; I cannot do otherwise*. There is something here which is humanely pure and which grips you. But each one of us who is not internally dead ought to find ourselves in that situation. The ethics of heart and the ethics of responsibility are not absolutely opposed but complementary, and only the man in whom they are joined has the political calling." [13]

It will be said that this talisman is a small thing, that it is only a question of ethics, that a major political viewpoint extends the history of a time, and that it gives it its formula. But this objection ignores the most certain conclusion Weber establishes. If history does not have a direction like a river but only a meaning, not a truth but only errors to be avoided, if practice is not deduced from a dogmatic philosophy of history, it is not superficial to base a politics on the analysis of the political man. After all, once a politics is separated from the official legends, what makes it important is not the philosophy of history which inspires it and which in other hands would only produce upheavals. It is the human quality that causes the leaders truly to love the political apparatus, and their most personal acts are the most important thing. It is this rare quality that elevates Lenin and Trotsky above the other authors of the 1917 revolution. The course of things is only meaningful to those who know how to read it, and the principles of a philosophy of history are dead letters as long as you cannot re-create them in contact with the present. But in order to succeed we must possess the capacity of living history of which Weber speaks. The truth of politics is only this art of inventing what will later appear to have been required by the times. Certainly Weber's politics will have to be elaborated. It is not by chance that the art of politics is found in some places and not in others. We can think of it more as a symptom of the "intentions" of history than as a cause. We can try to read the present more attentively than Weber did, to perceive "elective affinities" that escaped him. But that which he has shown definitively is that a philosophy of history which is not a historical novel does not break the circle of knowledge and reality and that it is more a meditation upon that circle.

We began this study with Weber because at a time when the Marxist dialectic was becoming an actuality he showed under what conditions a historical dialectic is possible. There had been Marxists who understood this, and they were the best. There had been a rigorous and consequential Marxism which also was a theory of the historical understanding of the *Vielseitigkeit* of the creative choice, and a philosophy which questioned history. It is only after Weber and this Weberian Marxism that the adventures of the dialectic of the past thirty-five years can be understood.

13. *Politik als Beruf,* p. 66.

7 / The Yogi and the Proletarian[1]

Translated by Nancy Metzel and John Flodstrom

KOESTLER is concerned with, but never really formulates, the true problem that emerges with the decline of ideology and the proletarian application of its principles. Can revolution avoid terror? Does the proletariat have a historic mission which is at the same time the moving force of the new society and the vehicle of the values of humanity? Or, on the contrary, is the revolution a completely voluntary enterprise, led by the authorities by means of executive power and suffered by the others? Hegel said that terror was Kant put into practice. Departing from freedom, virtue, and reason the men of '93 ended with pure authority because they believed that they were the bearers of the truth, that this truth embodied in men and in a government is directly menaced by the freedom of others, and that the governed, as the others, are *suspect*. The revolution of '93 is terror because it is abstract and attempts to pass immediately from principles to the forced application of those principles. This being the case, there are two solutions. Whether or not to let the revolution mature, to support it and no longer depend upon the decisions of a committee of public safety but on a movement of history. This is the solution that Hegel had perhaps envisioned in 1807. It is the one that Marx adopted. According to the German ideology, the revolution reduced the inevitable terror in the relations of men to a minimum and finally superseded terror because it is the political birth of the great majority of men and of a proletariat that is in itself a universal class. Hegel in his later years reserved this name for the functionaries of an authoritarian state who decide the meanings of history for all and who create humanity by force and by war. In sum he transformed terror into an institution. He renounced the hypocritical universalism of '93; and since, after all,

1. "Le Yogi et le prolétaire," *Humanisme et terreur, Essai sur le problème communiste* (Paris, 1947), pp. 161–91.

when reason is in power it becomes violence, he counted on violence alone to unify men. The problem today is to know whether the young Marx was right or the mature Hegel. It is not possible to postpone indefinitely the moment when we must decide whether the proletarian philosophy of history is accepted or not by history. The world in which we live is in this respect ambiguous. But although two or three or four grains of sand do not make a pile of sand, after a time the pile of sand is there, and no one can doubt it. You cannot indicate a moment when the compromises cease to be Marxist and become opportunistic. The formulas of the *Childhood Disease of Communism* can be applied to anything. But the moment arises when the detour ceases to be a detour, the dialectic a dialectic, and when we enter into a new order of history that has nothing in common with the proletarian philosophy of Marx.

We know Trotsky was attached to this philosophy to the point of deducing his tactics directly from it, without sufficient regard to facts as important as the existence of fascism or the U.S.S.R. It was for him *true history* that continued, even if it was only in the state of a "molecular process" under the diversions, the confusions, and the compromises of *everyday* history. However, he admitted in his last years that in the long run the distinction could not be maintained that if the proletarian philosophy of history is true this ought ultimately to appear in historical reality. *And he set a moment for the historic test of Marxism.* "The second world war had begun. It demonstrated without possible discussion that society could no longer live on the basis of capitalism. Thus the proletariat was submitted to a new and perhaps decisive test." If the war provoked a proletarian revolution, the world and the U.S.S.R. would return to the classical perspectives of Marxism. If, on the other hand, the proletariat didn't take the "direction of society into its own hands" the world could evolve toward a monopolistic and authoritarian capitalism. "As onerous as the second perspective is, if the proletariat of the world reveals itself to be in fact incapable of fulfilling the mission that has been conferred on it in the course of historical development, we must then realize that the socialist program founded on internal contradictions of capitalistic society has in the final analysis ended as a utopia." [2]

If Trotsky were alive today, could he simply maintain his critique of existing history in the name of the proletarian scheme of things? The proletarian platform permitted him to occupy for a long time (if not objectively and in the world struggle, at least in his own eyes) an independent position equally distant from the hard core and the counterrevolution. When he was killed, the moment came when

2. *The New International* (November, 1939). Cited by D. MacDonald, *Politics* (April, 1946), pp. 97–98.

history expelled him from that position. He would not have consented to capitulate before the course of events or to join with monopolistic capitalism or the regime of the U.S.S.R. His last writings show us that he tried to define, in opposition to both, the "minimum program" for the defense of the masses. But either this program would have been a variant of "humanistic socialism" and thus have played its role in the world conspiracy against the U.S.S.R., or else (and most certainly) Trotsky would have tried to base it on the movement of the masses and would have come into opposition with Communist parties. In his turn he would have been driven into a corner or would have found himself facing a dilemma. Since history has divorced that which Marxism united—the humanistic idea and collective production—either he would have had to decide in favor of an abstract humanism and against the country where, up to now, collective economy had been established, or else he would have taken the part of collective production and the country which represented it. Either the U.S.S.R. or the counterrevolution. A last declaration by Trotsky cannot be imagined. To challenge the present and appeal to the future would have been impossible for him, as he held the present experience to be crucial. Adherence to the government of the U.S.S.R. was improbable because he was, especially in his later years, too much a classical man, too much attached to the rationality of the world to live in contradictions and to enter into the romantic game of capitulations and uneasy conscience. The political life had become *impossible* for him.

Here one could doubtless say that, in effect, there is no political position for those who remain Marxists in the classical sense. But why grant a respite to this philosophy? It has not succeeded in becoming reality; it is a utopia. We should not let it continue to occupy our thoughts. This leads us to a last point which we must establish. The decline of proletarian humanism is not a crucial experience which annuls the whole of Marxism. It is still valid as a criticism of the existing world and of other humanisms. By virtue of this at least, it cannot be surpassed. Even if it is incapable of giving form to world history it remains strong enough to discredit the other solutions. Considered closely, Marxism is not just any hypothesis which can be replaced tomorrow by some other. It is the simple statement of those conditions without which there would be neither any humanism, in the sense of a reciprocal relation between men, nor any rationality in history. In this sense it is not a philosophy of history; it is *the* philosophy of history, and to give it up completely would be to strike out historical reason. After that there are no more dreams or experiences.

A philosophy of history presupposes, in effect, that human history is not simply a collection of juxtaposed facts—individual decisions and happenings, ideas, interests, institutions—but that there is in the present and in the succession of happenings a totality which is moving toward a privileged state which gives the whole its meaning. There will thus be no philosophy of history if certain categories of historical facts are insignificant—if, for example, history is the result of the projects of certain great men. History has a meaning only if there is, as it were, a logic of human coexistence, which does not make any experience impossible but which at least, as if by natural selection, eliminates in the long run those experiences which diverge from the permanent needs of men. Thus any philosophy of history postulates something like what is called historical materialism—namely, the idea that morals, conceptions of law and of the world, modes of production and of work are all internally bound together and throw light upon one another. A philosophy of history will be possible if all human activities form a system in which at each moment no one problem is absolutely separate from any other, in which economic and other problems form one large problem, and, finally, in which the productive forces of the economy have cultural significance, as, inversely, ideologies have an economic influence.

Very well, you may say, but the Marxist conception of history asserts even more. It asserts that economic history will become stable only through the collective appropriation of nature at the hands of the proletariat. From this perspective, it is the proletariat which is given a historical mission, and its struggle becomes of major importance. Isn't this but one hypothesis among many? Can we not imagine other philosophies of history which would bind the destiny of men to the wisdom of the prince or to that of the elders, or to that of scholars and intellectuals, or to that of government officials, or to that of saints, or finally to a system of "checks and balances" in the political and economic order such as the middle phase of capitalism has known? But a group of men cannot take on a historical mission—the mission of bringing history about and of creating humanity—unless they are capable of recognizing other men as such and of being themselves recognized by them. Now in the case of the prince, of elders, of sages, of government officials, or even of saints the historical role of these groups of men consists entirely in controlling others, whether by force or by kindness. And if civilization is defined by a wise balance of power, then civilization is still struggle, violence, and not reciprocity. It could be denied that the proletariat is in the position to fulfill its historical mission or that the situation of the proletariat, as Marx has described it, is sufficient to permit a proletarian revolution to be oriented toward a concrete humanism. It could also be denied that all the acts of violence in history can be imputed to the capitalistic system. But as long as this system is in existence and as long as the proletariat is proletariat, it is difficult to deny that humanity, as the recognition of man by man, remains a dream or a mystification. Perhaps Marxism does not have the power to convince us that one day, and by means of its methods, man will be the supreme being for man, but it retains the power to make us understand that humanity is humanity only in name as long as the greater number of men have abdicated their sovereignty and as long as some are masters and the others slaves. To say that history is (among other things) the history of ownership and that wherever there is a proletariat there is no humanity is not to advance a hypothesis which would later have to be proved, as one proves a law of physics. It is simply to enunciate that view of man as being in a certain position with respect to nature and to others which Hegel develops in his dialectic of master and slave and which Marx borrows from him. By dispossessing the masters, are the slaves in the process of transcending the alternative of master and slave? That is another question. But even if this development should not occur, it would not mean that the Marxist philosophy of history should be replaced by some other. It would mean that there is no history, if history is the advent of humanity and humanity the mutual recognition of men as men—and as a consequence that there is no philosophy of history. It would mean, finally, as Barrès has said, that the world and our existence are a senseless tumult. Perhaps no proletariat will come to exercise the historic function which the Marxist system recognizes as that of the proletariat. Perhaps the universal class will never appear, but *it is clear that no other class can ever replace the proletariat in this function.* Outside Marxism there is only the power of some and the resignation of others.

The reasons for which one holds to Marxism (and one does not leave it easily in spite of the "vicissitudes of experience") are now clear: put back within the perspectives of the unique philosophy of history, "historical wisdoms" appear as failures.

As Marxism is the only humanism which dares to develop its consequences, it has a first right, completely subjective, to receive a reprieve. But from this very fact a second right results, this time an objective one. Because the power of the proletariat has been realized nowhere in the world, some conclude that Marxism has been left behind by the fact that we can no longer ask whether "anyone today is still a Marxist." This is to suppose that the accounts of Marxism are closed and that, since it was not realized in institutions, is has nothing more to teach us. This assumption ignores many of the facts that show it to be continually alive, if not in the foreground of history at least in the background. Present history is not directed by a world proletariat, but from time to time it threatens to make its voice heard again. Leaders of states fear it, but each time that it relaxes its vigilance, universalism and the hope of a social transformation fade with it. This is a sufficient reason for continuing to consider the Marxist attitude not only as a moral criticism but as a historical hypothesis. Historical materialism is more proved than contradicted by the evolution of the U.S.S.R., since you can see there a strict hierarchy and a patriotic and religious compromise appearing together. If it is true that the rivalry of the U.S.S.R. and the U.S.A. explains a great number of things, it is to be remarked that in the countries of lesser importance it utilizes the struggle between the classes and is utilized by it. The two phenomena form an ambiguous whole in which now one and now the other dominates. The sympathies for the U.S.S.R. and the U.S.A. are distributed predictably enough according to the line which divides the classes. We saw how the British government during the war rallied the masses to the national effort through somewhat socialistic projects and abandoned these projects as soon as the danger was past. It knew well the Marxist law of history according to which class consciousness weakens the ties of patriotism. We have seen the Vichy and Madrid governments, at a time when the Communist Party was illegal and hunted down, denounce "internal Communism" as a danger greater than the victories of the Red army, thus recognizing the struggle of the classes as a spontaneous fact, in spite of all that they had attempted in order to mystify class consciousness. Without doubt they were interested in persuading the Anglo-Saxons that they formed a rampart against the proletariat, but at least one among them had not done so badly. Hitler's declarations concerning the dangers of a European Trotskyism belong to the same kind of propaganda.

But like all propaganda, this instance expresses in an ambiguous language one aspect of things under the pressure of its own problems—the permanent possibility of a proletarian movement in every country. It would be mistaken to accord less importance to the proletariat and to the class struggle as political factors than do their most resolute adversaries around the world. We have seen General de Gaulle, who first called down a great wave of revolution on his country, tranquilly disband it the moment he set foot in France—to return to power a group of discredited politicians, confidently decide military, economic, and judiciary problems without any popular participation; to moderate, discourage, and wear down his followers as if the problem of problems for him were to put the masses back in that state of passivity which makes governments happy. As if all change were necessarily revolution—which is exactly the Marxist thesis.[3]

3. It will be said that General de Gaulle was not concerned with the proletariat

The behavior of the French proletariat during the German Occupation is another one of those facts which Marxism clarifies and which confirms it. It can be said, as a whole and in particular, that the industrial proletariat, even when it had worked with or had commerce with the occupying forces, had remained remarkably insensitive to their propaganda, as elsewhere it had rebelled against chauvinism. Even the politically unaware opposed these forces, not with acts of heroism, of course, but with a deep, unshakable determination.

"All this does not concern us. This European socialism is not our socialism." As if the proletarian condition carried in itself an implicit and definitive refusal of reactionary ideas, even when they are disguised with a spontaneous wisdom truly in conformity with Marx's description!

If you consider contemporary history not statistically and broadly but at the level of individuals who live it, you see Marxist themes reappear that were believed to have been surpassed. Even now in physics there is no crucial experiment by means of which a theory could be said to be true or false. We see, rather, a decline of simplistic theories which become continually less capable of covering the whole range of known facts. This is even more true in history, where it is not a question of an external nature but of man himself and where, as a consequence, a theory does not cease to count as a historical factor, and in this sense to be true, until the day men cease to adhere to it.

That a Frenchman, despite the "contradictions in experience," remains attached to Marxist themes is, if you wish, only a psychological fact; but multiplied by many millions this "error" becomes a perfectly objective sociological fact and one which expresses a present reality of French history. Even when the Communist Party allows compromises, it is, because of its social composition, alone capable of effectively defending the farmers against the landowners, and it is very difficult to convince the peasants that they are wrong to vote for it. Likewise, whatever its politics of the moment, the country of the revolution ought to confirm the image that the masses have of it and introduce into the countries which it dominates the reforms that we have awaited for a century. In order to explain the fidelity of the urban and industrial proletariat which the party of compromises rejects, we need not have recourse to psychopathology, as Koestler does.

This proletariat remains in the party because it is there, and as long as it is there the Communist Party is the party of the proletariat. The

---

but with the Communist Party of the U.S.S.R. That is probable, but the fact is that in aiming at one he hit the other. All the distinctions in the world cannot disguise the fact that de Gaulle's government—to the extent that it was anti-Communist— restrained freedom, tried to play with suffering, and assumed a reactionary posture.

allegiance tends to be prolonged of itself. The anti-Communists say that a proletarian policy means the Russians. Yes, we answer, but the Russians mean a minimum of the proletarian policy which is not found elsewhere—at least as long as the proletariat does not view its fate as separable from that of the U.S.S.R. This is the ambiguous situation in which we find ourselves and which causes virulent anti-Communism to be conservative, even though the Communists have suspended or even abandoned revolutionary politics of the classical type.

Many former Communists closed their eyes to this residual or permanent truth of Marxism and as a consequence have taken up philosophical and political positions which are less than fully Marxist. They alienate themselves from a party that, for its members, is not quite like other parties. Nor is it a society of mutual aid, the instrument of a strictly delimited activity, but is the seat of all their hopes and the guarantee of human destiny. The break with the party is as complete as the break with a person, and follows the law of all or nothing. It does not leave intact the memory of what preceded. Former Communists are often less fair toward Marxism than those who have never made a profession of it because it belongs, as far as they are concerned, to a past which they have rejected with difficulty and which they do not wish to remember. If they did not fully understand in their Communistic period the real significance of Marxism, we cannot expect them to return to it now and ask themselves questions about a doctrine which they have rejected as they might have rejected a friend or a lover—that is to say, *in toto*. Perhaps they even keep the historical image that they had of it because it justifies their break. A man who has left a woman with whom he has lived is unable to believe that she could become dear to anyone else. He knew her better than anyone else through living with her each day, and the picture that someone else now has of her, so different from his own, can only be an illusion. He knows the others are mistaken. Thus it is not frivolous to compare political life with personal life. Our relations with ideas are inevitably, and with good reason, relations with people. This is why former Communists have long lacked lucidity with regard to certain questions.

This is verified by Koestler's example, judging from his talk about "scholastic Marxism" and "philosophical jargon."[4] We can presume that he never took seriously the philosophical evolution which, from the post-Kantians to Marx, showed the existence of the spirit in history. In fact, he began with the philosophy of the Commissar, the complex considered as a whole of simple elements, life as a modality of physical nature, man as a modality of life, consciousness as a product or even an

4. *The Yogi and the Commissar* (New York, 1961), *passim*. Citations from this book are taken from the most recent American edition.—*Trans.*

appearance, a homogeneous world stretched out flat without depth or interior, human action explained by causes like all physical processes, ethics, politics, subsumed under a technique of utilitarianism—in a word, the exclusive affirmation of the "exterior." Now he discovers freedom in the Cartesian sense as the indubitable experience of my own existence,[5] consciousness as the first truth. He is pleased to call attention to all in modern physics or psychology that contradicts the philosophy of the Commissar—the discontinuity of quanta, the fact that laws have only a statistical value, the strictly macroscopic validity of determinism,[6] and as a consequence the limitation of explicative thought and the rehabilitation of value judgment.[7] We realize that after breathing the suffocating philosophy of the Commissar so long, he is happy to leave it. What we understand less is that he blames Marxism for it and in so doing rejects Marxism itself. That quality is ultimately irreducible to quantitative difference. That the whole cannot be reduced to its parts; that it has a law of intrinsic organization, an *a priori* or an interior of life and history of which verifiable events are the visible unfolding and, as it were, the emergence; and that man is in the last analysis the source of history—all this Koestler could have learned from Hegel and from Marx, who is Hegel put into practice.

It would have been better if he had not exchanged one naïveté for another, and scientism for the oceanic feeling. Certainly he did not take the veil. He makes fun of those who believe they have found in the behavior of the electron the possibility of divine inspiration,[8] in the living cell a free will comparable to human freedom, and in the limits of exact science generally a proof for the Immaculate Conception.[9] What he wants to oppose to the philosophy of the exterior or the philosophy of the Commissar is not the philosophy of the Yogi or the philosophy of the interior. He dismisses both. The Yogi is wrong to neglect hygiene and antiseptics.[10] He lets violence happen and does nothing.[11] "To suppose that outside mechanism there were only the Church of England and that the only route to that which we cannot see or touch goes through the Christian dogma is a disarming naïveté."[12] What he is looking for is a "synthesis"[13] between the philosophy of the exterior, which reduces the world to the single plan of causal explanation, and the philosophy of the interior, which is restricted to describing

5. *Ibid.*, pp. 199–200.
6. *Ibid.*, p. 205.
7. *Ibid.*, pp. 216–20.
8. *Ibid.*, p. 205.
9. *Ibid.*, p. 205.
10. *Ibid.*, p. 16.
11. *Ibid.*, p. 220.
12. *Ibid.*, p. 221.
13. *Ibid.*, p. 221.

the levels of being in their unique difference and loses sight of their effective relations.[14] "The basic paradox of man's condition, the conflict between freedom and determinism, ethics and logics, or in whatever symbols we like to express it, can only be resolved if, while thinking and acting on the horizontal plane of our existence, we yet remain constantly aware of the vertical dimension. To attain this awareness without losing the other is perhaps the most necessary and most difficult task that our race has ever faced." [15] The formula is excellent, but as a matter of fact Koestler inclines toward the Yogi without even avoiding seizures of fanaticism which in the Yogi, as he himself indicates, alternates with the interior life.[16] We feel he is tempted, not perhaps by religion, which has a feeling for the problems of the world, but by religiosity and evasion. "The age of enlightenment had destroyed faith in a personal survival. The scars of the operation have never healed. There is a vacancy in every living soul, a deep thirst in all of us." [17] He makes Christianity responsible and appears to tie transcendental beliefs to the idea of a plurality of levels where the lower doesn't explain the higher.[18] All this is exaggerated if we remember Aristotle. Koestler declares coldly that science has usurped the place of "the other mode of knowledge" for almost three centuries—which is extreme if we recall the Descartes of the *Meditations* or Kant or Hegel. He calls this "other mode of consciousness" contemplation, and declares that it has survived only in the East and that to learn it we must turn to the East.[19] We would like to refer him again to Hegel, who explained the East as the dream of a natural infinite without historical mediation and as the idleness of death.

We thus get the impression of a philosophy in retreat: Koestler withdraws from the world; he takes leave of his youth and retains almost none of it. For example, when he speaks of Freud, it is not in order to extricate the acquisitions of Freudianism from its now outmoded framework or from the scientific prejudices which Freud shared with his generation. It is in order to preserve a pure realm of values, beyond all corporeal and historical conditioning. The smile of the *Mona Lisa* must be separated from any association with Leonardo's youth,[20] just as courage and self-sacrifice must be separated from masochism and the death instinct.[21] When he should look even into masochism and the death instinct, or into childhood conflicts for an

14. *Ibid.*, pp. 219–20.
15. *Ibid.*, pp. 221–22.
16. *Ibid.*, p. 222.
17. *Ibid.*, p. 197.
18. *Ibid.*, pp. 213–14.
19. *Ibid.*, p. 222.
20. *Ibid.*, p. 215.
21. *Ibid.*, p. 218.

indication and first sketch of the human drama which will be most clearly expressed in the actions and works of the adult (who can never abstract himself from them) and when he should bring values and mind down to the supposedly "biological" facts—Koestler claims for them a distinct methaphysical realm and thereby closes the path to psychological analysis and criticism of ourselves and turns us over to the mystifications of our good conscience. Koestler discredits history and psychology, whereas he should retain all the psychological or historical conditions of a work or of a life and simply integrate them into a total situation which presents itself to the individual as the theme of his whole life and which he is, in other respects, free to treat in several ways—as man reads into the givens of his life whatever he is pleased to find there. Whereas he should recognize the human significance of the libido as an undetermined power of "fixation" and of "integration," in accord with the spirit of Freud's concrete studies—even though against Freud's own statements when necessary —Koestler prudishly asks that love of neighbor be put beyond somatic conflict.[22]

Because he too long believed in a life without values and without spirit—as he still does—he can now reintegrate them only on a higher level. We must see how Koestler dismisses "dialectic"[23] and reinstates supposedly clear thought in the name of "elementary laws of logic," several contemporary examples of which—ready-made beliefs[24] and thalamic reasoning[25] and the schizoid mentality—furnish a terrifying counterproof. Koestler does this as if it were possible to surmount life's contradictions by forgetting about one of the two terms which make them up, as if the cause of the abuse of dialectic were to be found in dialectic itself and not in the increasing contradictions which humanity experiences, and as if the rules of thinking could stop with clear and distinct ideas at the risk of failure to understand what is happening. Finally, in the order of moral judgment, Koestler wages war against the formula "To understand all is to forgive all." He pulverizes it by means of that abstract logic which he shares with

22. He cites the works of de Sade (p. 217) as a good example of an ethics which is submitted to "biology," whereas to all appearances de Sade proves, rather, that on the human level the biological, like the sociological, is charged with a will for the absolute. In the statement of Kirilov in *The Possessed* (p. 216) ("When he believes he does not believe that he believes, and when he does not believe, he does not believe that he does not believe") Koestler does not find the echo of Descartes' evil genius, the expression of an ever possible doubt about the authenticity of our assertions and our decisions—to be transcended, as Descartes teaches us, through the experience of thought in act. No, for Koestler we must forget the doubt by forgetting psychology and history, and by granting once and for all that we transcend them.

23. *Ibid.*, p. 206.
24. *Ibid.*, p. 112.
25. *Ibid.*, p. 120.

the collaborators of *Polemic*. In effect, what he says is either that I understand an action in itself—and this understanding can only lead me to condemn it more severely if it is bad—or else that to understand is to explain it by such external causes as environment, heredity, circumstances (but then I would be treating action as a simple product of nature—which would not affect my judgment of action as a free activity). But what if our actions were neither necessary in the sense of natural necessity nor free in the sense of a decision *ex nihilo*? In particular, what if, in the social order, no one were innocent and no one absolutely guilty? What if it were the very essence of history to impute to us responsibilities which are never entirely ours? And what if such freedom determined itself in a situation which it had not chosen, even though it had assumed it? We would then be in the difficult situation of never being able to condemn with a good conscience, though it is inevitable that we do condemn.

This is what Koestler does not want. For fear of having to forgive, he prefers not to understand. Enough of ambiguities, he thinks; enough of problems and of puzzles. Let us return to absolute values and clear thoughts. Perhaps, as far as he is concerned, it is a question of his own [mental] health, and nobody likes to interrupt a cure. But we should not let him set forth a remedy for his uncertainties as the solution to the problems of our time. He condemns the philosophy of the Commissar, which he adored. This does not give us much confidence in his present statements. We find in Koestler's essays a "back and forth" style, shared by many former Communists, which annoys others. After all, we do not have to atone for the sins of Koestler's youth; and if at the age of twenty he felt disposed toward "rationalism, superficial optimism, cruel logic, arrogant self-confidence, the Promethean attitude," this is no reason to liquidate with them the advances of the nineteenth century and now incline toward "mysticism, romanticism, irrational moral values, and medieval twilight" or to furnish the masses who continue to lead their sacrificial existence with an "antimaterialistic nostalgia" which they are incapable of understanding and which is as vain as materialism itself.[26] We don't like these beautiful, recently discovered truths. As Montaigne says, "Just between us, I have always seen a remarkable accord between supercelestial opinions and subterranean morals." [27] A certain ostentatious cult of values, of moral purity, and of the interior man is secretly akin to violence, hatred, fanaticism. Koestler knows this, for he warns us about "mysticism which acts like an inverted commissar." [28] We like a man who changes

26. *Ibid.*, p. 21–22.
27. *Essais*, III, XIII.
28. *The Yogi and the Commissar*, p. 221.

because he has matured and understands today more than he understood yesterday. But the man who reverts to his older position has not changed; he has not got beyond his errors.

It is in the area of politics that Koestler's humanism shows its vicious side. Here as elsewhere he does not progress; he breaks with his past. In other words, he remains the same. In only one passage in his book does he mention that type of Marxist revolutionary that the nineteenth century produced, a type which lies between the Commissar and the Yogi. "Since Rosa Luxemburg," he says, "there has arisen no man or woman endowed with both the oceanic feeling and the momentum of action." [29] This leads us to understand that neither Rosa Luxemburg nor any of the great Marxists of this century have professed, or in any case experienced, the sordid philosophy of the Commissar. If, then, we find that today's Communism departs from its original inspiration, this is something that must be admitted; but the *remedy will not consist in any case in reverting to the game of the completely interior life,* of which Marxism has once and for all shown the mystifications. Koestler forgets what he should have retained from his Communist past, the sense of the concrete; and he keeps what he should have forgotten, the disjunction of interior and exterior. He is both too faithful and not faithful enough to his past, like those patients of Freud who remained fixed in their experiences and just for this reason could not understand them, assume them, and eliminate them.

Koestler calmly praises British "socialism." "The constitutional framework of the British democracy gives us at least the chance of a relatively smooth transition towards socialism." [30] "One of the basic teachings of Marxism is that of the importance for the proletariat of preserving certain democratic liberties in the State." [31] The fact that "socialism" and British democracy rest upon the exploitation of a part of the world—this objection is not mentioned. Even more, Koestler apprehends that one has taken away from the English socialists any scruples they might still have, and from the conscientious proletarians, if there be any, whatever they might be able to retain of universalism. "That famous sentence in the *Communist Manifesto* 'The workers have no fatherland' is inhuman and untrue. The farm laborer, miner or road sweeper is bound to his native village or street, to the traditions of language and habit, by emotional ties as strong as those of the rich. To go against these ties is to go against human nature—as doctrinaire socialism with its materialistic roots so often did." [32]

If a proletariat emerges from provincialism and chauvinism, we

29. *Ibid.,* p. 19.
30. *Ibid.,* p. 196.
31. *Ibid.,* p. 195.
32. *Ibid.,* p. 191.

can count on Koestler to plunge it back into them. And we do not easily understand why, in a recent interview, his sole reproach against the Labour Party was that it had not created an International (and this reproach was made without concerning himself with what the reasons for such a regrettable omission might be). After the famine of Karkov, we understood that Koestler took the moral climate of beautiful and melancholy England at its proper value. Of course no one likes restrictions or police. No one with any sense has ever doubted that it is more agreeable to live in those countries which, thanks to their historical advantage and thanks to their natural resources aided by the revenues of a usurious state, assure their citizens a standard of living and certain liberties which a collective economy in the formative stage denies to its citizens. But that is not the question. Even if tomorrow the United States were to become the master of the world, it is quite obvious that neither its prosperity nor its system would thereby be extended everywhere. Even if France were politically tied to the United States, it would not for that reason have known the relative prosperity which the Belgians, for example, owe to the possession of the Congo. France would have had to pay for the importation of U.S. products, which are the most costly in the world. In the same way, in the area of Russian affairs we must evaluate the Soviet problems and solutions. Koestler's tone in speaking of the famine of Karkov and electric-power failures recalls that of certain French journalists who, before the war, spoke of rationing, of bread lines, and of poverty in the U.S.S.R. Since then we have experienced the same things, and for nothing. Certain American soldiers, when presented with the spectacle of our sordid life, did not show any compassion but rather a kind of contempt and shock; they were probably convinced that no one could be so unfortunate unless he had sinned a great deal. Something analogous happened among certain of our compatriots who spent the period of the Occupation in the United States. Symmetrically, there is among many continentals a sort of sympathy for those people who go hungry and who have experienced need.

It is not by an appeal to feelings that we will resolve the question— which is, once more, not to find out whether one is better off here or there but to discover whether one of the systems (and which one) is endowed with a historical mission. We have asked the question with regard to the U.S.S.R. We must also ask it with regard to British "socialism." We must ask ourselves if a "socialism" which abandons internationalism, at least "in its doctrinaire form," and accepts without scruples the succession of Churchill's policies, is of any interest at all to men of other countries and whether "socialism" thus understood is not just another name for imperialistic politics. The French voters, say the anti-Communists, are voting for Marxism and are playing the Russians' game. But can they not see that "humanistic socialism" is exactly the disguise that Western imperialism ought to take if it wishes to claim a historical mission? Since he is so conscious of the first equivocation, we are amazed to see that Koestler is so little aware of the second. He appeals to the "revolutionary humanism of the West." [33] But in other respects he finds no fault with the internal policies of the Labour Party, whose revolutionary spirit we have felt for some time. As far as humanism is concerned, he hopes for peace; but the whole question is to know how he hopes to obtain it and, as they say in the schools, by what *means* we are going towards this honorable *end.* In this regard *The Yogi and the Commissar* shows well that anti-Communism and humanism have two ethics: that which they profess, celestial and uncompromising, and that which they practice, terrestial and even subterranean.

> How convincingly the Left columnists proved during the days of Munich that appeasement leads not to peace but to war—and how thoroughly they have forgotten the sermons which they preached! In the case of Russia as in that of Germany, appeasement is based on the logical fallacy that an expanding Power if left alone will automatically reach a state of saturation. But history proves the contrary. A yielding environment acts as a vacuum, a constant incentive to further expansion, and gives the aggressor no indication how far he can go without risking a major conflict; it is a direct invitation to him to overplay his hand and stumble into war by sheer miscalculation. Both world wars actually arose from such miscalculations. Appeasement transforms the field of international politics from a chessboard into a poker table: in the first case both partners know where they are, in the second they don't. Thus the opposite of appeasement is not bellicosity, but a clearly outlined, firmly principled policy which leaves the partner in no doubt how far he can go. It does not eliminate the possibility of war but prevents the danger of stumbling blindly into it, and that is as much as political wisdom can achieve. It is highly unlikely that any great Power will commit an act of aggression against a small nation if it is clearly and definitely understood by all concerned that a new world war will be the inevitable consequence.[34]

This is how so many scrupulous meditations on means and ends conclude. The last sentences bestow upon the whole the benediction of *si vis pacem.* Alas! If the pacifism of the leftist journalists makes Koestler recall today this policy of appeasement of the years 1938 and 1939, the *si vis pacem* of Koestler also reminds us of something. In 1939 there were two ways of making light of the world. One was to say

33. *Ibid.,* p. 196.
34. *Ibid.,* pp. 193–94.

that Germany would be disarmed by making certain concessions; the other was to say that Germany was bluffing and that firmness would prevent a war. The year 1939 taught us that appeasement leads to war but also that firmness is not serious unless it is already a consent to war, perhaps even a will to war. For an act of consent, being conditioned, is only an inclination, and the adversary who senses this acts accordingly. The "firm" powers may devote themselves entirely to preparation for war, and then their threats count—but no matter how peaceful their *ends* may be, these are overlooked by the adversary who sees only the tanks, the artillery, the fleet and deduces the consequences of this situation. Or else the powers may be loath to use belligerent means, and then their diplomatic firmness is ineffectual. Is it, then, necessary that starting today England and the United States should prepare for war, as they prepared for the invasion of 1940 to 1944? Must we from now take it for granted that the U.S.S.R. cannot coexist with the rest of the world? That is the question, for it is impossible to present the threat of a world war as a means of assuring peace when we saw Germany in 1941 wage war in the East and fight against an almost general coalition without having beaten the West. It is also impossible to evoke a united front among the powers which would leave the aggressor by himself; for an aggressor is never without accomplices, the interests of the powers being too various to let them all side together against him at the first onset.

True firmness takes the state of war for granted. This is certainly a policy but one which could not be called a humanism without abusing language. Moreover, the danger is still present that the means may devour the ends. When the United States will have annihilated the U.S.S.R. (which won't be without a battle), Koestler (if he survives) will need only to propose to the people of Western Europe (if any remain) a new policy of "firmness" toward the United States as an "expanding power." We can very well imagine a new essay of Koestler's under the title *Anatomy of a Myth* or *The End of an Illusion*, this time consecrated to the Anglo-Saxon countries. He would peremptorily establish that the United States, land of anti-Semitism, of racism, and of the repression of strikes, is now only in name the "land of the free," and the "ideological bases" of the socialism of the worker which remained intact would not be enough to justify the foreign policy of the British Empire. Perhaps the Yogi, after this double detour by way of shameful means, would at last be able to proceed directly toward the humanistic goals.

Perhaps Koestler will say that we are criticizing him with the language of radical pacifism, which is today that of the Soviet fifth column, as it was that of the Hitlerian fifth column in 1939. But it is not we who profess abstract humanism, purity of means, and the oceanic feeling; it is he. We are using his own argument against him. We will show that the uncompromising application of his principles is on the same grounds a condemnation of Anglo-Saxon and Soviet politics and makes it impossible to define a political position in the present world. We will also show, on the other hand, that if one wishes to spread them throughout the world by means of the Anglo-Saxon power which sustains them and makes a show of them, he as well as they will reenter into the working out of eternal history and the principles will be transformed into their opposites.

Communism cannot be justified simply by showing that violence is a component of Western humanism because the type of violence used by Communism is "progressive," as Marx thought it was. Even less is this enough grounds for us to give to it that spineless assent which pacifism, whether it means to do so or not, historically gives to political systems which employ violence. But this is to take away from the Western policies that unembarrassed good conscience which is so astonishing in the writings of so many contemporary Anglo-Saxons. It is to put the discussion between the Western democracies and Communism back into its true domain—a discussion which is not that between the Yogi and the Commissar but rather between one commissar and another. If the events of the last thirty years permit us to doubt that the proletariats of all countries are uniting and that the proletarian power in any single country establishes reciprocal relations among men, they do not take any truth away from this Marxist idea: that the humanism of capitalistic societies, no matter how real and precious it may be for those who benefit from it, does not filter down from the citizen to the common man and does not eliminate either unemployment or war or colonial exploitation, and that consequently this humanism, having been put back into the history of *all men,* is, like the freedom of the ancient cities, the privilege of the few and not the property of all. What can we reply when an Indochinese or an Arab draws our attention to the fact that he is well acquainted with our arms but not our humanism? Who would dare to say that, after all, the advances of humanity have always been brought about by the few and sustained by delegation of authority and that we are that elite and the others have only to sit back and wait? This would nevertheless be the only frank reply. But this would also be to avow that Western humanism is a *humanism in intension:* a few are the guardians of the treasure of Western culture; the others obey. It would be to admit that Western humanism subordinates factual humanity to a certain idea of man and to the institutions which support this idea, just as the Hegelian state does, and that in the end it has nothing in common with *humanism in extension,* which admits that there is in each man—not in so far as he is an organism endowed with such and such distinctive characteristics but in so far as he is an existence capable of determining himself and situating himself in the world—a power more precious than his products.

Western humanism in its own eyes is the love of humanity, but for others it is only the customs and the institutions of a group of men, their password and sometimes their battle cry. The British Empire has not sent into Indonesia, nor has France into Indochina, missions of Yogis to teach them "change from within." The least that one can say is that their action in these countries has been a "change from without," and it has been rather crude. If they should reply, "Our arms are being used to defend freedom and civilization," then they would be relinquishing absolute morality. They would thereby give the Communists the right to say, "Our arms defend an economic system which will stop the exploitation of man by man." It is from the conservative West that Communism has received the notion of history and learned to make moral judgments relative. It has not forgotten its lesson and has sought, at least in the given historical milieu, those forces which nonetheless had the chance to make humanism a reality. If one does not believe that the power of the proletariat is able to establish itself or that it can achieve the goals that Marxism had set for it, the capitalistic civilizations which have the merit of existing, no matter how imperfectly they may do so, may perhaps represent the least horrible fruit which history has produced. But between them and other civilizations, or between them and the Soviet enterprise, the difference is not that between heaven and hell or good and evil; it is only a question of the different ways of using violence. Communism should be considered and discussed as an attempt at a solution of the human problem and not treated as an epithet.

It is a definitive merit of Marxism and an advance in the Western conscience to have learned to confront their ideals with the social functions they are reputed to animate, to have confronted our viewpoint with those of others, and our ethics with our politics. Any defense of the West which forgets these fundamental truths is a mystification.